COMPUTATION
IN LINGUISTICS
A CASE BOOK

CONTENTS

Albert Schütz. The material for this study was collected in the
    Fiji Islands from November, 1960, to August, 1961, and in
    January, 1963. The first field trip was sponsored by the
    National Science Foundation and directed by Charles F. Hockett
    of Cornell University. The second trip was supported by the
    Research Committee of the University of Hawaii. Thanks are
    due to other members of the Language Data Processing Seminar
    for their suggestions, and to Howard P. McKaughan and George
    W. Grace, of the University of Hawaii, for their comments on
    Section 1 of the paper.

Roger W. Shuy. I would like to thank Paul L. Garvin and the mem-
    bers of the 1964 Linguistics Institute Research Seminar in
    Language Data Processing for their helpful discussion of this
    paper. In addition, I am indebted to William Card, who gave
    many helpful suggestions and criticisms.

Bernard Spolsky. I am indebted to Paul L. Garvin and members
    of the 1964 Linguistics Institute Research Seminar in Language
    Data Processing for suggestions and criticisms.

Richard L. Venezky. I am indebted to Paul L. Garvin and to the
    other members of the Linguistics Institute Research Seminar
    in Language Data Processing for suggestions and criticisms
    on this work. While many of the ideas presented here were
    developed subsequent to the summer session in Bloomington,
    the major part of the work was aided by the continual discus-
    sions throughout the summer months.

Oswald Werner. This work, including the author's stay at the 1964
    Linguistic Institute at Indiana University and participation in
    the Language Data Processing Seminar was supported by an NSF
    postdoctoral fellowship. This support is acknowledged with
    gratitude. Thanks are also due to Ken L. Hale and James D.
    McCawley for criticism and many suggestions.

S. N. Jacobson.* Initial stimulus to the work reported in the
    paper was given by the unpublished paper 'Shipibo Paragraph
    Structure' by James Loriot. I am especially indebted to
    Loriot for several discussions concerning his paper. I should
    also like to acknowledge gratefully the detailed criticisms of
    earlier versions of this paper by Erica Garcia, Edward Green-
    glass, and Russell Kirsch. An earlier version of this paper
    was delivered at the 1964 meeting of the Association for
    Machine Translation and Computational Linguistics. This
    work was supported in part by the U. S. Air Force, Rome
    Air Development Center. Acknowledgement for copyright
    material is made to Lawrence Pollinger Limited, and the estate
    of the late Mrs. Frieda Lawrence.

Mary Lu Joynes. The work carried on in 1960 on the paper was
    supported by a University of Wisconsin Faculty Summer Grant.
    I am grateful to Paul L. Garvin for his many helpful suggestions
    and to Laura Trout for her invaluable advice on the preparation
    of the flowcharts.

Dan M. Matson. This work was supported in part by a research
    contract between the U. S. Office of Education and the Univer-
    sity of Wisconsin.

Fred C. C. Peng. This study was supported in part by the Infor-
    mation Processing Laboratory of the Rome Air Development
    Center of the U. S. Air Force, under Contract AF 30(602) -
    3462. I am grateful to Paul L. Garvin for many constructive
    suggestions.

Paul O. Samuelsdorff. I am indebted to Paul L. Garvin for criti-
    cism and suggestions, and to Bernard Spolsky and Gene M.
    Schramm for discussing with me some points of ambiguity in
    modern Hebrew. I am grateful to Laura Trout and Steven I.
    Laszlo for advice on the possibilities of programming the
    flowcharts and to Gerhard Stickel of the Deutsches Rechenzen-
    trum, Darmstadt, for programming the analysis of the arti-
    ficial sentences. I am especially indebted to the persons and
    institutions that made it possible for me to participate in the
    Seminar.

---

* The tragic death of S. N. Jacobson during the summer of 1965
prevented his reading the proofs of his paper.

ACKNOWLEDGEMENTS

This book is the result of the 1964 Linguistic Institute Research Seminar in Language Data Processing, directed by Paul L. Garvin at Indiana University, under the sponsorship of the U. S. Air Force Office of Scientific Research, Directorate of Information Services, under Grant AF-AFOSR-574-64.

Reproduction by agencies of the Federal government is authorized.

The following contributors to this volume held research stipends under the above AFOSR Grant: Ranan Banerji, William C. Crossgrove, Dan M. Matson, Fred C. C. Peng, Paul O. Samuelsdorff, Albert J. Schütz, Roger W. Shuy, Bernard Spolsky, and Richard Lawrence Venezky.

Acknowledgement for support for other contributors participating in the Seminar is included in individual acknowledgements below. After the termination of the Seminar, the following sponsoring agencies and institutions made the creation of this volume possible:

The editorial work by Paul L. Garvin, including the authorship of the Introduction, was sponsored by the U. S. Air Force Office of Scientific Research of the Office of Aerospace Research, under Contract No.. AF49(638) - 1516 with the Bunker-Ramo Corporation.

The editorial work by Bernard Spolsky, the drawing of the flowcharts by the Graphic Arts department of the Indiana University Audio-Visual Center, and the retyping of some manuscripts, were supported by the original grant referred to in the first paragraph.

Acknowledgements by individual contributors follow:

Ranan B. Banerji. This work was carried out while I was on leave from Case Institute of Technology to which I am grateful for having made time available. Thanks are due to the United States Air Force Office of Scientific Research for allowing me to transfer my activities during the summer of 1964 from work supported by grant AFOSR-125-63 to the Language Data Processing Seminar.

William C. Crossgrove. I am indebted to the members of the Language Data Processing Seminar for many useful criticisms which were offered during my work. I have especially profited from the comments of Paul L. Garvin and the editorial assistance of Bernard Spolsky.

THE AUTHORS

Paul L. Garvin, Manager, Language Analysis and Translation, The Bunker-Ramo Corporation.

Ranan Banerji, Associate Professor of Engineering, Case Institute of Technology.

William C. Crossgrove, Assistant Professor of German, Brown University.

S. N. Jacobson, (formerly) Member, Natural Language Group, Radio Corporation of America.

Mary Lu Joynes, (formerly), University of Texas.

Dan M. Matson, Assistant Professor of South Asian Languages and Linguistics, University of Wisconsin.

Fred C. C. Peng, Member, Technical Staff, The Bunker-Ramo Corporation.

Paul O. Samuelsdorff, Research Associate, Seminar für Vergleichende Sprachwissenschaft der Universität zu Köln.

Albert J. Schütz, Department of Linguistics, University of Hawaii.

Roger W. Shuy, Associate Professor of English and Linguistics, Michigan State University.

Bernard Spolsky, Assistant Professor of Linguistics, Indiana University.

Richard Lawrence Venezky, Assistant Professor of English and Linguistics, University of Wisconsin.

Jerome Wenker, (formerly) Programmer, Linguistics Research Project, Indiana University.

Oswald Werner, Department of Anthropology, Northwestern University.

COMPUTATION IN LINGUISTICS

A CASE BOOK

PAUL L. GARVIN
EDITOR

BERNARD SPOLSKY
ASSOCIATE EDITOR

INDIANA UNIVERSITY PRESS
BLOOMINGTON AND LONDON

Contents

Descriptive Problems — Syntax

Applied Problems — Machine Translation

Applied Problems — Content Processing

Applied Problems — Programmed Instruction

INTRODUCTION

The computer is a problem-solving tool, and the use of computing equipment in linguistics has brought about an increased emphasis on problem-solving. Consequently, the more the research takes on a problem-solving aspect, the more the use of computers becomes meaningful.

It is useful, therefore, to give some thought to the nature of linguistic problems and to the methods and tools required for their solution, and in this context, to assess the application of the computer as a problem-solving tool in linguistics.

Most usually, linguistic problems are organized on the basis of the conventional divisions of the field of linguistics such as the best known of these, into historical and descriptive linguistics. In historical linguistics then, problems are those of comparison and reconstruction, etymology, historical dialectology, and the like. A problem can here most often be defined in terms of the description or interpretation of a given historical process, or of the origin and historical background of a particular phenomenon.

In descriptive linguistics, problems are most often classified in terms of the different levels of description that a particular linguistic researcher accepts. Within the well-known division of phonemic, morphological, and syntactic problems, an individual problem will be concerned with the description or interpretation of a given aspect of phonology, morphology, or syntax in a particular language.

In both major branches of linguistics, the formulation of a problem will of course be strongly controlled by the particular theoretical frame of reference that the researcher adhers to. Thus, in historical linguistics, his frame of reference may either be comparative in the older tradition, or structuralist. In descriptive linguistics, the older descriptivist or one of the more recent approaches such as transformational theory may be chosen.

A further area of linguistic problem-solving is that of theory itself. Here, the problem is not posed primarily in terms of a given set of data that are to be described and/or interpreted, but in terms of a theoretical position that has to be further developed and applied to a body of data. In most theoretical work, the problems turn out to be more philosophical than operational in nature, since the question here is one of greater depth of explanation.

With the introduction of the use of computing equipment into linguistics, it has become possible to describe and categorize

linguistic problems in less conventional terms. Instead of the
subdivisions of the field of linguistics, the nature of the process
required for the solution of a problem may be used to define the
the problem. This new type of categorization of problems, based
on the problem-solving process, is necessary if one is to assess
properly the role of the computer as a problem-solving tool in
any discipline.

Two important characteristics of computing equipment can
aid in such an assessment. On the one hand, the memory capacity
of modern computers, as well as their speed of operation, make
possible the processing of extremely large bodies of data. Data
of great bulk can now be processed within a finite span of time
whereas earlier this analysis would have required decades of work
by human researchers. The second important characteristic of
computing equipment is its mechanical logic, that is, the well-
known fact that data-processing machines carry out every single
instruction to the letter. They lack the human capacity for overriding instructions spontaneously, a capacity which makes human
beings both more original and less reliable than computing equipment.

The first-named characteristic of computers can be called
their data-processing capability, the second, their logical capability.
The data-processing function and the logical function can be used
as the two poles of a continuum on which the nature of linguistic
problems and their solution with the aid of computing equipment
can be discussed. I have written on this subject on a previous
occasion under the heading of 'Computer Participation in Linguistic
Research', (Lg. 38. 385-9 [1962]). My basic point concerned the
varying degree to which computation is an intrinsic part of the linguistic research process in which it is applied. Three fundamental
degrees were posited there: 'language data collection, which is
essentially a form of bookkeeping; computer programs using the
results of linguistic research; and automation of linguistic research
procedures' (p. 385). These degrees can be placed along the above-
mentioned continuum. The lowest degree relies almost entirely
on the data-processing capability, the highest degree almost entirely on the logical capability. The criterion is the extent to which
the computer program 'exercises' linguistic 'judgment'. 'The
"judgment" of a computer program thus consists in the increasing
diversity of conditions which it is capable of taking into account
in making its string of yes/no decisions' (p. 389).

It is possible to take still another view of this question of the
'judgment' exercised by the computer, namely, in terms of the
stage in the application of the equipment at which the fundamental
research decisions are made. Are the decisions made in the
manual preparation of the input for processing by the computer?
Are the decisions made in the program itself? Are the basic
decisions made in the interpretation and further consideration by
humans of the output?

It is clear that the work of the computer is most closely associated with the research process when the basic research decisions are written into the program. That is, the researcher uses
the computer as an extension of his intellect rather than as an
accelerator of his filing cabinet. The logical function of the computer manifests itself here in giving back to the researcher the
exact consequence of his assumptions. This allows him to verify,
with a degree of precision not achievable without the use of computing equipment, the exact consequences of his assumptions. It
is for this reason that this highest degree of computer participation
has great theoretical as well as practical significance for the field
of linguistics.

The papers in this volume exemplify various degrees of computer participation in several fields of linguistics. The book, organized basically in terms of the two fundamental capabilities of
the computer, falls into two categories: data-processing problems
and systems problems (i. e. problems of logical design). Within
each of these categories, the further classification of the contri-
butions follows the more conventional subdivisions of the field of
linguistics.

Paul L. Garvin

The Bunker-Ramo Corporation
Canoga Park, California
November, 1965

FIELD DATA

Chapter 1
===== =

Computers and Anthropological Linguistics

Oswald Werner

1.0 INTRODUCTION

This paper discusses the role of computation in anthropological
linguistics on the basis of experience gained with Navaho.

The fulcrum of the Navaho sentence is the verb. The thirteen
prefix categories before the stem[1] mark a large number of dependencies to other constituents of the sentence. A particularly interesting aspect of Navaho grammatical research is the determination
of the structure of these dependencies.

One of the aims of such research is an automatic parsing
program of Navaho sentences. This requires the solution of at
least three interrelated problems: (1) the structural description
of Navaho sentences; (2) the form of the dictionary entries which
accompany the grammar, and (3) the grammar codes to be attached
to the entries in the dictionary. The latter is the problem of the
nature of the nonterminal vocabulary and of subcategorization of
word classes, in other words, the problem of the effect of word
categories on Navaho grammatical constructions.

A corollary of the parsing problem is a treatment of Navaho
derivational prefixes. Yet their complexity, their limited distribution, and their present obscure lexical productivity make their
treatment considerably more difficult than that of inflectional
prefixes. The discussion of these prefixes is postponed.

The approach to the problem of this paper is transformational
generative. There will be no attempt at defending this point of
view. Both defense and criticism have been presented in numerous
papers. This approach has been selected as a matter of personal
preference. The emphasis on personal preference should put the
choice of theoretical orientation beyond controversy — needless
to say, this does not apply to the substance.

This theoretical bias puts one at a disadvantage in a discussion
of automatic parsing of sentences in any language. Such a parsing

program must be based on a minimally adequate grammar of the language to be parsed. In other words, a parsing program is subsequent to a grammar of the language, regardless of how preliminary or putative such a grammar may be. As shall be seen later, the definition of grammatical units in a transformational generative grammar is not independent of the aims of the grammar, which is the production of grammatical sentences. Hence, the entire problem of subcategorization cannot be treated independently of such a grammar.

The opinion has been voiced frequently (in private conversations more than in public discussions) that transformational grammar is not empirical. Whatever the reasons for holding this view may be, this author agrees with Longacre that 'generative grammars are by no means uninterested in linguistic analysis'. [2]

It has been previously stated that the ultimate aim of this work is an automatic parsing program. It was also said that the prerequisite for such a program is a minimally adequate transformational generative grammar. Following this sequence of priorities, an attempt will be made to answer questions concerning the usefulness of a computer for the construction of a transformational generative grammar. Parts of the process will be illustrated by examples from Navaho. In particular, those linguistic computer programs which are easily available will be considered.

The author is in agreement with Longacre that techniques of discovery 'are guess-and-check procedures'. [3] Trial and error plays an important part among the techniques of any science. The linguist has in addition several aids at his disposal: his typological knowledge or his experience, be it formal or intuitive, with other languages of the world. [4] The transformational grammarian is in addition aided by his basic assumption that the deep structure, the output of the constituent or phrase-structure component of the grammars of the languages of the world, is similar. [5] That is, with the knowledge of the deep structure of English and other well-known languages, one can draw likely conjectures about the structure and processes in the phrase-structure part of the theory or grammar of any language of the world.

In the following sections the author will also discuss the field techniques of the anthropological linguist and the extent to which these are modified by the theoretical orientation toward transformational generative grammar. He hopes to support in detail the notion that there is close analogy and even an overlap between the techniques and procedures of analysis used in finding the units of a taxonomic grammar and the construction of transformational

generative grammars. The reassuring closeness of the analogy
should not be interpreted as a defense or justification of the
taxonomic theoretical stance.

It was inevitable that the preoccupation of the taxonomic grammarians with more or less automatic discovery procedures should
lead them to general and probably universal analytic techniques
which are applicable, as laboratory techniques are, regardless of
one's theoretical bias. This is in no way demeaning the achieve-
ments of taxonomic grammarians. On the contrary, an attempt
will be made to demonstrate that their successes in analyzing languages are very important to anthropological linguists dealing
with little-known languages.

2. 0 HEURISTICS

The following heuristic principle was proposed by Katz and
Postal: 'Given the sentence for which a syntactic derivation is
needed, look for simple paraphrases of the sentence which are
not paraphrases by virtue of synonymous expressions; on finding
them, construct grammatical rules that relate the original sentence
and its paraphrases in such a way that each of these sentences has
the same sequence of underlying P- (phrase) markers. Of course,
having constructed such rules, it is still necessary to find independent syntactic justification for them. '[6] This principle, as it
stands, complicates the picture by leaving unexplained a number
of factors which would make derivation simpler. It assumes (see
'the same sequence of underlying P-markers') that most sentences
encountered in the eliciting situation are complex, consisting of
more than one underlying phrase marker. This is generally true
of sentences in texts. However, the specific advantage of eliciting
with a knowledgeable informant is the linguist's awareness of the
metatheoretical fact that complex sentences consist of simple sentences and that it is, therefore, possible and more efficient to start
eliciting 'simple sentences' even though some may later turn out to
be complex.[7] It is best to make some ad hoc assumptions about what
simple sentences are, and to try for nonsynonymous paraphrases
of these. This is analogous to eliciting for morphemic analysis as
it was stated by the Voegelins.[8] The objective is to 'postulate
what common underlying sentences occur in what constructions'.
('[F]ind what common morphemes occur in what sequences' has
here been replaced by 'postulate what common underlying
sentences...') Although quite apart in theoretical orientation,

close analogies are seen in the techniques of analysis (see the
following discussion).

The eliciting procedure is based on the fact that formal grammatical relationships exist among sentences of quite different
superficial structures.[9] It must be added that there exist quite
similar superficial structures which have no formal relationships.
Hale's statement can be restated: 'formal relationships often do
not exist among sentences of quite similar superficial structure'.
The objective of field technique is to keep these two cases apart.
The former is a case of nonsynonymous paraphrase, the latter a
case of structural ambiguity.

There is a close analogy between eliciting for a transformational
grammar and eliciting for a taxonomic grammar. The notion of
'emic' and 'etic' may be extended to eliciting techniques for transformational generative grammars: The objective is a general statement of the 'emic' abstract underlying sentences of the constituent
structure component of the grammar. Such a statement takes into
account transformational varieties. The transformational varieties
of sentences are derived from 'emic' underlying strings. The deep
structure of a sentence is its 'emic' representation, whereas the
transformations are responsible for the generation of 'etic' 'allo-
forms' of the surface structure. This represents a relationship
of invariance, which is preserved across transformation: it is the
invariance of the semantic interpretation of the sentences. This
is the discovery of Katz and Postal, that transformational generative grammars can be constructed in such a way that transformations
do not change the semantic interpretation of the sentences. This
strategy is motivated by considerations of simplicity and intuitive
preference.[10] The 'emic' deep structure is postulated on the basis
of 'independent syntactic justification'.

The striking feature of this analogy is that many statements
which were made concerning the discovery of taxonomic units in
taxonomic grammars are, with slight modification, applicable as
eliciting techniques for transformational grammars. Garvin's
statement, 'the input to the morphological analysis is thus a set
of behavioral units, namely, informant responses elicited by a
form-meaning technique in ordered sets under controlled conditions',[11] may be applied to syntactic analysis.

'Controlled conditions' I interpret as the requirement that
ungrammatical sentences are not permitted, unless so marked.
In other words, in the eliciting situation, there is sufficient time

to permit postediting by the informant, i. e. there is a closer
check on grammaticality than in 'natural' situations.[12]

'Ordered sets' are unordered sets of paraphrases of sentences.
The 'form-meaning relationship' is interpretable as those sets of
sentences which are nonsynonymous paraphrases of each other and
which must preserve their semantic interpretation across all
possible transformations. The sentences of the surface structure
(plus phonetic interpretation) are 'behavior units' considerably
closer (because 'precooked') to behavior than the abstract char-
acterization of the underlying strings. The behavioral units are
modified and abstracted by postediting (see note 12) and transcription. Finally, the 'input' is not to morphemic but to transformational generative analysis.

Garvin goes on to say that two aspects of linguistic analysis
are 'often termed segmentation... and... distributional analysis'.
Again with slight modification the gist of these terms is applicable
here. The purpose of the analysis is the isolation of sentences or
parts of sentences which are nonsynonymous paraphrases of each
other. An important addition is, however, that the informant's
help is required in order to determine which sentences or parts
of sentences conform to this requirement, or preserve the invariance of the semantic interpretation. The distributional analysis is analogous to the search for syntactically justified and
economical ways of stating transformational relationships. Whereas
in distributional analysis the 'etic' environment is the overriding
factor, the central concerns here are the 'emic' conditions which
trigger the desired transformational outputs. The treatment is
distributional in the sense that certain transformations only apply
in certain environments. For example, if a sentence of a given
structure is embedded in a matrix sentence of a given structure
most transformations may not apply.

One can further illustrate this analogy by applying Garvin's
five steps comprising an analytic cycle.[13]

1) 'The formulation of the immediate analytic objective'. In
the transformational generative view the analytic objective is
given by metatheoretical considerations. We know that we are
dealing with sentences, and we know that sentences are very often
composed of other sentences. The analytic objective is to establish
the nature of simple sentences, and the nature of transformations
by which certain sets of simple sentences are related to each other.
This involves relating the deep structure to the surface structure.
It must be emphasized that appeal is made to the informant's
Sprachgefühl.

2) 'Preparation of data base by elicitation, study of text or reorganization of existing data'. This problem will be discussed in detail in the next section. However, neither study of texts, nor elicited data, nor reorganization of existing data is a priori excluded.

3) 'Impressionistic examination of data to observe pertinent units and relations'. All procedures require careful examination of the data, not only by the analyst but also by the informant who has to be trained for this task. Garvin's 'observe pertinent units' must be restated as 'postulate pertinent units'. The postulation of units and their structural relationships is an important part of transformational and generative grammar construction. It is essential to observe the difference: units are postulated, rather than observed. That the units of taxonomic grammar (e.g. morphemes) are postulated rather than observed is noted by Koutsoudas.[14] The distinction is important because it affects the definition of these units. Although one may define linguistic units by diagnostic environments, the selection of 'diagnostic environment' is not automatic and can be applied only 'if the answer is in a sense already known'.[15] Transformational grammar defines its units by rules.[16] 'Rewrite N as' followed by a number of lexical items on the right-hand side defines the members of this list as units called 'noun'. Such a definition is necessary but not sufficient. How one has discovered this rule is relatively unimportant, except perhaps for the fact that taxonomic techniques can and should be utilized. Whether the definition is adequate becomes apparent only if sentences generated by the grammar do not meet the requirement of grammaticality. Such a definition is sufficient only if the grammar will generate grammatical and only grammatical sentences.

4) 'Operational tests when necessary to verify impressionistic observation leading to attestation of relations and definitions of units.' At this point in the analytic cycle of a transformational generative grammar, a first tentative formulation of the rules and categories of the grammar has been made. The operational test is the generation of sample sentences either randomly or by some other procedure. The attestation of relations and the definition of units follows: if the grammar is inadequate it will produce other than grammatical sequences, and the rules, or categories, or both, have to be adjusted accordingly.

5) 'Collection and examination of additional data to cross-check relations and definitions.' The grammarian's work is never done. There exists no complete grammar of any language. The

examination of additional data will reveal parts of the grammar which either inadvertently or intentionally have been by-passed and left out. Although relations and definitions are crosschecked at this point, more is involved in formulation. General formulations are preferable and should replace particularistic ones. General rules are preferable to specific rules, covering one or just a few cases. Extending a grammar to new sentence-types may lead to new relationships, and adjustments will be necessary. These should make the rules of the grammar more comprehensive.

It is useful to look upon the construction of grammar in terms of certain priorities. The formalism underlying the theory of grammar is well suited to partial solutions or subgrammars. These deal with subsets of rules and categories of some ultimate grammar. Such a subgrammar generates only a certain type of subsets of sentences.[17] The choice of some sequence of priorities in the study of sentence-types may be based on linguistics universals. Other priorities may vary from language to language. Equational sentences, if present in a given language, are probably the simplest structures. In ascending order, intransitive sentences, transitive sentences, double transitive sentences and their derivatives, are increasingly more complex. Rather than attacking a language frontally one may with less effort procede from simpler structures to the more complex.

Subgrammars are limited not only by sentence-type. Sentences of a given type may contain (as they do in Navaho) future, imperfective, perfective, iterative, optative, or other subsentence types.

In the next section a Navaho morphophonemic class of verbs is considered in detail. These verbs of the imperfective paradigm have been selected because the syncretism or morpheme overlap is simpler than in the perfective. The relationship of the imperfective to the future or any of the other paradigms was not checked. A further simplification of the Navaho example is achieved by considering only the simplest of the imperfective morphophonemic class of verbs. These are verbs without derivational affixes, or the so-called disjunct imperfectives.[18]

Among the list of priorities is also the problem of subcategorization, which plays an important part in the assignment of grammar codes (grammatical markers)[19] or labels to the modes of the structural description. The subcategorization in a transformational generative grammar is finer than in traditional grammars, certainly more so than in most taxonomic grammars.

As Chomsky has shown, at least one aspect of grammaticality can be expressed in terms of subcategorization.[20] The lexical entries of the grammar are subcategorized componentially. The use of grammatical components is an efficient way of dealing with intersecting classes. Componential solution is an important aspect of recent formulations.[21]

An arbitrary level of grammaticality for early formulations may be decided in advance. This will simplify the first stages of analysis. Subcategorization may be represented as a taxonomic rooted tree. It is the 'depth' of this taxonomy that can be arbitrarily fixed and decided upon in advance.

A zero level of subcategorization, in this view, contains only words. A first level of subcategorization separates words into such classes as nouns, verbs, particles, etc. A second level of subcategorization may separate nouns into count nouns and mass nouns, and so on. The level of subcategorizations, if the branchings are always binary, and if set arbitrarily at five, gives 32 categories, at six, 64 categories, or at seven, 128 categories of classes of words. An example of some arbitrary limit of subcategorization is one which permits sentences of the type John spoke softly and The horse spoke softly, but excludes sentences of the form The orange spoke softly. It does not make the complete distinction between animate, human and nonhuman nouns. The lack of this distinction may be due to an arbitrary restriction of the taxonomic depth to perhaps four or five.

3.0 INFORMANT VERSUS TEXT

There is no doubt that all human beings have an innate genetic predisposition that enables them to learn at least one human language. The information that goes into learning a language is vast. To speak is perhaps the most complicated task that a human being learns during his lifetime. 'Since each speaker is a finite organism, this knowledge (of his native language) must be finite in character, i.e. learnable'.[22] In fact we are forced to assume that such learning involves the breakdown of the finite external linguistic information into a set of elementary rules (or some hypothetical complex neural connections) which are capable of reproducing and/or interpreting an infinite set of sentences which a speaker of a language may produce or encounter. It follows that this innate ability to analyze language, however implicitly and nonselfconsciously, is a corollary to the innate ability of being able to learn

a language. This observation is important to the anthropological
linguist because no matter how strange a human culture may be
or how strange the language spoken in that culture is, native
speakers can be taught to become efficient linguistic technicians
or linguists. That is, they can be taught to make the notions of
an implicit nonselfconscious linguistic analysis explicit and hence,
verbally public.

Linguists who work on well-known languages usually analyze
their own language. They combine in one person the native speaker
and the analyst. The anthropological linguist is rarely that lucky.
It is for this reason that he is eternally preoccupied with techniques
of discovery. The best recourse of the anthropological linguist is
close cooperation with a native speaker. That this cooperation
assumes a special character should be evident from this discussion.[23] It is inevitable and necessary for eliciting toward the
'discovery' of the grammatical structure of a language. The native
speaker becomes considerably more central to the linguistic investigation than he has been in eliciting for taxonomic grammars.[24]
There are two reasons for the native speaker to be central to
transformational generative analysis:

1) Because of his knowledge of the language he is capable of rec-
    ognizing partial and total similarities between sentences and
    parts of sentences, i. e. he is capable of establishing the fact
    quickly and efficiently that a given sentence and another are
    paraphrases of each other, he can state the nature of the para-
    phrase relationship (synonymous vs. nonsynonymous) or can
    recognize that they are not related at all. The native speaker
    is also capable of taking his entire knowledge of the language
    into account while making these judgments. It is on the basis
    of this total knowledge that he is capable of making decisions
    about the plausibility of a proposed source sentence. It should
    be noted that it is a requirement of descriptive adequacy[25] that
    these skills of the informant be explicitly accounted for.
2) (Not entirely independent of 1)) A great asset of the native
    speaker is his capacity to recall large bodies of linguistic
    material on demand by virtue of his memory and fluent knowl-
    edge of his language.

The emphasis on the native speaker or the participant-consultant
in a project of writing a grammar of a given language raises the
question of the usefulness of texts. The place of texts in the taxonomic grammatical analysis was discussed in detail by the Voegelins
in Hopi Domains.[26] The technique of ancillary eliciting is based

on the availability of a text. '(It) starts with translation eliciting
(i.e. texts read to the informant who then translates them into the
language of the analyst), but once the English gloss of the word is
obtained, "how do you say" questions are asked in an attempt to
discover combinatorial possibilities, to find what common morphemes occur in what sequence', and '...ancillary eliciting generates numerous texts...'.[27] Ancillary eliciting according to this
view was carried on until all the morphemes — particularly the
minor morphemes or affixes of the language — had been identified.
Ancillary eliciting in itself controverts the claim that a text can
be analyzed without recourse to ancillary data. Anthropological
linguists never subscribed to that extreme in practice, but in their
theoretical orientation the corpus was considered closed when all
morphemes were assumed to be listed, particularly the minor morphemes or affixes. There was no further reason for more data.

   The technique of ancillary eliciting with minor modification
and specific attention to sentence structure can be applied to the
eliciting of transformational generative grammars. The basic
assumption of the Voegelins, that the text is primary and subsequent eliciting is ancillary, however, must be reversed. Eliciting
becomes primary and the use of text is ancillary. The Voegelins
state that ancillary eliciting is time-consuming.[28] So is general
grammar construction. However, to the anthropological linguist
the procedure suggests a general technique of analysis.

1) It is useful to start work in an unknown language with a text.
    The text may function as an ancillary data base. In addition
    it may perform a useful function in the training and education
    of informants (see below).
2) If the corpus is large enough it will be possible to find in it
    related sentences. These can be brought together and presented
    to the informant as evidence that related sentences do exist in
    his language.[29] The informant can be taught what nonsynonymous
    paraphrases of sentences are and how they are to be used in
    the analysis. In order to expalin the type of relationship that
    the linguist is interested in, it is most useful to bring together
    examples, and demonstrate with these the objectives of the
    linguist. In an entirely unknown language, and working with
    an unsophisticated informant, such illustrative examples may
    be the quickest and perhaps the only effective method of
    demonstrating the relatedness of sentences. Once this is
    accomplished, it becomes easy to transcend the text and to

elicit related sentences directly from the informant. Hale has
remarked that it is useful to teach the informant to respond to
metatheoretical linguistic labels such as, 'would you please
now give me an equational sentence', etc. This greatly facili-
tates the informant's ability to 'perform operations on given
linguistic material'. [30]

3) As the eliciting of new varieties of sentences proceeds, it is
useful to add the new sentences to the original text as expansions
of the corpus.

4) A further advantage of the presence of the large text is that
there are sentence-types which are infrequent in ordinary dis-
course and which may elude the memory of the informant. A
file of sentences from elicited texts or elicitations based on
elicited texts may perform the useful function of a memory base.
Such a file becomes more and more important 'as the questions
become more sophisticated (and) the informant's responses become more and more difficult to control, and his memory becomes less and less reliable'. [31] Transformational generative
grammar construction certainly meets this requirement of
sophisticated responses which are increasingly more difficult
to control. It is in the treatment and manipulation of such
large bodies of data, which can be accumulated in amazingly
short periods of time, that a computer processing of linguistic
information can be used as an aid in the construction of the
rules, transformations, categorization and selection restrictions
which hold in a transformational generative grammar of a
given language.

4.0 THE USE OF COMPUTERS

According to the view taken in this paper 'discovery procedures'
have no place in linguistic theory. There is no a priori way in
which we can determine how discoveries are made. However, no
one doubts the utility of various analytic techniques which can be
used to manipulate the 'raw' data and by means of which one can
gain understanding. Such understanding is the raw material of
creative intuition. Some analytic techniques are more useful and
more appropriate for the manipulation of data or for information
processing. Among the various techniques and trial-and-error
procedures which one can use to cull understanding from the data,
some by their very nature promise greater reward than others. It
is obvious that in a list of priorities of analytic usefulness, the

ouija board, familiar spirits, or a solar eclipse will have a lower priority[32] than the vast memory capacity and speed of modern electronic computers. This does not mean the linguistic analysis cannot be performed without a computer. It can be done and has been done by trained linguists who may or may not be native speakers of the language analyzed.

To the anthropological linguist who knows the language to be investigated poorly, if at all, the information-processing capacity of a modern computational device may be a tremendous asset. If there is a considerable body of data available, there is a second reason for computers. They may serve as data organizers and make previous works available for quick recall or look-up.

Computers and human beings have a common feature. They are both complicated information-processing devices. The speed and accuracy of computers makes it a device for the extension of human capabilities. Computers have been programmed as general problem solvers of highly structured simple games or of theorems of logic and geometry. [33] However, at least at present a computer program which can automatically analyze a previously unknown language and furnish structural descriptions of its sentences and a lexicon with a grammar code is beyond reach. [34]

Computers may be used as check on exhaustiveness. 'In eliciting complex sentences', according to Hale, 'some sentence types are inevitably missed'. He proposes that by sensitizing the informant to questions of the kind, 'What is the simple sentence which underlies sentence X?' and by explaining to him what 'underlie' or 'source' means, some of the hiatus can be filled in. [35] In spite of the effectiveness of this technique there is no procedure which will guarantee the exhaustiveness of a grammatical investigation. This is an inevitable by-product of the infinitely many sentences which constitute the repertory of a speaker of a natural language.

The greater the variety of source texts and of techniques of discovery the higher the degree of exhaustiveness. Without artificial stimulation of some kind or proper sociophysical contexts, no informant will be able to provide all possible sentence-types occurring in his language. Computer programs processing texts can function as artificial stimulants in this sense.

A grammarian, even if he does not know the language too well, can use concordances and very simple search programs. More complex programs (see other articles in this volume) require a vast amount of sophisticated linguistic information before they become feasible or economical. Simple concordances and search

programs with various extensions and adaptations may perform
much more effectively because of the generality and independence
from linguistic analysis.

In spite of sophisticated additions (see discussions below) concordances are inefficient information-retrieval devices. The contexts of most key words in long texts contain more sentences than
are needed at any stage of the analysis. Fortunately, the number
of context sentences is much smaller than the entire corpus. The
separation of sentences with the relevant features can easily be
done manually.

There are two types of concordance programs which are easily
accessible to linguists: so-called unblocked concordances, and
blocked concordances. The first gives an arbitrary amount of
context for each key word.

Martin Kay's (RAND) CRUDEN unblocked concordance provides
one line of 130 characters (including spaces) for the key word and
its context. The key word is centered on the printout page. I found
this format useful with Trader Navaho texts. I had difficulty in
establishing sentence boundaries, however; in most cases, the
130-character line included more than a single sentence of context.
(See Fig. 1.1.)

Blocked concordances have the advantage that the unit of context can be chosen in terms of its relevance to the linguistic objective. A grammarian intending to write a grammar of the sentences
of a language will prefer the sentence as the extent of 'the block'.
The boundary of the block is marked by boundary symbol, usually
an identification number. There is no reason to limit context always
to one sentence. It can easily be extended to include larger, or
smaller units.

Unblocked concordances are generally easiest to use with one
line of text, which for the anthropological linguist will rarely suffice. More often than not, he needs English translation labels
along with the original sentence. Although the CRUDEN concordance
program allows for multiple lines (see Fig. 1.1), the count of items
between spaces (i.e. the words) of the text and the English sentences
must coincide. Such matching requires very careful and exacting
proofreading, hence, extra time. With more than two lines (say,
interlinear and free translation) this task becomes most cumbersome.

Blocked concordances have the advantage that precise matching
of items on each interlinear line is unnecessary. The blocks are
keypunched in a special format which automatically assures the
proper sequence and proper placement of the lines.

Some blocked concordances have provisions for an unlimited
number of parallel lines. Lines may be subgrouped into several
classes. For example, the BIDAP (Bibliographical Data Processor)
program developed by Professor James Aagaard at Northwestern
University has four classes of lines. Each line can have up to 99
continuation cards (see Fig. 1.2).

Northwestern University's TRIAL, programmed by William Tetzlaff,
can handle eight classes of cards, each with up to 99 continuation
cards. Multiple classes of lines can be utilized in various ways: for

#ABINDATA7

7GI7I7 . 02004 #E7E7 , #E7E7 , NAAGI YISK8A7A7NGCC #AYGISII . 02005 SOSE7D DAASKE7N #E7NDA .02006 #AA
D . 02004 HESIT , HESIT , TWO DAYS VERY . 02005 SEVEN O#CLOCK THEN .02006 #AA
#ABINDATA7A7 #E7E7 KWE7E7 . 02005 SOSE7D DAASKE7N #E7NDA .02006
MORNING HESIT HERE . 02005 SEVEN O#CLOCK THEN .02006

1 OCCURRENCE OF THIS WORD.

#ACE7E7DE7E7

DILHKID .09018 NII DAACI HADII #CC HCLNI QUE .09019 #AWE7E7 . 09020 D07C7 KAD #E7E7
SKED .09018 YOU MAYBE WHAT JST TELL QUE .09019 BABY . 09020 AND NOW HESIT
#ACE7E7DE7E7 #ALSI7I7SI7I7 DAACAA , 09020 D07C7 KAD #E7E7
FIRST A-LITTLE SICK , 09020 AND NOW HESIT

1 OCCURRENCE OF THIS WORD.

#ACI7I7SI7I7GI7I7

7E7 NADZA7A7HC7C7 4 #E7NDA #E7E7 RIZHE7E7 HC7L8C7C7NII #ACI7I7SI7I7GI7I7 LHAYE WO7SHDE7E7 . 08009 #AA#C7C7LE7 DC7C7DEDA •
008 HESIT COMING-BACK THEN HESIT BEER A LITTLE SOME BRING . 08009 WELL EXCLAM •

.06019 TA7A7DC7C7 #ALHNII#AI7GI7I7 SHASHIN QUE .06020 DEEGCC #ACI7I7SI7I7GI7I7 DAACI QUE , DEEGCC NE7ZI7GI7I7 DAACI QUE .06021
.06019 THREE-AND A-HALF-CNE THINK QUE .06020 HIGHT MAYBE QUE , HIGHT TALL-CNE MAYBE QUE .06021

BINA7A7GAYI7GI7I7 QUE .06012 L8AA .06013 #E7E7 TLAZHI#E7E7 #ACI7I7SI7I7GI7I7 SHBAA QUE .06014 HAG8CC7N QUE .06015 DC7C7
CLD QUE .06012 CK .06013 HESIT TROUSERS SHORTCNES EH QUE .06014 ALLRIGHT QUE .06015 ALSO

17 .05010 SI7LF/LHI7 D27C7 QUE .05011 L8AA . 05012 #AKA7A7N #ACI7I7SI7I7GI7I7 DC7C7 QUE .05013 L8AA .05014 BILHE7E7#ILIN
.05010 MATCHES ALSO QUE .05011 CK . 05012 FLCUR SMALL ALSO QUE .05013 CK .05014 BAKINGPOWDER

. 05005 DC7C7 HADI7I7 DC7C7 QUE .05006 DIDE7CCC YAADIIZI7N #ACI7I7SI7I7GI7I7 DAACI QUE , N9CA7A7YI7GI7I7 DAACI QUE .05007 L8AA
. 05005 AND WHAT ELSE QUE .05006 PEACH TIN-CAN SMALL MAYBE QUE , BIG MAYBE QUE .05007 CK

N9CA7A7YI7GI7I7 #E7E7 DCC DA , SIKI7S .04004 #A7A7 #E7E7 #ACI7I7SI7I7GI7I7 .04005 #AAKEDE HA#NILHE7E7 BIKE7E7GCC #A7A7
BIG-CNE THAT NCT GCCD , FRIEND .04004 HESIT HESIT SMALL-CNF .04005 SADDLE BLANKET SIMILAR-TC HESIT

6 OCCURRENCES OF THIS WORD.

#ACI7I7SI7I7

N9NIZN9 QUE .05003 NC7C7MASI DC7KWI7I7GCC QUE .05004 #AZIS #ACI7I7SI7I7 #ADE7E7Z2BIN #AYLHAY BE7E7SCC BAYIL8I7I7 •
YOUWANT QUE .05003 PCTATCES HCW-MUCH QUE .05004 BAG SMALL FULL CNE DOLLAR COST •

1 OCCURRENCE OF THIS WORD.

#ADE7E7Z2RIN

E7 NE7HC7C7N . 12010 TCC#ARED SHRAA QUE . 12011 #E7E7 TC #ADE7E7Z2BIN , YAA QUE , .12012 #A7A7YII NE7HC7C7NEE •
IT PRETTY . 12010 THE-PCNO EH QUE . 12011 HESIT WATER IS FULL . ISIT QUE . 12012 EI PRETTY

#ADE7E7D

```
7YASH  QUE .  10009 LRAA .  10010 HAYISHDE7E7GI7I7 QUE .  10011 #ADE7E7D BIKEEYI7SH QUE .  10012 DC7KWI7I7 BITT7GHA QUE .
LY     QUE .  10009 CK   .  10010 WHAT-KIND        QUE .  10011 GIRLS   HERSHOE-EH QUE .  10012 HOW-MUCH  FIIS    QUE .
                                                                          1 OCCURRENCE OF THIS WORD.
```

#ADE7E7RIN

```
.05003 NC7C7MASI DC7KWI7I7GCO QUE .05004 #AZIS #ACI7I7SI7I7 #ADE7E7RIN #AYLHAY BE7E7SCO BAYIL8I7I7 . 05005 DC7C7 HADI7I7
.05003 POTATOES  HOW-MUCH     QUE .05004 BAG   SMALL         FULL       ONE     DOLLAR  CCST       . 05005 AND
                                                                          1 OCCURRENCE OF THIS WORD.
```

#AGHA7A7

```
DCC HOSHNI DA   . 07004 #E7E7 AYLHA#AY DAM8C7C7 #E7NDA DAACI #AGHA7A7 NAYISNI7I7GI7I7 BIBELAGATA7NA #E7E7 SIDA7  . 07005
NOT I-SELL NOT  . 07004 HESIT ONE      WEEK     HENCE  MAYBE WCCL     WHITE-MAN      HESIT        THERIS        . 07005
                                                                          1 OCCURRENCE OF THIS WORD.
```

#AGHAA

```
.06025 07001 JIDRA7A7 SHII BEEDI7I7D SINILEE GC7C7 . 07002 #AGHAA HOSHINI BEENIGI7I7 . 07003 #E7E7 DCC HOSHNI DA .
.06025 07001 TODAY    I    ALBU      QUERQUE GO    . 07002 WCCL   I-SELL  REASON-FCR . 07003 HESIT NOT I-SELL NOT .
                                                                          1 OCCURRENCE OF THIS WORD.
```

#AG07C7

```
#E7NDA DAAIDAADILH#ALH . 10005 SHII #AYGISII JE7E7 DEEYA7A7 #AG07C7 . 10006 SRE7E7LHCC NAYISNII . 10007 HA7A7DI7I7SH
THFN   CLOSE           . 10005 I    VERY     TIRED AM       SC-THEN . 10006 HURRY      BUY      . 10007 WHAT
                                                                          1 OCCURRENCE OF THIS WORD.
```

#AKA7A7N

```
BAYIL8I7I7 .05010 SITILE7LHI7 IC7C7 QUE .05011 LRAA . 05012 #AKA7A7N #ACI7I7SI7GI7I7 DC7C7 QUE .05013 LRAA .05014 BILHE7E7#IL
CCST       .05010 MATCHES     ALSO  QUE .05011 CK   . 05012 FLOUR    SMALL          ALSO  QUE .05013 CK   .05014 BAKINGPOWD
                                                                          1 OCCURRENCE OF THIS WORD.
```

Figure 1.1 The Output of the CRUDEN Concordance Program

text; interlinear translation; free translation; grammar code; etc.; or as in the case of my Navaho dictionary work, for identification number; stem; prefixes; nouns, postpositions, and examples; and English translations (see Fig. 1.2).

The two Northwestern programs are equipped for the use of logical operators (AND, OR (exclusive), and NOT) for special search procedures. This feature permits searchers for cooccurrence or noncooccurrence of 'words' or parts of words. [36] The investigator is not restricted to a simple concordance but can ask for a concordance of two or more items simultaneously occurring in the same sentence or block.

In the following section some Navaho examples and problems are discussed including the applicability of computer programs to their solution.

4.1 <u>Examples of computer applications</u>. Garvin calls the phonemic fusion of two morphs morpheme overlap. 'The difficulty of separating morphs increases with the amount of morpheme overlap present in the language'. [37] In Navaho the morphemes of the verb mode and the person markers tend to fuse, making analysis difficult.

The incorporated person markers represent an important feature of the verb: the person marked within the verb must be in agreement with the nominal subject and nominal object of the sentence. This dependency relationship between the nouns and verbs of the Navaho sentence is a clear-cut and natural place to begin analysis.

Two paradigms have been investigated in detail: the imperfective and the perfective. The complexities of the perfective are overwhelming and will not be dealt with further in this paper.

Note to Fig. 1.1 <u>The output of the CRUDEN concordance program.</u>
Note the discrepancy in the spelling of 'ADE7E72BIN and 'ADE7E7ZBIN (due to a change to CDC equipment at Northwestern ' is printed as ≠) as well as 'AGHA7A7 and 'AGHAA. Concordances are ideal for locating inconsistencies in the transcription (first example) or free variations (second example) of speech. (The Trader Navaho transcription follows the Indian Service alphabet of Young and Morgan (op. cit.) with the following changes: ts = C; ł = LH; ń = N6; ñ = N9; if V = vowel, then V7=high vowel, VV=long vowel, V7V7=long high vowel, and 8V7V7=nasalized long high vowel. This sample of Trader Navaho is spoken by Sam Drolet of Carson's trading post. Trader Navaho is a marginal language spoken by white traders, usually of pioneer stock, who are engaged in trading with the Navaho Indians of Arizona, New Mexico, and Utah. Because they are isolated from each other every trader has his own version of Trader Navaho. For details see my dissertation, 'A typological comparison of Four Trader Navaho Speakers' (Indiana University, 1963).

```
UU1U5YMA                                                            010 0001
'A7ADI                                                              013 0001
'A7ADI NIIT'A7AZHGO 'I7NDA 'ADIID8I7I7LH                            023 0001
THERE ( AT )                                                        014 0001
WE'LL EAT AS SOON AS WE ARRIVE THERE                                024 0001
UU106YMA                                                            010 0002
'AADI ,, 'AADI SIDA7                                                013 0002
THERE (AT ) ,, THERE HE SITS                                        014 0002
UU107YMA                                                            010 0003
'A7A7DO7O7 ,, SHASH YIYIISX8I7 'A7A7DO7O7 SHI7 NI7SE7LH'AH          013 0003
FROM THERE ON ,, AND THEN ,, HE KILLED THE BEAR AND THEN I S        014 0003
KINNED IT                                                           024 0003
00108YMA                                                            010 0004
'A7A7DO7O7 BIK'IJI' ,, 'A7A7DO7O7 BIK'IJI' NIKINI7YA7               013 0004
AFTER THAT ,, AFTER THAT I WENT HOME                                014 0004
00109YMA                                                            010 0005
'AAHASTI' ,, BAAHASTI'                                              013 0005
CARE , RESPECT ,, CARE OR RESPECT TOWARD IT                         014 0005
00110YMA                                                            010 0006
'AAHWIINI7T'8I7 BA7 HOOGHAN                                         013 0006
COURTHOUSE                                                          014 0006
00111YMA                                                            010 0007
'AA'8A'II                                                           013 0007
MAGPIE                                                              014 0007
00112YMA                                                            010 0008
'A7A7HSITA'                                                         013 0008
CERVICAL                                                            014 0008
00113YMA                                                            010M0009
'AA 'ADINIIH                                                        013M0009
BAA 'ADINIIH                                                        023M0009
VENEREAL DISEASE                                                    014M0009
HE HAS VENEREAL DISEASE                                             024M0009
00114YMA                                                            010 0010
'AA 'A7HA7LYA7ANII                                                  013 0010
BODYGUARD                                                           014 0010
00115YMA                                                            010 0011
'A7A7LH   F          'AAH   I              'A7A7LH   PRG            011 0011
'8A7   P             'A7A7H  R             'A7A7LH   O              021 0011
DIDEESH(1F) DIDI7I7(2F) YIDIDOO(3F) JIDIDOO(4F) DIDIIT(21F)         012 0011
DIDOOH(22F) DIDOOT(P2F) * DISH(1I) DI(2I) YIDI(3I) JIDI(4I)         022 0011
DIIT(21I) DOH(22I) DIT(P2I) * YISH(1PRG) YI7(2PRG) YOO(3PRG)        032 0011
JOO(4PRG) YIIT(21PRG) GHOH(22PRG) * DE7(1P) DI7I7NI(2P) YID         042 0011
EEZ(3P) JIDEEZ(4P) DEET(21P) DISOO(22P) DEEST(P2P) * N6DI7SH        052 0011
(1R) N6DI7(2R) NE7IDI(3R) NI7ZHDI7(4R) N6DIIT(21R) N6DO7H(22        062 0011
R) N6DI7T(P2R) * DO7SH(1O) DO7O7(2O) YIDO7(3O) JIDO7(4O) DOO        072 0011
T(21O) DOOH(223) DO7T(P2O) *                                        082 0011
BIZE7E7' BECOMES YIZE7E7' IN 3                                      013 0011
TO PLOT AGAINST HIM                                                 014 0011
00116YMA                                                            010 0012
'A7A7LH   F          'AAH   I              '8A7   P                 011 0012
'A7A7H  R             'A7A7LH  O                                    021 0012
HA DIDEESH(1F) DIDI7I7(2F) IDIDOO(3F) ZHDIDOO(4F) DIDIIT(21F        012 0012
) DIDOOH(22F) BIDI'DOOT(P2F) * HA DISH(1I) DI7(2I) IDI(3I) Z        022 0012
HDI(4I) DIIT(21I) DOH(22I) BI'DIT(P2I) * HA DI7I7(1P) DI7I7N        032 0012
I7(2P) IDI7I7(3P) ZHDI7I7(4P) DIIT(21P) DOO(22P) BI'DOOT(P2P        042 0012
) * HA N6DI7SH(1R) N6DI7(2R) NE7IDI(3R) NI7ZHDI(4R) N6DIIT(2        052 0012
1R) N6DO7H(22R) NA7BI'DIT(P2R) * HA DO7SH(1O) DO7O7(2O) IDO7        062 0012
(3O) ZHDO7(4O) DOOT(21O) DOOH(22O) BI'DO7T(P2O) *                  072 0012
SIN                                                                013 0012
```

Figure 1.2 The BIDAP Input from the Young and Morgan Navaho
Dictionary

Young and Morgan list five morphophonemic classes of imperfectives: one disjunct imperfective, with no derivational affixes,
and four conjunct imperfectives, which cooccur with various
derivational prefixes. [38]   It appeared on the basis of Young and
Morgan's work that it should be possible to write a relatively
simple search program for an electronic computer which would
recognize the five classes of Navaho imperfectives. In the process
the program should also recognize the subject and object markers
incorporated in the verb and assign the 'person' of the subject
and object to the verb construction. [39]

Such a program would have a dual function. (1) It could be
utilized to search the keypunched version of the Young and Morgan
Navaho Dictionary[40] in order to check the exhaustiveness of the
five postulated classes of imperfectives. Residual forms, i. e.
imperfectives which the program could not identify, could then
be analyzed and the program refined accordingly. Experience
gained in this operation could then be applied to the more complex
paradigms of Navaho. (2) As soon as a corpus of Navaho sentences becomes available for computer processing (again the
greatest bottleneck is, of course, keypunching), the program may
be applied to such data. The assignment of the 'person' of the
incorporated subject marker would be a small but important step
in the assignment of a grammar code to the constituents of Navaho
sentences.

Unfortunately neither one of these approaches is rewarding.
In the first instance the programming time is considerable and the
gain relatively small. The same objective can be achieved more
exhaustively by a concordance program. In order to retrieve this
kind of information about the structure of the prefixes of the Navaho
verb, the Northwestern BIDAP program was modified in the following manner (see Fig. 1. 2).

The BIDAP card format contains five classes of cards. Class
Ø (marked by Ø in column 75) contains the identification number of
the dictionary entry. The first three digits are the page number
in the dictionary, the next two digits are the number of the entry
on a given page, YMA designates the first dictionary of Young and
Morgan. The two digits in column 73 and 74 are used as continuation numbers for each class, i. e. from 1-99 continuation cards.

On the lines of class 1 (marked by 1 in column 75) and all
other classes only column 1-60 are used for data. In class 1,
the 60-character line is divided into fields of 20 characters.
These fields are used for the stems of the various paradigms.

Column 1-20 is reserved for the future stem, 21-40 for the imperfective, 41-60 for the perfective, etc., the stems are continued
on the next continuation card of class 1 if necessary. In addition
to its position, each stem is marked by a letter following two spaces
after the last symbol of the stem. The abbreviations are F: Future,
I: Imperfective, P: Perfective, R: Repetitive, O: Optative, PRG:
Progressive, U: Usitative, CI: Continuative Imperfective, and SP:
Si-Perfective.

The lines of class 2 contain all the prefix combinations of the
dictionary entries. The paradigms are separated by asterisks and
each prefix complex is marked by a symbol for paradigm (same as
above) and by 1, 2, 3, 4, for first, second, third, and fourth person[41] subject, 21 and 22 for first and second person dual, and P1
and P2 for the two 'passives'. In this class there are usually
several continuation cards.

Class 3 cards contain three types of information: (1) postpositions if they precede the verb, (2) illustrative sentences, and (3)
entries which are not verbs and consist of only one construction.

Class 4 cards contain all the English equivalents given in the
Young and Morgan dictionary as well as translation of the sample
sentences.

A 'key word from context' concordance can be compiled on any
one of the five line classes (see Fig. 1. 3). Instead of printing out
the full contexts the entries may be simply indexed according to
their location in the Young and Morgan dictionary. (Fig. 1. 4)

The alphabetic sorting performed on all the prefixes contained
in the dictionary provides all the information contained in the above
described search program. It provides considerably more detail
because the sorting is performed on all Navaho paradigms contained
in the Young and Morgan dictionary. All identical prefix forms
marked for person and paradigm are brought together. Since in
the case of the search program and the BIDAP program the entire
dictionary must be keypunched to assure exhaustive exploitation of
the source dictionary, nothing is to be gained by such a specially
programmed search routine.

The failure of the search program in its application to texts
is even more serious. Figure 1. 5 indicates what such a search
routine may look like in the form of a schematic search tree. The
search procedes from right to left through the Navaho word and
follows the stem recognition and enclitic-stripping routine (see
note 41). Although the diagram is restricted to the disjunct
imperfectives, it is a representative example of paradigmatic

```
       1R) N6DO7H(22R) NA7BI'DIT(P2R) * HA DO7SH(10) DO707(20) IDO7
       (30) ZHDO7(40) DOOT(210) DOOH(220) BI'DO7T(P20) *
       SIN
       TO START IT ( A SONG )
       CORRECTION TO BE INSERTED BY KB 00116YMA
DIDI7I7LH(2F                                          09511YMA
       HASH  F              HA7A7SH  I           HAZH  P
       HASH  R              HA7A7SH  O
       BI DIDEESH(1F) DIDI7I7LH(2F) DIDOOLH(3F) ZHDIDOOLH(4F) DIDII
       L(21F) DICOOLH(22F) DI'DOOL(P2F) * BI DISH(1I) DI7LH(2I) DIL
       H(3I) ZHDILH(4I) DIIL(21I) DOLH(22I) 'DIL(P2I) * BI DI7I7LH(
       1P) DI7I7NI7LH(2P) DI7I7LH(3P) ZHDI7I7LH(4P) DIIL(21P) DOOLH
       22P) 'DOOL(P2P) * BI NI7DI7SH(1R) NI7DI7LH(2R) NE7IDILH(3R)
       NI7ZHDILH(4R) NI7DIIL(21R) NI7DO7LH(22R) NI7DI7L(P2R) * BI D
       O7SH(10) DO707LH(20) DO7LH(OO) ZHDO7LH(40) DOOL(210) DOOLH(2
       20) 'DO7L(P20) *
       TO TAKE A BITE OF IT
DIDOOH(22                                            00115YMA
       'A7A7LH  F           'AAH  I              'A7A7LH  PRG
       '8A7  P              'A7A7H  R            'A7A7LH  O
       DIDEESH(1F) DIDI717(2F) YIDIDOO(3F) JIDIDOO(4F) DIDIIT(21F)
       DIDOOH(22F) DIDOOT(P2F) * DISH(1I) 'DI(2I) YIDI(3I) JIDI(4I)
       DIIT(21I) DIT(P2I) * DOH(22I) DIT(P2I) * YISH(1PRG) YI7(2PRG) YOO(3PRG)
       JOO(4PRG) YIIT(21PRG) GHOH(22PRG) * DE7(1P) DI7I7NI(2P) YID
       EEZ(3P) JIDEEZ(4P) DEET(21P) DISOO(22P) DEEST(P2P) * N6DI7SH
       (1R) N6DI7(2R) NE7IDI(3R) NI7ZHDI7(4R) N6DIIT(21R) N6DO7H(22
       R) N6DI7T(P2R) * DO7SH(10) DO707(20) YIDO7(30) JIDO7(40) DOO
       T(210) DOOH(223) DO7T(P20) *
       BIZE7E7' BECOMES YIZE7E7' IN 3
       TO PLOT AGAINST HIM
DIDOOH(22F                                           00116YMA
       'A7A7LH  F           'AAH  I              '8A7  P
       'A7A7H  R            'A7A7LH  O
       HA DIDEESH(1F) DIDI7I7(2F) IDIDOO(3F) ZHDIDOO(4F) DIDIIT(21F
       ) DIDOOH(22F) BIDI'DOOT(P2F) * HA DISH(1I) DI7(2I) IDI(3I) Z
       HDI(4I) DIIT(21I) DOH(22I) BI'DIT(P2I) * HA DI7I7(1P) DI7I7N
       I7(2P) IDI7I7(3P) ZHDI7I7(4P) DIIT(21P) DOO(22P) BI'DOOT(P2P
       ) * HA N6DI7SH(1R) N6DI7(2R) NE7IDI(3R) NI7ZHDI(4R) N6DIIT(2
       1R) N6DO7H(22R) NA7BI'DIT(P2R) * HA DO7SH(10) DO707(20) IDO7
       (30) ZHDO7(40) DOOT(210) DOOH(220) BI'DO7T(P20) *
       SIN
       TO START IT ( A SONG )
       CORRECTION TO BE INSERTED BY KB 00116YMA
DIDOOLH(22F                                          09511YMA
       HASH  F              HA7A7SH  I           HAZH  P
       HASH  R              HA7A7SH  O
       BI DIDEESH(1F) DIDI7I7LH(2F) DIDOOLH(3F) ZHDIDOOLH(4F) DIDII
       L(21F) DIDOOLH(22F) DI'DOOL(P2F) * BI DISH(1I) DI7LH(2I) DIL
       H(3I) ZHDILH(4I) DIIL(21I) DOLH(22I) 'DIL(P2I) * BI DI7I7LH(
       1P) DI7I7NI7LH(2P) DI7I7LH(3P) 7HDI7I7LH(4P) DIIL(21P) DOOLH
       22P) 'DOOL(P2P) * BI NI7DI7SH(1R) NI7DI7LH(2R) NE7IDILH(3R)
       NI7ZHDILH(4R) NI7DIIL(21R) NI7DO7LH(22R) NI7DI7L(P2R) * BI D
       O7SH(10) DO707LH(20) DO7LH(OO) ZHDO7LH(40) DOOL(210) DOOLH(2
       20) 'DO7L(P20) *
       TO TAKE A BITE OF IT
DIDOOLH(3F                                           09511YMA
       HASH  F              HA7A7SH  I           HAZH  P
       HASH  P              HA7A7SH  O
```

Figure 1.3 BIDAP Output: Concordance on Line of Class 2 —
Verb Prefixes

Figure 1. 4. Sample of a Partial Index of Navaho Verbal Prefixes
from the Young and Morgan dictionary by BIDAP

DIDI7I7LH(2F	09511YMA	DI7I7(1P	00116YMA
DIDOOH(22F	00115YMA	DI7I7LH(1P	09511YMA
DIDOOH(22F	00116YMA	DI7I7LH(2F	09415YMA
DIDOOLH(22F	09511YMA	DI717LH(2F	09502YMA
DIDOOLH(3F	09511YMA	DI7I7LH(2F	09510YMA
DIDOOT(P2F	00115YMA	DI7I7LH(3P	09511YMA
DIIL(21F	09415YMA	DI7I7NI(2P	00115YMA
DIIL(21F	09502YMA	DI7I7NI(2P	00116YMA
DIIL(21F	09510YMA	DI7I7NI7LH(2P	09511YMA
DIIL(21I	09511YMA	DI7LH(2I	09511YMA
DIIL(21P	09511YMA	DOH(22I	00115YMA
DIIT(21I	00116YMA	DOH(22I	00116YMA
DIIT(21P	00116YMA	DOLH(22I	09511YMA
DILH(3I	09511YMA	DOO(22P	00116YMA
DISH(1I	00115YMA	DOOH(220	00116YMA
DISH(1I	00116YMA	DOOH(220	00115YMA
DISH(1I	09511YMA	DOOL(2 10	09511YMA
DISOO(22P	00115YMA	DOOLH(22F	09415YMA
DIT(P2I	00115YMA	DOOLH(22F	09502YMA
DI7(2I	00116YMA	DOOLH(22F	09510YMA

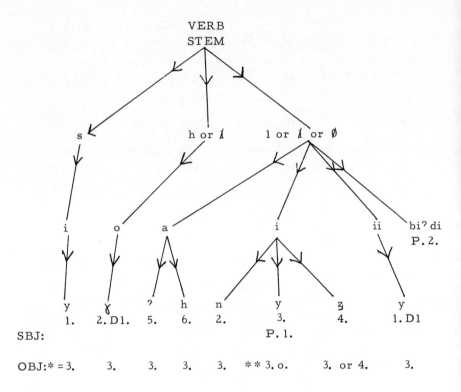

SBJ:

OBJ:* = 3.   3.   3.   3.   3.   ** 3. o.   3. or 4.   3.

* Object if verb stem is transitive.
** Obviative.

Figure 1.5 A Schematic Search Tree of the Navaho Disjunct
Imperfective

information given in the source dictionary. The Young and Morgan
Navaho dictionary is not a dictionary of lexical items in the usual
sense of the word. It is apparent (see sample page of the dictionary,
Fig. 1.2) that it is a paradigmatic dictionary. Instead of giving
only the 'naming units'[42] each entry of a verb contains a partial
paradigm. If the verb is intransitive the entry is usually restricted
to the 1, 2, 3, 4, person singular and the 1, and 2, person dual.
If the entries are transitive, the third or obviative form of the
object is implicit, while the subject person markers are the same
as in the intransitive. Whenever possible, passive forms are
added.

   This paradigmatic limitation of the entries makes the proposed
search program unsuitable for texts. The object may assume any
number of 'persons' which are not contained in the dictionary. The
extension of the search to objects marked for other than third person is not selfevident nor automatic and must be ascertained by
work with an informant. The matrix of Fig. 1.6, presumably
exhaustive (except for the reciprocal and reflective incorporated
pronominal forms), represents the entire set of marked subjects
and objects in the disjunct imperfective. The situation is complicated by the fact that verb stems place selectional restrictions on
the noun classes of subject or object. In most cases only part of
the matrix (Fig. 1.6) is utilized.

   One verb stem selection restriction not noted in the Navaho
literature is the animate-inanimate distinction: e.g. yi-λóóh 'third
person animate is cold'[43] versus yi-tin 'third person inanimate is
cold'. First, second, and fourth person forms given by Young
and Morgan are ungrammatical.[44] The pairing of animate vs. inanimate stems is a prevalent feature of the Navaho stem vocabulary.

   The problem of selection restrictions between the nominals of
the subject and object of the sentence and the verb stem raises the
question of the dependencies and selection restriction holding between the verb stem, and the subject and object nominals of the
sentence and the subject and object markers incorporated in the
verb construction. The following eleven sentences illustrate the
scope of the problems.

Eleven Related Navaho Sentences

(i)   ʔasƶání   diné   yit'ood

      woman   man   she wiped him (with a rag)

(ii)   ʔasẓání   diné   žit'ood

        woman   man   she wipes him (with a rag)
        (one or both human beings)

(iii)   diné   ʔasẓání   hat'ood

        man   woman   she wipes a human being
        (with a rag)

(iv)   diné   ʔasẓání   bit'ood

        man   woman   she wipes an animate being
        (with a rag)

(v)   ʔasẓání   diné   hožit'ood

(vi)   diné   ʔasẓání   hožit'ood

        woman   man
                                      she wipes him or he wipes her
        man   woman
        (with a rag — both human beings)

(vii)   diné   biʔdit'ood

(viii) diné   hoʔdit'ood

        man   is wiped (with a rag — by 'indefinite')
        (object of first sentence must be animate, of second
        sentence must be human)

(ix)   ʔasẓání   ʔat'ood

        woman   she wipes 'indefinite' (with rag)

(x)   ʔasẓání   ʔažit'ood

        woman   she wipes 'indefinite' (with rag)
        (subject must be human being)

(xi)   ʔat'ood

        (there is) wiping (of 'indefinite' by 'indefinite' with a rag.)

        (someone definite) is wiping (something indefinite) (with a
        rag)

OBJECT

	1.	2.	3.	4.	5.	6.	1.D1	2.D1.
1.	*	niš	yiš	haš	ʔaš	haš	-	nihiš
2.	ší	*	ni	hó	ʔí	hó	nihí	-
3.	ši	ni	yi / bi	ha	ʔa	ha	nihi	nihi
4.	šiži	niži	ži	hoži	ʔaži	hoži	nihiži	nihiži
5.	šiʔdi	niʔdi	biʔdi	hoʔdi	ʔa	-	nihiʔdi	nihiʔdi
6.	-	-	-	-	-	ha	-	-
1.D1.	-	niid	yiid	hʷiid	ʔiid	-	*	nihiid
2.D1.	soh	-	oh	hoh	ʔoh	-	nihoh	*

SUBJECT

* Reciprocal and reflexive forms are excluded.

Legend: 1. & 2. second and first person ; 3. noncommittal third
person ; 4. human third person marker ; 5. 'indefinite' third
person marker ; 6. 'time — place' marker ; 1. D1. & 2. D1.
first and second person of the dual. Narrow vertical box contains
person markers usually given by Young and Morgan.

Figure 1. 6.   The Full set of Subject and Object Person Markers of
the Navaho Disjunct Imperfective

The verb stem t'ood '(to) wipe (with a rag)' requires a human subject, but is noncommittal and may apply to any object nominal. The 'any' to be interpreted as 'at present possible finer subcategorization is not known'.

These eleven sentences are not synonymous paraphrases of each other since they differ in their lexical makeup. However, they have the same underlying structure. The rules for the generation of these eleven sentences and a great many like them, are as follows:

$$(1) \quad S \longrightarrow \quad \begin{array}{c} NP\,(1) \\ \left[\begin{array}{c} +\text{emphasis} \\ -\text{emphasis} \end{array}\right] \end{array} \quad + \quad \begin{array}{c} NP\,(2) \\ \left[\begin{array}{c} +\text{emphasis} \\ -\text{emphasis} \end{array}\right] \end{array} \quad + \quad VERBAL$$

This rule gives a three-way division of the Navaho sentence. It is needed to account for the later transformational permutation of the two-noun phrases. The two-noun phrases are numbered. The numbering may be interpreted as 1 = subject and 2 = object; however, the main purpose for the numbers is to simplify the statement of certain later environmental restrictions. A component of emphasis (+) or no emphasis (-) must be attached to every noun phrase. This component will later determine the order of the noun phrases in the sentence, as well as the selection of the incorporated person markers within the verb. Any noun phrase with the components of emphasis and humanity (see rule 7) refers to a person psychologically close to the speaker. Ken Begishe explains this feature as: 'if the person is well known'.

$$(2) \qquad VERBAL \quad \longrightarrow \quad P\,(2) \quad + \quad P\,(1) \quad + \quad VERB$$

The VERBAL consists of the two incorporated person markers. They are numbered for a more simple later environmental statement. Again they mark the incorporated subject person marker (1) and the object person marker (2). The numbering corresponds to the numbering of the two-noun phrases.

$$(3) \qquad VERB \quad \longrightarrow \quad MOD \quad + \quad CLASS \quad + \quad STEM$$

The verb proper consists of a modal MOD which is marked in this class of disjunct imperfective verbs by a morpheme yi (the so-called yi-imperfective). (Other classes are considerably more complex.) The classifier of t'ood is zero ($\emptyset$). With other stems

in this class it may be '1' or 'Ɬ'. The function of the classifiers
is not too well understood. This class has a membership of
about twenty stems.

(4)   NP (∝)   ⟶   N   (∝ = 1 or 2)
        ⎡+emphasis⎤   ⎡+emphasis⎤
        ⎣-emphasis⎦   ⎣-emphasis⎦

                                    . . .
                                  ⎡+emphasis⎤
                                  ⎣-emphasis⎦

One type of noun phrase is a noun. There are other possible noun
phrases symbolized here by the three dots '...'. Whatever constituent structure the noun phrase may have, the component of emphasis
is carried across the rewrite rule and is attached to the componential
structure of the right side of the rule. The exact nature of this rule
is not important because complex noun phrases consisting of more
than a noun are not considered.

The next three rules expand the componential structure of the
Navaho nouns:

(5)   N   ⟶   ⎡+definite⎤
        ⎡+emphasis⎤   ⎣-definite⎦   Not if: N
        ⎣-emphasis⎦   ⎣-emphasis⎦

(6)   N   ⟶   ⎡+animate⎤
        ⎣+definite⎦   ⎣-animate⎦   Not if: N
                                                                  ⎣+emphasis⎦

(7)   N   ⟶   ⎡+human⎤
        ⎣+animate⎦   ⎣-human⎦

Nouns are divided into definite and indefinite nouns. All indefinite
nouns must be emphasized. The definite nouns are divided into
animate and inanimate nouns, but there is no way to emphasize inanimate nouns. All animate nouns may be human or nonhuman
nouns.

Two transformations are necessary to account for this set of
sentences:

$$(8) \quad T\,(OBL): \quad P\,(\alpha) \quad \longrightarrow \quad \frac{NP\,(\alpha)}{P\,(\alpha)} \quad if: \quad [Q] \quad and \; \alpha = \alpha$$
$$[Q]$$

So far only nouns (or noun phrases) have components. This transformation attaches a duplicate of the components of the nouns to
the corresponding incorporated person markers P. The environmental statement in this rule is simplified if the noun phrases are
numbered. (See rule (1)).

$$(9) \quad T\,(OBL) \quad \# \; X + \; NP\,(1) \qquad + \, Y \; \longrightarrow \; \# \; NP(1) \qquad + \, X + \, Y$$

where the NP brackets contain
$$\begin{bmatrix} +\text{emphasis} \\ R \end{bmatrix}$$

If there is a noun phrase in noninitial position in the sentence which
contains any set of components R <u>and</u> a component of emphasis,
then it must obligatorily assume the initial position in the sentence.
    The remaining rules are lexical:

$$(10) \quad P\,(\alpha) \quad \longrightarrow \quad ?\,a \quad if \quad \alpha = 1: \quad \begin{array}{c} P\,(2) \\ \end{array} \quad + \; \underline{\quad\quad}$$

with left side $\begin{bmatrix} +\text{emphasis} \\ -\text{definite} \end{bmatrix}$ and right side $P\,(2)\begin{bmatrix} +\text{emphasis} \end{bmatrix}$

The indefinite incorporated person marker P (2) requires the
emphasis of the object of the sentence. The morpheme ? a can
occur as P (1) only if it is preceded by an emphasized P (2). This
restricts the occurrence of this ? a to the following sequence:
? a + ? a, bi + ? a, and ha + ? a (see rule (14) and (15)). Sentence
(ix) is hence unambiguous and can signify only 'the woman she
wipes "indefinite" (with a rag) '. A sentence

(xii) *   čidí   ? at'ood

has no interpretation. čidí 'car' cannot be the subject of the
stem t'ood which requires a human actor; it cannot be its object
because all inanimate nouns are nonemphasizable.
    The selection restrictions governing the indefinite cannot be
ascertained by sentences of the form:

(xiii)(some indefinite   (some other inde-   ? at'ood
        nominal)   finite nominal)

Such sentences cannot be elicited. There are no nouns or pronouns
which can occupy the position of object or subject in an indefinite

sentence. This can be demonstrated by the following sentences.

(xiv)   haišį́į́   ?at'ood

   'someone definite wiped (with a rag) the "indefinite" '

(xv)   diné   ła?   ła?   náádiné   yit'ood   [never   ?at'ood]

   'some man wiped (with a rag) some other man'

(xvi)   diné   ła?   ła?   náádiné   žit'ood   [never   ?at'ood]

   'some man wiped (with a rag) some other man'

The indefinite nouns are place-holders. Their existence can only be inferred indirectly. They are deleted after the feature of indefiniteness is transferred to the appropriate P (α) by transformation (8).

(11)   P (1)
       $\begin{bmatrix} +\text{emphasis} \\ +\text{human} \end{bmatrix}$ $\longrightarrow$ ži

(12)   P (1)
       $\begin{bmatrix} -\text{emphasis} \end{bmatrix}$ $\longrightarrow$ $\emptyset$

(13)   P (1)
       $\begin{bmatrix} +\text{emphasis} \\ -\text{human} \end{bmatrix}$ $\longrightarrow$ $\emptyset$ Not if: P (2) $+$ _____
                                                              $\begin{bmatrix} +\text{emphasis} \end{bmatrix}$

An emphasized psychologically close human person marker P (1) is to be replaced by ži. The nonemphasized person marker P (1) is replaced by a zero morpheme. All emphasized nonhuman person markers P (1) may be replaced by a zero morpheme, but can never occur in the environment following an emphasized P (2). Only the occurrence of two emphasized human person markers (1) and (2) permits this kind of ambiguity as reflected by sentences (v) and (vi) (see next rule (14)).

(14)   P (2) $\longrightarrow$ ha   if: _____ $+$ P (1)
       $\begin{bmatrix} +\text{emphasis} \\ +\text{human} \end{bmatrix}$ $\begin{bmatrix} +\text{human} \end{bmatrix}$

The selection of ha requires that the subject of the sentence be human, i.e. the subject marker may be ∅ (rule (12)) if it is not emphasized, or ž̦i if it is emphasized. In the latter case the sentence is ambiguous because according to transformation (10) either one of the two NP may be interpreted as either subject or object of sentences (v) and (vi).

(15) P (2)   ⟶   bi   Not if: ____ + P (1)
      ⎡+emphasis⎤   ⎡+emphasis⎤
      ⎣+animate ⎦   ⎣+human   ⎦

Any human or animate object P (2) may be denoted by bi. It cannot occur in the environment preceding the emphasized, close human subject marker ž̦i.

(16) P (2)   ⟶   yi
      ⎡-emphasis⎤

In all cases where the object is not emphasized the morpheme is yi.

Once the noun phrases are marked by the incorporated person markers they may be optionally deleted. All noun phrases with the component of indefiniteness must be deleted obligatorily. Sample derivations of sentences (ii), (iii), (v), (vi), (ix), and (xi) are given in the diagrams on the following pages.

According to the proposed solution, sentence

(xvii)   yit'ood

          'someone definite wipes someone definite
          (with a rag)'.

is two-way ambiguous, because of the two sources of zero morphemes (rules (12) and (13)). This ambiguity is caused by the asymmetry of bi which has no P (1) analog. There are two possible solutions:

A.   A transformational rule which eliminates the component combination of rule (13), i.e. which changes

          ⎡+emphasis⎤   to   ⎡-emphasis⎤
          ⎣-human   ⎦   ⎣-human   ⎦

B.   There is some reluctance on the part of Ken Begishe to extend P (2) bi to animals (animate objects). If bi is restricted

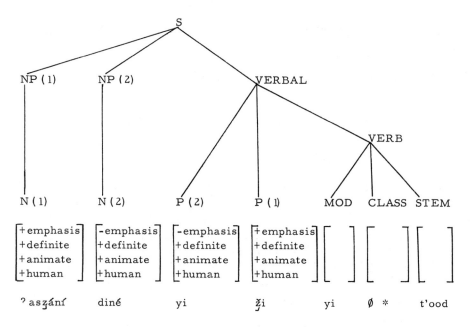

which after the application of the phonological rule

yi + ž̦i + yi ⟶ ž̦i   gives :

(ii)   ʔasz̦ání diné ž̦it'ood

* In this and the following phrase markers rules for the deletion of the zero morphemes are assumed but not explicitly stated.

Sentence (ii)

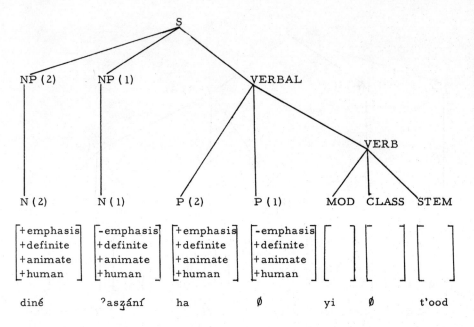

which after the application of the phonological rule

ha + yi ⟶ ha   gives :

    (iii)   diné   ʔasʒání   hatʼood

NP(2) was moved into the initial position by transformation (9)

Sentence (iii)

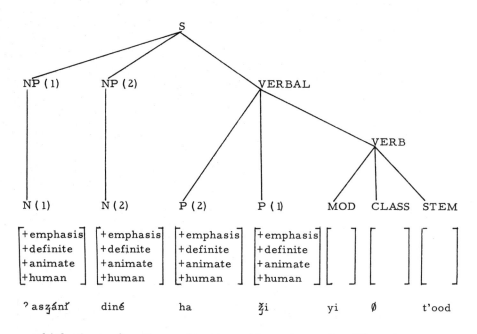

which gives after the application of transformation (9) and the phonological rule ha + ǯi + yi ⟶ hoǯi   two sentences:

(v)   ʔasẓání   diné   hoǯit'ood

(vi)   diné   ʔasẓání   hoǯit'ood

Sentences (v) and (vi)

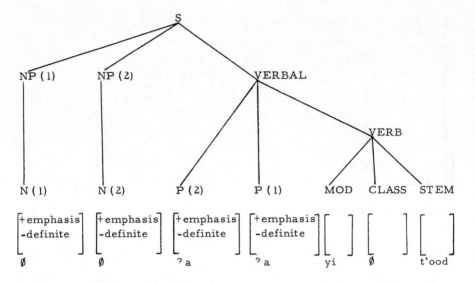

which gives after the application of the phonological rule

ʔa + ʔa + yi ⟶   ʔa   :

(xi)   ʔat'ood

with the first interpretation of this sentence

Sentence (xi)

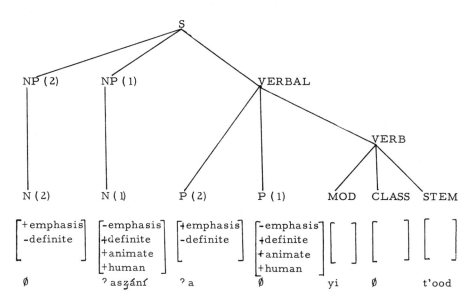

which gives after the application of the phonological rule
ʔa + yi ⟶   ʔa   :

(ix)   ʔ asǯání   ʔ at'ood

and by a rule permitting the optional deletion of the subject

(xi)   ʔ at'ood

with the second interpretation of this sentence (see p. 25).

Sentences (ix), (xi)

to human beings, a component of closeness has to be introduced
to distinguish bi from ha. However, if an environmental restriction is added to rule (7) to the effect that the component of non-
humanity can occur only with nonemphasis, the ambiguity of
sentence (xvii) is eliminated.

The ambiguity of this sentence has no overt effect and is not
serious, except perhaps for esthetic considerations. Because of the
potential extension of bi to animals the present solution is retained.
It remains to be seen if and how the feature of emphasis affects
transformations which will be added in a more complete solution of
Navaho.

The introduction of the 'place-holder' indefinite nouns is independently motivated by the possessive construction which is, in the
form here given, already transformationally derived.

Apparent neologisms of Navaho such as ši? abe? 'my indefinite
possessor's milk' for store bought milk (versus šibe? 'my milk
(from my own breast)') and ši? ažéí 'my indefinite possessor's heart
= my (car) battery)' (versus šižéí 'my own heart'), become easily
explainable:

(xviii)   ši   POSS-N   POSS-be?
                       [-definite]

becomes transformationally (possibly in two steps)

(xix)   ši   ši-N   ? a-be?
                       [-definite]

and, after the necessary deletions,

(xx)   ši? abe?

This solution is supported by constructions with definite
nouns:

(xxi)   šibέέgašii   bibe?

               'my cow   its-milk'

and (xxii) šimá   bibέέgašii   bibe?

               'my mother her cow   its milk
               (my mother's cow's milk)'

This extended example is intended to illustrate two points: first, that selection restrictions in Navaho are complicated; second, to demonstrate that postulation of the abstract underlying grammatical structure of sentences is hardly aided directly by the use of computers.

5.0 CONCLUSIONS

The preceding discussion and the examples indicate that the computers currently in use are not ideally suited for linguistics. Since the texts must be viewed as ancillary to work with informants, the problem of constant updating of the text with newly elicited materials prevails.

The anthropological linguist, accustomed to small operations, is limited not only by the present cumbersome technique of keypunching elicited material on IBM cards, but by the expense of this operation. The fact that the text is mere nonsense syllables to the English-speaking keypuncher, impairing his speed and accuracy, is another drawback. The anthropological linguist is not alone in his difficulties of reading linguistic data into the computer. The technology has not yet caught up with the problem.

The ultimate computers for linguistic analysis have not been built. One could easily imagine a machine which accepts spoken or at least written sentences in its memory banks without the tedious recourse to punched cards. Equally imaginable is a system where a native speaker-linguist or linguist-native speaker team would sit at the console of the computer with a large corpus of texts in its memory, carrying on a conversation with the machine — a conversation in the sense that the computer would, in short order, not only provide requested information but immediately store and make available new materials from the lips of the informant, and also try out proposed generative formulas.

My goal in this paper was to explore the utility of easily available existing programs for linguistic analysis. I focused particulary on the problems faced by the anthropological linguist. The utility of the programs is information retrieval in one way or another rather than what has been called automatic linguistic analysis.[45]

NOTES

1. H. Hoijer, IJAL 11. 193-203 (1945)

2. R. E. Longacre, Grammar Discovery Procedures 10 (The Hague, 1964). Although the author agrees with the spirit of this quote, it is more to the point if paraphrased as 'generative grammarians are by no means uninterested in linguistic analysis'. This paper hopes to demonstrate that this is so.

3. Longacre, 11.

4. As this applies to phonology, see for example, C. F. Voegelin and Florence M. Voegelin, 'Guide to the Transcribing of Unwritten Languages in Field Work', AL 1:6. 1-28 (1959).

5. This is the interpretation given to R. B. Lees' 'shocking' statement that 'all languages are dialects of English'.

6. J. J. Katz and P. M. Postal, An Integrated Theory of Linguistic Description 157 (Cambridge, Mass. , 1964).

7. This observation is from an unpublished paper by K. L. Hale, 'On the Use of Informants in Field Work' 3 (1964).

8. C. F. Voegelin and Florence M. Voegelin, Hopi Domains 3 (1957).

9. K. L. Hale, 1.

10. Katz and Postal.

11. P. L. Garvin, On Linguistic Method 66 (The Hague, 1964). Garvin's 'ordered set' is not to be construed in the set-theoretical sense of the word.

12. It is interesting to note that such postediting of informant responses is in general unconscious, on the part of the informant as well as the investigator. That this is so can easily be ascertained by comparing informant responses with recorded spontaneous conversations or occasionally with spontaneous texts which do not require formal delivery in the culture whose language is under study. That this observation was missed in the past is probably due to the fact that tape recorders are relatively recent innovations of linguistic field technique. The author has noted on several occasions, for example, the bewildered amusement of Navahos when selected texts from E. Sapir and H. Hoijer, Navaho texts (LSA, 1942) were

read to them. They claim that no Navaho speaks in such short, choppy sentences. The brevity of the sentences was most certainly due to the limitations of the unaided memory span of the transcribers. Among American Indian languages there are few examples of recorded live conversations.

13. P. L. Garvin, 64.

14. A. Koutsoudas, IJAL 29. 160-170 (1963), see also R. B. Lees, Lg. 33.375 - 408 (1957) and J. J. Katz, Lg. 40. 124-37 (1964).

15. R. B. Lees, Lg. 36. 210 (1960).

16. The fact that some of these rules are nonarrow rules will for the moment be disregarded.

17. Such subsets may also be infinite.

18. R. W. Young and W. Morgan, The Navaho Language 77 (U.S. Indian Service, 1943).

19. E.g., J. J. Katz and J. Fodor, Lg. 39. esp. 207-10.

20. N. Chomsky and G. M. Miller, 'Finitary Models of Language Users', Handbook of Mathematical Psychology esp. 2. 443-49 (New York, 1963).

21. N. Chomsky 'Topics in the Theory of Generative Grammar' (1964, to appear).

22. Paul M. Postal, 'Underlying and Superficial Linguistic Structure', Harvard Educational Review 34. 246-66 (1964).

23. For a discussion of this point in semantic eliciting see Oswald Werner, 'Semantics of Navajo Medical Terms: I', IJAL 31. 1-16 (1965).

24. It is for this reason that the designation of participant-consultant or participant-informant is more appropriate. Oswald Werner, 8-9.

25. N. Chomsky, 'Current issues in Linguistics', The Structure of Language esp. 66-76 (Englewood Cliffs, N.J., 1964).

26. C. F. and Florence M. Voegelin, Hopi Domains (1957).

27. Voegelin and Voegelin, Hopi Domains 3.

28. Voegelins, ibid.

29. When informants are not confronted by examples and if the linguist fails to explain the tasks with sufficient clarity, the informant will sometimes say 'You can't do that in my language'. Examples from a text may alleviate this danger. Needless to say, there are times when the informant is right and one 'can't say it that way' in his language.

30. Ken Hale, 3 (1964).

31. Garvin, 8 (1964).

32. The author is indebted to Bruce Dikson for these examples.

33. See for example E. A. Feigenbaum and J. Friedman, Computers and Thought (New York, 1963).

34. I cannot agree with Garvin that, 'data processing equipment allows the processing of very large bodies of texts using the same program, with the program assuming the role of the linguistic analyst'. Garvin, 80 (1964) emphasis added. If we accept the fact that it takes a competent native speaker to perform the operations which lead to the postulation of the structure of a language, then a program which can allegedly replace an analyst would need to be superior to the capabilities of human beings in the following sense: It is implicitly assumed that such a program could perform linguistic analysis without the aid of the speaker's knowledge of his native language. That is, it is claimed that the computer program is capable of performing complicated judgments comparable to the native speaker's without mastery of the language under investigation.

35. K. Hale, 9.

36. This feature is at present restricted to 'prefixes' or 'words' minus suffixes, i. e. a search for Navaho stems is at present not possible.

37. Paul Garvin, 25.

38. Young and Morgan, 77-81.

39. In the following discussion it is assumed that two problems of Navaho automatic grammatical analysis have been solved: (1) Every Navaho verb may take from one to three enclitics following the last morpheme of the verb, which is the stem. The morpheme overlap between stem and enclitics is relatively simple. A sufficiently large number of enclitics are known (possibly all) so that an 'enclitic-stripping' program seems to present little difficulty; (2) Similarly, a 'stem-recognition' routine is also required. Since

all stems are of the form CVC or CV (V representing one or two
vowel segments), and since the morpheme overlap between the
stem and the prefix immediately preceding it is relatively simple,
such a stem-recognition routine should be easy to construct.

40.   The Young and Morgan dictionary is being keypunched at the
present time by Kenneth Begishe under a grant awarded to me by the
American Philosophical Society.

41.   The Navaho fourth person is a special third person restricted
to human beings (see p. 30).

42.   Madeleine Mathiot, 'A Procedure for Investigating Language
and Culture Relations' 4 (ms. 1963).

43.   Apparently deleted from the Young and Morgan dictionary by
a printer's error on page 55.

44.   Young and Morgan, 209, and Kenneth Begishe, personal
communication.

45.   Validation of the results of analysis is another very important
application.   That is, computer generation of sentences (for example
by a COMIT program) or of phonological units.   COMIT is a compiler program designed for programming generative grammars.
For a brief introduction to COMIT see V.H. Yngve, 'The COMIT
system for Mechanical Translation', Information Processing 183-87
(Paris, 1960) and the two COMIT manuals (Cambridge, Mass.,
1963).

Chapter 2

A Syntactic Concordance for Middle High German

W. C. Crossgrove

1. INTRODUCTION

This paper discusses a method of preediting Middle High German texts as a first step in preparing a concordance which can provide statistics about Middle High German syntactic patterns. The concordance will consist of a computer input which contains text plus a coded grammatical analysis, but which requires reasonably little time spent by scholars in preparation of the input. The paper begins with some discussion of the need for a syntactic concordance as an aid to research in historical linguistics. The chief variables which control the selection of a suitable preediting procedure are discussed in terms of a specific language, Middle High German. A tentative coding system for Middle High German is presented. Finally, two programs are flowcharted to demonstrate how the syntactic concordance might be used to answer specific questions. While much of the discussion deals with Middle High German, it is assumed that similar considerations apply to all languages which are extant only in written texts.

2.0 DESCRIPTION OF DEAD LANGUAGES

Most work in computational linguistics has derived either directly or indirectly from the widespread interest in machine translation, which is a practical goal only in the case of those languages where a large and growing body of material is available for translation. There is, however, a large class of languages which consist of written texts but which have no living native speakers. Historical linguists are attempting to provide adequate descriptions of some of these languages. This paper explores at least one way in which computational linguistics can aid the production of adequate descriptions of these so-called dead languages by providing distributional data for syntactic patterns.

2. 1 Limited goals. Automatic analysis programs which start
with unedited corpora are not likely to be practical at the present
stage of research. Historical linguists who study a particular 'dead'
language are generally a small group by comparison with the number of linguists working on a living language such as Modern
English or Russian. Furthermore, there is no particular reason
why a government agency or private foundation should want to en-
courage an increase in the number of researchers. Thus if computation is to play a role in historical linguistics, these limitations
must be taken into account and goals which are somewhat short of
completely automatic analysis of natural language adopted.

2. 2 Written texts. A second point, which is obvious but nevertheless often overlooked, is that methods for the description of
languages preserved only in written texts are necessarily somewhat different from methods used in describing languages with living
native speakers. Native-speaker intuition is not available to historical linguists. On the other hand, the fact that a language exists
only as a set of written texts is an invitation for computational linguistics, especially since one of the most obvious limitations of
computational linguistics is that its application is as yet restricted
mainly to the written language. Exclusive reliance on the written
language becomes a necessity rather than an inadequacy when
working with languages which are attested only in written form.

2. 3 Available information. Thirdly, while one might deplore
the fact that much of the work in historical linguistics is out of
date or in some sense methodologically inadequate, it is also true
that a large body of knowledge has been accumulated. Any researcher
who does not attempt to include a maximum amount of the available
knowledge in any proposal for further research runs the risk of
rediscovering the already known or overlooking previously gained
insights. Available information should be put to use in furnishing
better descriptions than those currently provided.

2. 4 Syntactic research. Finally we are faced with the curious
situation that work in historical linguistics has been concentrated
more on lexicography and phonology than on syntax. Yet it is
obvious that in a language which is preserved only in written form
syntax is intrinsically more accessible to study than sound systems
or meaning. We have no direct access to the way in which the
native speakers pronounced their language nor do we know exactly

what they 'meant' when they used it. On the other hand we do have
a more or less exact record of how they manipulated the signs of
their language, or at least some portion of it. One practical limitation on progress in syntactic studies has been the amount of data
which must be grasped and worked through by the researcher when
no native speaker is available to answer specific questions. Large-
scale data manipulation is one of the most obvious abilities of the
digital computer, so it is not surprising that computational linguistics has a potential application in simplifying the problems
which are encountered by historical linguists in conducting syntactic
research.

3.0 MIDDLE HIGH GERMAN

Middle High German is an example of a language which has
been intensively studied using methods which are now regarded as
outdated.[1] A large body of knowledge has been accumulated in
more than a century and a half of research. At the lowest level
of understanding there is general agreement about certain grammatical categories. For example, in the sentence dâ lâgen zwei
kreftigiu her (Parzival 16.28) 'two powerful armies were camped
there', dâ is an adverb, lâgen is a verb in the past tense, her is
a neuter plural noun in the nominative case and is the subject of
the sentence, and zwei and kreftigiu modify her.
There may be widespread disagreement on the appropriateness
of some of the terminology which is used in the traditional approach
to Middle High German grammar, and there may even be doubts
about the descriptive validity of many of the categories. Certainly
rigorous criterial tests will fail in many instances. At the same
time it is also true that if a small set of traditional categories is
furnished and scholars are asked to use them in classifying forms
which occur in a text, there will be general agreement, as in the
example above. This information is too valuable to be wasted and
offers the basis for preediting texts in order to construct an input for a digital computer. The input will consist of the text plus
a code which will include information about grammatical categories
and dependency relationships within the sentence. The grammatical analysis which will be built into the input will be a first approximation toward a more complete description of the grammar of the
language. The grammatical information can be used to acquire
statistics about Middle High German syntactic patterns as an aid
in furnishing better descriptions of Middle High German.

Nearly every university in the United States that offers a Ph.D. degree in German has a specialist in Middle High German, but the majority of these scholars are interested primarily in Middle High German literature; they study and teach the language in preparation for literary research. In German-speaking areas of the world, Middle High German literature is regarded as an important part of the cultural tradition, and even students in the Gymnasium receive some exposure to it. University students who specialize in German ordinarily take several courses in Middle High German and acquire a basic understanding of the language. One can estimate that the number of students who intensively study Middle High German is substantially larger than a thousand annually. Linguistic research, however, is carried on by only a handful of scholars.

One typical Middle High German 'beginner's' grammar contains the following divisions: 'Lautlehre', pp. 7-56; 'Flexionslehre', 57-119; 'Zur Satzlehre', 120-126.[2] More thorough grammars contain long sections on syntax (in Paul-Mitzka 'Syntax' is the longest section in the grammar), but the information is of little help to anyone who wishes to know which syntactic patterns are productive, which are nonproductive but in widespread use in certain constructions, and which are isolated occurrences. It is clear that even for pedagogical purposes statistical information about patterns which occur would be most helpful. Such information can also contribute to the study of style, which is of interest to the literary scholar as well as the linguist.

4.0 LIMITATIONS OF THE CODING SYSTEM

In order for preediting to be feasible for a large corpus, it is obvious that the amount of time required to analyze the sentences of the corpus must be kept to a minimum. Therefore, while it is desirable to include as much information as possible, it is also necessary to keep the categories broad enough to reduce decision-making to a minimum. For this reason, rigor will often have to be sacrificed for speed, and some information will have to be arbitrarily excluded as potentially less interesting than other. Thus, gender is not marked in the system of coding proposed in this paper, on the grounds that little additional information is likely to be derived from further analysis based on gender. Categories need to be specified as carefully as possible, but there will be cases where classification will have to be done with recourse to 'general agreement among students of Middle High German' or a

similar appeal to tradition or authority. If general agreement
proves to be illusory, then the analysis will have to be changed.
The method of classification which is offered here represents a
first step and will need modification before it can be actually
employed. In order to be a useful procedure, the system of analysis will have to be easy to teach to scholars and students who are
familiar with Middle High German for it is clear that many thousands of lines of Middle High German will have to be analyzed before meaningful results are obtained. Attempts to teach the coding
system will presumably indicate what kind of changes is necessary
to make the code usable.

    4. 1 <u>Coding system.</u> The preedited computer input could be
stored on magnetic tape or a similar form of permanent storage,
which will contain the text and grammatical information. Each
word of the text will be entered, followed by a number of slots
which will be filled as described in Table 2. 2. The information
which is built into the input tape can be clarified by a phrase-
structure grammar of the type described in Table 2. 1. Such a
phrase-structure grammar does not attempt to describe the word
order of Middle High German sentences, but information about
word order is already present in the input tape since the text is
entered from left to right in the order in which it occurs in texts.
    The main reason for including Table 2. 1 in its present form
is to make the code used in Table 2. 2 more readily comprehensible.
The rules given in Table 2. 1 are meant to describe the dependency
relationships which are indicated in the coding system.
    The rules of Table 2. 1 cannot be freely used to generate Middle
High German strings because the rules as they now stand would
permit far too many nonoccurring sequences. Restrictions on application of the rules can be determined by what actually occurs. In
fact, one of the potential uses of the input tape might be to determine what cooccurrence restrictions will need to be written into
the rules in order to convert them into a real generative grammar
of Middle High German. The first approximation to a grammar
which is provided here might conceivably be used as the basis for
a discovery procedure for refining the grammar.

    4. 2 <u>Defining word classes.</u> It is important to note that the
traditional system of analysis which is used as the basis for the
coding system contains word classes which are defined in rather
different ways. The categories <u>noun</u>, <u>adjective</u>, <u>verb</u>, <u>pronoun</u>,

and <u>determiner</u> (see Table 2.2, Column 12) can be defined largely
by inflectional criteria. At the present stage of research these
inflectionally determined categories can be regarded as rather
clearly defined. There are residual problems and borderline cases,
but for the most part one can furnish defining criteria. The cate-
gories <u>adverb</u>, <u>conjunction</u>, <u>sentence</u>-word, and <u>preposition</u> contain forms which are not subject to inflection. The definitions of
the noninflected categories depend entirely on syntactic information.
Thus a given form might be classified as a conjunction or an adverb
depending on whether or not it was the first item in a subordinate
clause. The class <u>adverb</u> in particular has long been a catch-all
category for items which do not fit into any other category. It is
used in the present coding system in just this fashion. One of the
uses of the syntactic concordance may well be to reclassify some
of the syntactically defined categories, or at least to provide more
rigorous definitions for them.

4.3 <u>Sentences of unusual complexity</u>. It is clear that the rules
in their present form will not account for all the data of Middle
High German.[3] It will probably prove most feasible to analyze as
many sentences as possible with the machinery provided by the
code, and to append to each text a supplementary list of sentences
which cannot be readily analyzed. When a program is run to answer
a specific question using a coded corpus, the researcher can examine the unanalyzed sentences by hand for any additional data which
they might contain. A procedure of this sort is surely more
practical than an attempt to make the code complex enough to
handle all data from the very start. If some simplifying generali-
zation should later be discovered, it would always be possible to
modify the code to take account of the new information.

4.4 <u>Practical problems</u>. The main concern of this paper is
to develop a code which is economically feasible and yet adequate
for providing useful data. My experience with the code as it is
now formulated indicates that a maximum speed of about 50 lines
of hand-coding per hour can be expected if one is familiar with the
text and does not dwell too long on constructions which do not fit
readily into the coding system. ('Line' means the equivalent of
an average line from a courtly epic — about six or seven words.)
At best then it would require 2,000 hours of skilled analysis plus
additional clerical costs, keypunching, programming, and computer time to get a corpus of 100,000 lines, which would seem to

be a minimum corpus for answering questions of a statistical nature.
The initial investment in a program of this size would clearly be a
substantial one, but once the coding job was completed, the corpus
would be useful for an indefinite time and would render unnecessary
a large number of data-gathering tasks which were formerly done
by hand if at all.

5.0 SAMPLE FLOWCHARTS

It remains to give some examples of the kind of information
which can be provided using a code of the type described above.
Figures 2.1, 2.2, and 2.3 contain flowcharts showing how two
questions might be answered using the data available in the coded
corpus. Both questions can be answered in a straightforward manner, but this does not preclude the possibility of more complicated
kinds of programs. The two flowcharts are intended to give only
an idea of the possibilities.

5.1 Impersonal clauses. Figure 2.1 contains a flowchart for
counting the number of clauses which do not have subjects and the
number of those which do. One-word clauses, clauses with imperative verbs, and clauses with no verbs are not counted. Clauses
without subjects are presumed to be impersonal clauses similar
to Modern German Mir ist kalt. We now read, e.g. in Paul-
Mitzka 186: 'Unpersönlich werden im Mhd. im allgemeinen die
gleichen Verben gebraucht wie im Nhd. Ausserdem noch manche
andere...' With the information provided by a program such as
that proposed in Figure 2.1 it would be possible to say something
like: 'x per cent of the multiword clauses in the test corpus which
have nonimperative verbs contain verbs with no subject'.

5.2 Position of finite verbs. Figures 2.2 and 2.3 give a
flowchart for calculating the position of the finite verb in Middle
High German sentences in terms of four positions: initial, second,
final, other. The statistics are further broken down according to
clause-type. This information is relevant to statements in the
existing grammars which are notably vague on the location of the
finite verb in various clause-types. Phrases such as 'in general'
and 'frequently' abound. A program similar to the one outlined
in Figures 2.2 and 2.3 would permit exact statements to be made.

5.3 Usefulness of analyses. Both of the programs outlined
in the preceding paragraphs could give information which would

allow us to speak more precisely about Middle High German than
we now can. Neither question is of enough importance in itself
to merit a great deal of scholarly effort in trying to answer it. If,
however, a large number of such questions can be answered using
the same corpus, then a sizable contribution can be made to the
study of Middle High German without overburdening the few
scholars engaged in its study.

6.0 ADDITIONAL USES

Several further uses of the corpus can be foreseen in addition
to the main purpose of providing distributional data about syntactic
patterns. Since the text is included along with the grammatical
information, it would be possible to write a program which would
produce an alphabetized and parsed word list of the entire corpus
or individual parts of it.[4]

The text component could also be used, without the grammatical information, for performing the kinds of analysis which are
ordinarily done on unanalyzed text.[5] The syntactic concordance
would then serve both as a corpus of written language and as a
source of statistics about syntactic patterns.

NOTES

1. Further information on the chronological and spatial delimitation of Middle High German can be found in Hermann Paul,
Mittelhochdeutsche Grammatik, 18th edition by Walther Mitzka
16-31 (Tübingen, 1959). This work is henceforth cited as 'Paul-
Mitzka'.

2. K. Weinhold, G. Ehrismann, and H. Moser, Kleine
mittelhochdeutsche Grammatik[13] (Vienna and Stuttgart, 1963).

3. To give just one example, it is assumed when dealing with
discontinuous constituents that an intervening constituent is enclosed within the larger constituent. If both constituents are to
be coded in the same column, one might get a sequence I M I
M F F (see Tables 2.2 and 2.3). The code can be looked at as
equivalent to a right-facing parenthesis before I and a left-facing
parenthesis after F. The sequence would then be bracketed as
(I M (I M F) F) and the parentheses would be resolved starting

with the innermost ones. Such a situation is typical for relative
clauses which are included within main clauses. There are, however, also constructions in which two clauses share a common
element such as the following example: dô spranc von dem gesidele
her Hagene alsô sprach (Kudrun 538, as cited in Paul-Mitzka 279)
'then jumped from his seat Lord Hagen, (Lord Hagen) spoke as
follows'. At the clause level the following position-markers
would be assigned (Column 2, Table 2. 3): I M M M M I F M F.
According to our convention for bracketing this would represent
(I M M M M (I F) M F), but the wrong interpretation would be derived with unlabeled parentheses. The correct bracketing would
have to be represented by e. g. (I M M M M [I F) M F]. On the
other hand constructions where unlabeled parentheses give wrong
analyses are extremely rare, and the added complication of
providing for constructions such as the one discussed above seems
impractical if one wants to keep the code manageable.

    4. See R. Wisbey, 'The analysis of Middle High German texts
by computer — some lexicographical aspects', Transactions of
the Philological Society 28-48 (1963), for a discussion of word
lists and concordances for Middle High German. Wisbey concludes
that it is wasteful to include grammatical information with running
text (p. 33). Since his interests are primarily lexicographical,
this is probably true. The kind of program which he describes
would, however, contain no information about word order. At the
same time it should be emphasized that the concordances which
Wisbey proposes are likely to be in use far sooner than anything
similar to the plan outlined in this paper. Time is a factor which
is worth considering as pointed out by John C. Wells, 'A word-index
and glossary to the Old High German glosses', IBM literary data
processing conference proceedings 148-59 (1964), to justify his
work with the Old High German glosses.

    5. The text component could serve the same function as for
example the million-word corpus of English prepared by W. N.
Francis. See the Manual of information to accompany A standard
sample of present-day edited American English, for use with digital computers (Providence, 1964) for a description of this corpus.

Table 2. 1[1]

Rules To Explain the Grammar Code of Tables 2. 2 and 2. 3

1 Sentence ⟶ Main Clause

2 Main Clause ⟶ $\begin{cases} \text{sentence-word} \\ \text{(conjunction)} + \text{Nonverbal} + \text{Verbal [14]} \end{cases}$

3 Nonverbal ⟶ (Concord-Element) + (Element) [13]

4 Concord-Element ⟶ Nominal

5 Nominal ⟶ $\begin{cases} \text{Nominal Clause [2]}^2 \\ \text{(Modifier)} + \text{Nucleus [11]} \end{cases}$

6 Modifier ⟶ $\begin{cases} \text{Relative Clause [2]}^2 \\ \text{Adverbial [8]} \\ \text{(determiner)} + \text{(Adjectival)} \end{cases}$

7 Adjectival ⟶ $\begin{cases} \text{(Adverbial)} + \text{adjective} \\ \text{Nominal [5]} \end{cases}$

8 Adverbial ⟶ $\begin{cases} \text{Adverbial Clause [2]}^2 \\ \text{Adverb Phrase [10]} \\ \text{Prepositional Phrase} \end{cases}$

9 Prepositional Phrase ⟶ preposition + Nominal [5]

10 Adverb Phrase ⟶ $\begin{cases} \text{adverb} + \text{(Adverbial) [8]} \\ \text{adverb} + \text{preposition} + \text{(Nominal Clause) [2]} \end{cases}$

11 Nucleus ⟶ $\begin{cases} \text{pronoun} + \text{(Nominal) [5]} \\ \text{adjective} \\ \text{noun} \\ \text{Infinitive Phrase} \end{cases}$

12 Infinitive Phrase ⟶ (ze) + infinitive + (Element)

13 Element ⟶ (Nominal) [5] + (Adverbial) [8]

14 Verbal ⟶ $\begin{cases} \text{nonpast} \\ \text{past} \\ \text{nonpast subjunctive} \\ \text{past subjunctive} \\ \text{imperative} \end{cases}$ + $\begin{cases} \text{nonpast participle} \\ \text{past participle} \\ \text{infinitive} \\ \text{Infinitive Phrase [12]} \end{cases}$

15 Main Clause ⟶ Main Clause + (conjunction) + Main Clause[3]

Notes to Table 2.1

1. The following conventions are used in the presentation of
the rules. Braces { } are used to indicate that any of the paths
to the right of the left brace are possible. The right side is closed
only if there are further items to be added. Parentheses ( ) are
used to enclose items which may be optionally selected. When all
items to the right of an arrow are in parentheses, it is assumed
that at least one item must be chosen. Square brackets [ ] are
used to refer to the proper rules for expanding nonterminal symbols,
unless they are dealt with by the next rule in regular sequence.
Nonterminal symbols are indicated by labels with upper-case first
letters; terminal symbols by lower-case first letters. Underlining
indicates the graphemic representation of a Middle High German
form. For purposes of simplification, case and number markers
are not included. In a grammar of Middle High German case and
number as well as gender would have to be marked, perhaps by a
system of subscripts plus transformational rules. See Emmon
Bach, 'The order of elements in German', Lg. 38.264-5 (1962).

2. Relative Clause, Nominal Clause, and Adverbial Clause
reenter the rules at Rule 2 and expand like Main Clause.

3. Rule 15 is an optional, recursive rule which allows for
coordination or series. Most items can be expanded in the same
way, but there are many constraints which need not be discussed
here. In an actual grammar of Middle High German such rules
would prove cumbersome and inadequate. They would probably
have to be replaced by rules of transformational complexity.

Table 2.2

Slot Fillers for the Grammar Code

1 Clause type: Main, Adverbial, Nominal, Relative[1]

2 Clause position: Initial, Medial, Final, Word[2]

3 Concord-Element: Initial, Medial, Final, Word, Blank[3]

4 Element: (same as 3)

5 Constituent of an element: (same as 3)

6 Constituent of 5: (same as 3)

7 Constituent of 6: (same as 3)

8 Verbal position: (same as 3)[4]

9 Verbal: past, nonpast, past subjunctive, nonpast subjunctive, past participle, nonpast participle, infinitive, imperative, Blank[5]

10 Case: Nominative, Accusative, Dative, Genitive, Dative or Genitive, Indeterminate, Blank[6]

11 Number: Singular, Plural, Indeterminate, Blank

12 Word class: noun, pronoun, preposition, determiner, adverb, Verb, adjective, sentence-word, conjunction[7]

---

1. See Note 2 to Table 2.1. The parts of the entries which are underlined are the designations which will be used for hand-coding as in Table 2.3.

2. The entries in Column 2 refer to the position within the clause of the item being coded. Initial means leftmost in the clause, Medial means neither rightmost nor leftmost, Final means rightmost, and Word means that the clause contains only one item.

3. Columns 3-8 have the same entries as Column 2 with similar reference to position within constituents smaller than the clause. In addition, Columns 3-8 are not always applicable, so the category Blank must be added. In Table 2.3 Blank is marked by leaving the column blank, but in a computer code it would of course require a designation just like any other entry.

4. Column 8 is based on the branching provided in Rule 2, Table 2.1. An infinitive phrase derived by Rule 14 will be included

in Column 8, but one derived through Rule 11 will not be included in Column 8.

5. See Rule 14 in Table 2.1. Column 9 can also have <u>Blank</u>
as an entry for obvious reasons.

6. See Note 1 to Table 2.1. The entries <u>DG</u> and <u>Ind</u> are provided to deal with occurrences of case syncretism where it is difficult to arrive at a decision. <u>DG</u> reflects a special category for the
frequent syncretism of the dative and genitive singular of feminine
nominals. These categories are used only as a last resort. Even
where there is formal syncretism a decision will be made if it is
plausible.

7. Column 12 always has an entry. All entries except <u>Verb</u>
are terminal symbols. Verbal nouns (see Rule 11, Table 2.1) are
indicated by the entry <u>noun</u> in Column 12 plus the appropriate designation in Column 9.

Table 2.3[1]

Line	Text	1	2	3	4	5	6	7	8	9	10	11	12
1	Mîn	M	I	I							N	S	det
	herze	M	M	F							N	S	noun
	hât	M	M						I	np		S	Verb
	betwungen	M	M						F	pp			Verb
2	dicke	M	M		W								adv
	mîne	M	M		I						A	S	det
	zungen	M	F		F						A	S	noun
3	daz	A	I										con
	si	A	M	W							N	S	pron
	des	A	M		I	W					G	S	pron
	vil	A	M		F						A	S	noun
	gesprochen	A	M						I	pp			Verb
	hât	A	F						F	np		S	Verb
4	daz	R	I	W							N	S	pron
	nach	R	M		I								prep
	der	R	M		M	I					G	S	det
	werlde	R	M		M	F					G	S	noun
	lône	R	M		F						D	S	noun
	stât	R	F						W	np		S	Verb
5	daz	M	I	W							A	S	pron
	rieten	M	M						W	p		P	Verb
	im	M	M		W						D	S	pron
	diu	M	M	I							N	P	det
	tumben	M	M	M							N	P	adj
	jâr	M	F	F							N	P	noun
6	nû	M	I		W								adv
	weiz	M	M						W	np		S	Verb
	ich	M	M	W							N	S	pron
	daz	M	M		W						A	S	pron
	wol	M	M		W								adv
	vür	M	M		I								prep
	wâr	M	F		F						A	S	adj

1. The text consists of lines 1-6 of <u>Gregorius</u> by Hartmann von Aue, edited by Hermann Paul in the <u>Altdeutsche Textbibliothek</u> series, No. 2. The ninth edition prepared by Ludwig Wolff (Tübingen, 1959) was used. A free rendering of the passage is: 'My heart has often forced my tongue to say a great deal which is aimed towards earthly reward. My lack of experience gave it that advice. Now I well know that to be true.' See Table 2.2 for identification of the columns. The sequence of derivation is partially indicated by the system of coding. Coding <u>nach der werlde lôn</u> (line 4) in Column 4 as constituent followed by <u>der werlde</u> in Column 5 means that <u>der werlde</u> can be derived only after a second pass through Rule 11.

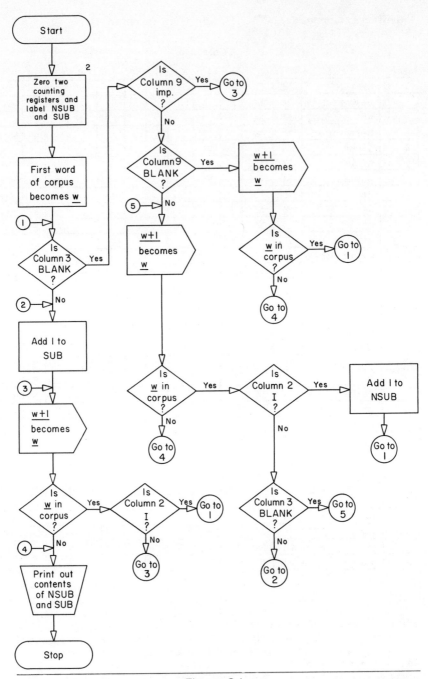

Figure 2.1

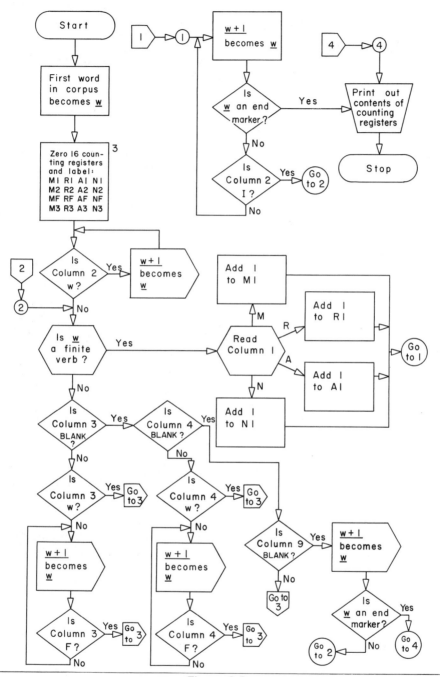

Figure 2.2

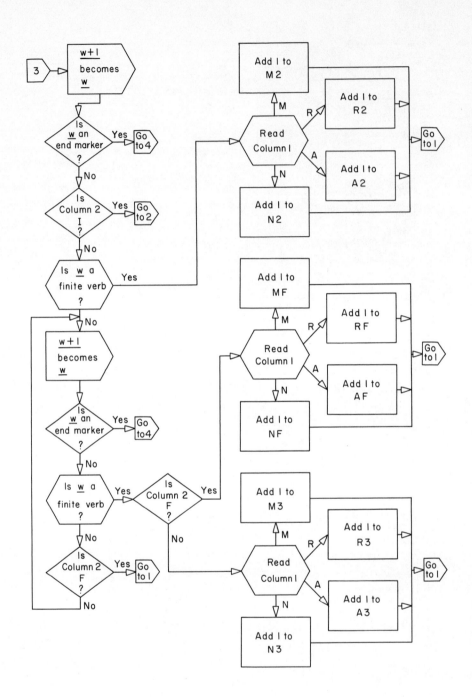

Figure 2.3

Notes to Figures 2. 1, 2. 2, and 2. 3

1.   The mechanics of the form in which the text and the grammar code would be put into the computer are not discussed.   The
code would be some sort of linear representation of Table 2. 3.
The first two words of the sample text might be represented by
something like: 1 Mîn M I I O O O O O O N S det herze M M F O
O O O O O N S noun.   Appropriate boundary markers would also
have to be included.

2.   The labels SUB and NSUB indicate 'subject' and 'no subject'.

3.   The labels are formed from the following components: M =
main clause, R = relative clause, A = adverbial clause, N = nominal
clause, 1 = finite verb in initial position, 2 = verb in second position, F = verb in final position, and 3 = verb in other position.

Chapter 3

An Automatic Retrieval Program for the Linguistic Atlas of the United States and Canada

Roger W. Shuy

1.0 THE NEED FOR A RETRIEVAL SYSTEM

1.1 Accessibility of Atlas data. It is indisputable that the
collections of The Linguistic Atlas of the United States and Canada,
valuable and well organized as they are, present the researcher
with many difficulties. To begin with, the files of each regional
Atlas are usually located in only one place. The investigator must
either work at that place or have the field records copied and sent
to him. Secondly, the Atlas questionnaire is filed by pages; that
is, all the page sevens of all the interviews in one state are filed
together. Likewise, all the page 22's and so on. This is as efficient
a system of its kind as one can develop (more effective, in fact,
than the British system), but the fact remains that a great deal of
page turning must accompany any extensive research in which the
Atlas files are significant.

1.2 Problems of collecting Atlas data. Not only are the Atlas
data difficult to get at, but they are also difficult to collect. Thus
far the Director of the Atlas has insisted, and rightly so, that only
highly skilled field workers may gather the data. The informant's
every response is recorded in a narrow phonetic transcription by
a person thoroughly trained to hear perceptively and to record
accurately. There is a general lack not only of qualified field
workers but also of financial support for research and publication.
Furthermore, the length and thoroughness of the questionnaire and
the size of the country have necessarily limited the quantity of
field records in the Atlas files.

1.3 The focus of Atlas research. Up to this time, moreover,
the attention of linguistic geographers in the United States has
focused on the relationship of dialect variables to education or

culture level and to geography. Critics of American linguistic
geography have strongly suggested that more emphasis should be
placed on other bases of group identification such as occupation,
age, sex, church affiliation, political party, and so on.[1] Although
dialectologists have not been blind to the possible effects of these
forces on current dialects, they have not been successful in utilizing
the vast body of information that has been gathered to answer such
questions. In short, with a more efficient tool for getting at the
data that dialectologists have collected and are still collecting,
they could say a great deal more about the diversity of sociolinguistic features which characterize American speech.

　　1.4 The scope of this paper. With these problems in mind, I
looked to electronic data processing for whatever solutions it might
offer. Then I set to work on what is essentially a punched-card
problem to be done on relatively simple tab equipment. The accessibility of the data has been foremost in my mind in this study,
although it has also suggested some valuable insights on the collection of data.*

2.0 THE COMPARTMENTALIZED ATLAS RETRIEVAL SYSTEM

　　2.1 Complexity of data. It is obvious that a retrieval system
able to handle a wide variety of possible responses to a 750-item
questionnaire would be a complex and impressive tool. I have felt
that the place to begin such a study was not the whole questionnaire.
The complexity of symbolizing pronunciations for electronic data
processing is, in itself, enormous. Add the problems posed by
vocabulary and morphology-syntax variations and the formulation
becomes even more imposing. If the entire Atlas evidence is not
to be handled in a single retrieval program, compartmentalization
into separate programs of pronunciation, vocabulary, and morphology-
syntax seems to be the most obvious cut to make.

　　2.2 Previous Atlas data processing. Such compartmentalization seems particularly relevant in that electronic handling of Atlas
vocabulary data has been begun by the late E. Bagby Atwood and by
Gordon R. Wood.[2] Since William Card and Virginia McDavid[3]

---

*I am greatly indebted to William Card for his general help through-
out the preparation of this paper. His suggestions concerning style,
content, and application were particularly useful. It should be noted,
however, that his generous concern makes him in no way responsible
for all aspects of the paper.

have outlined a similar program involving verb forms, it seemed
wise to limit the present research to the programming of the remaining aspects of grammar, exclusive of verbs. The problems
involved in programming Atlas pronunciation data will not be dealt
with in this paper but must, of course, be faced in the near future.

2. 3 The usefulness of this research. The nonverb grammatical
items are a natural beginning point for accurate, contemporary
statements about usage. The immediate usefulness of such an automated program would be appreciated by several organizations such
as The National Council of Teachers of English and the American
Dialect Society, both of which are vitally interested in American
English usage.

3. 0 SELECTING DATA FOR THE PROGRAM

3. 1 Lexical vs. grammatical vs. phonological. Some Atlas
responses appear to be useful both as vocabulary and as grammatical
items. For example, the response sick (to/at/on/in/of) your
stomach is at the same time lexical and grammatical. Likewise,
all information gathered in the Atlas files has phonological significance. Since this program treats grammatical items only, it became my task to deal only with the grammatical status of selected
responses. What is done with the phonological evidence is the
focus of another problem. At a later time, an analyst will have to
decide whether some or all of the grammatical items treated in this
program are to be included in a phonological analysis.

To avoid possible overlap between lexical and grammatical
items, I carefully chose items which were clearly structural rather
than lexical. The following types of items were included in this
study: prepositions, matters of agreement, noun plurals, pronouns,
adjective suffixes, adverb suffixes, conjunctions, and articles.
These categories were selected because the field records yield
consistent information in these areas. Though the field workers
recorded much other interesting grammatical information not
asked for in the questionnaire, it is too sporadic to be susceptible
to programming.

3. 2 Backgound data. It was relatively easy to determine
which background data aboutinformants to include in this study.
For the sake of scientific accuracy, nothing that appears systemat-
ically and that can be readily coded should be excluded. It is of
great importance to avoid throwing away data of any kind. The
Atlas field records include background material about the informants'

State, community, education, age, sex, ethnic association, occupation, and family history, as well as the field worker's name and the
year in which the field work was done. All of this information was
coded on the data card for each informant.

3. 3 Grammatical data. Fortunately, there is a limited range
of response possibilities for nonverb grammatical items, a fact
which makes the task of coding in this program relatively simple.
The number of recurring variants for most items was quite limited.
Occasionally an unusual response appeared. It was necessary, in
this investigation, to determine whether to include all answers that
have ever been given or to lump this small number of unusual
responses into a category called 'other'. Involved in this question
are the definition of idiosyncrasy, an evaluation of the accuracy of
evidence which includes only the most common answers, a definition
of economy, and an understanding of the limited storage capacity
of the equipment. In the end I grouped forms into categories of
variants rather than into separate items, partly on the basis of
known occurrence and inclusion in the Atlas field records, partly
on the word-of-mouth agreement among field workers, and partly
on intuition. This problem did not turn out to be very extensive in
the study of nonverb grammatical items. Originality or idiosyncrasy of structure is undoubtedly more restricted than, say,
that of lexicon or pronunciation. Consequently, the categories of
variants were determined here with relative ease.

3. 4 Items in this study. In all, 78 nonverb grammatical items
were selected from The Linguistic Atlas of New England as a basis
for this study. Since the New England field workers used a longer
questionnaire than the one used in most other parts of the country,
there will not be complete congruence of items in various Atlas
collections. My decision to include items that are in the New
England Atlas, whether or not they appear in other Atlas question-
naires, was made for two reasons. First, I wanted to retain as
much data as possible. Second, it is probable that these (and other)
data will be included in future collections. The number of items
(not variants) included in this study is broken down as follows:

prepositions	18
agreement items	9
noun inflections	16
pronouns	22
adjective suffixes	2
adverb suffixes	5

conjunctions	5
article	1
total	78

4.0 CLASSIFYING THE DATA FOR THE PROGRAM

4.1 Standardization. One of the advantages of a program for
the automatic retrieval of nonverb grammatical items is its usefulness both to other investigators of the same data and, as we
shall see, to researchers in other compartments of Atlas data such
as pronunciation, verb forms, and vocabulary. It is very important,
if the programs of various compartments are to be interchangeable,
that we agree upon a standard format of data input. For this reason,
I wrote a code book which is, in effect, a detailed table of contents
for the arrangement of all the various kinds of data included in the
nonverb grammatical program. Further standardization is being
established for background data. For example, there should be
agreement among all Atlas programs on the numbering system for
States, communities, field worker identification, occupations, and
so forth.

4.2 Atlas classification systems. In setting up the code book
for nonverb grammatical items, I tried, as much as possible, to
follow the order of previously published retrieval systems in
American dialectology. E. Bagby Atwood, in his The Regional
Vocabulary of Texas, set a precedent for future machine handling
of Atlas materials. I have followed his ordering in the first few
columns of the code book but have supplemented it with additional
background material in keeping with my belief that no useful and
codable information should be excluded.[4] In the end it will be
necessary to involve a larger body in the decisions, including
particularly the directors of the various regional Atlases.

4.3 Classifying data in this program. Punched-card columns
1 through 35 in the code book deal with background information for
each field as follows:

columns		
	1-2	State
	3-5	County
	6	Type
	7-8	Informant by type
	9-10	Age
	11	Sex
	12-13	Ethnic

14-15	Field worker
16-17	Year of field work
18-19	Occupation
20-21	Father's birthplace
22-23	Mother's birthplace
24-25	Paternal grandfather's birthplace
26-27	Paternal grandmother's birthplace
28-29	Maternal grandfather's birthplace
30-31	Maternal grandmother's birthplace
32-35	Item identification

Beyond the matter of background information, there is no precedent for ordering the coded responses. Arbitrarily I separated the items by natural grammatical types. That is, prepositions are all in one place, items of agreement are grouped together, and so forth. The researcher who wishes to add other items to his study can easily put them at the end, for there are available programs that will bring the new item back to its category-mates at the printout stage.

One last matter concerning the classification of data involves card identification. Columns 73-80 of each card are used for identification in the following manner:

columns		
	73-74	program identification
	75-76	State identification
	77-79	informant identification
	80	card number

Thus, if columns 73-80 read 30010012, we may understand that in the Atlas program for nonverb grammatical items (30), we have a card for Maine(State 01), informant number one (001), card number two (the last number). The compartmentalized approach to the analysis of Atlas data will require a standardized numbering system of States and informants as well as an agreed-upon symbol of program identification. The number 30 was arbitrarily chosen for the program here, pending such standardization.

We have identified the columns reserved for background information of the informants and the columns reserved for card identification. The following is a description of the remainder of the classification by columns:

card 1, columns	36-66	prepositions
	67-72	blank
card 2, columns	1-7	agreement items
	8-22	noun inflections

23-42	pronouns
43-44	adjective suffixes
45-49	adverb suffixes
50-57	conjunctions
58	article
59-72	blank

5.0 RESOLVING PROBLEMS OF CODING

5.1 Coding the data. The essential problem in utilizing electronic language data processing is the matter of coding the data. This, in turn, is related to the nature of the equipment to be used, the criterion of simplicity, the code's usefulness to other people who work with the same data, and the convertibility of the raw data to punched-card input.

The linguist will know best what constitutes simplicity and how useful this program may be to other linguists. The computer specialists will know best which equipment and/or program suits the specific linguistic problem most adequately. One of my primary goals in this project was to obtain frequency distributions. After consultation with professional programmers at the Indiana University Research Computing Center, I decided to use the Indiana University Research Computing Center's IBM 709-1401 Program for 101 Simulation. Its primary function is to tabulate the number of units falling into various categories according to classification variables.

The unit record for the simulator is one to eight IBM cards. The information is placed on magnetic tape via the 1401 computer and is then processed on the IBM 709.

5.2 Special problems. Getting the raw data coded involves special problems which will not be our major concern in this paper. Such a special problem is illustrated by the field work in Maine for The Linguistic Atlas of New England, the source of the data in this study, which was done by only one field worker, the late Guy Lowman. Other field workers in other States frequently recorded responses that were repeated at the field worker's request, responses that were heard-of but not used by the informant, responses of auxiliary informants, suggested responses, responses considered archaic by the informant, and corrected responses. Very few facts of this type were recorded by Lowman in Maine, and in this study I arbitrarily excluded them. This does not mean that I consider such responses irrelevant or unimportant. I was

simply not interested in complicating the coding system at this
time by making provisions for these possibilities. It appears, in
fact, that it might be easier to run two separate programs in such
a study: one for the type of responses which concern us here and
another for such modifications as repeated, suggested, or auxiliary
responses. The two kinds of information could then be brought
together for whatever significance they might show in juxtaposition.

5.3 <u>Problems of identification.</u> There are several problems
of coding which must be mentioned. Identification of grammatical
items and variants is one such problem. The 709-1401 Program
for 101 Simulation permits identification of each item in eight
alphanumeric columns and variants in six. It is impractical to
try to identify the item by the field worker's question. For
example, the investigator might ask the informant to fill in the
missing part of this sentence: <u>When trouble hits, it comes ———.</u>
One of the sets of possible answers includes the response <u>all at
once</u> and its variations such as <u>all to once.</u> But the informant
might also offer an alternate type of answer to this clue. He
might respond with <u>in bunches</u> or <u>quickly.</u> The clearest way to
identify the item, therefore, is not by the field worker's question
but by the answer set, as long as the set is comprehensible under
that identification. Therefore I have used ALLXONCE as the
item identification for that set. Since the program will not permit
dashes, X has been used to indicate the position in which the variant appears.

Identification of variants follows much the same procedure
except that the program allows for only six alphanumeric characters for this purpose. There is no particular problem with
readability until we are faced with the need for compressing
three variants in one six-character slot. For example, the frame
<u>I wonder what he died ——</u> has 16 possible responses:

1.	of	9.	with, for
2.	with	10.	from, for
3.	from	11.	of, with, from
4.	for	12.	of, with, for
5.	of, with	13.	of, from, for
6.	of, from	14.	with, from, for
7.	of, for	15.	of, with from, for
8.	with, from	16.	other

The coding of the responses with one and sometimes two variants
is relatively clear and readable. But when the entire set is coded,

the printout looks like this:

1.	OF	9.	WTHFOR
2.	WITH	10.	FRMFOR
3.	FROM	11.	OFWHFM
4.	FOR	12.	OFWHFR
5.	OFWITH	13.	OFFMFR
6.	OFFROM	14.	WHFMFR
7.	OFFOR	15.	ALL
8.	WTHFRM	16.	OTHER

5.4 <u>The problem of complexity</u>. The problem of identification
leads to the second coding problem to be mentioned here, that of
complexity. It is clear that if there are five possible variant
single responses, there will be a total of 32 responses including
single responses, combinations, and a slot for other responses.
The coding of as many as four possible responses in a six-column
space is possible but the outcome will hardly be readable. For
example, the item elicited from the frame <u>I won't go — he does</u>
might be coded as follows:

response	code
1. unless	UNLESS
2. without	WTHOUT
3. 'lessen	LESSEN
4. 'thout(n)	THOUTN
5. 'douten	DOUTEN
6. unless, without	UNLWHT
7. unless, lessen	UNLLSN
8. unless, thout(n)	UNLTHN
9. unless, douten	UNLDTN
10. without, lessen	WHTLSN
11. without, thout(n)	WHTTHN
12. without, douten	WHTDTN
13. lessen, thout(n)	LSNTHN

* * *

18. unless, lessen, thout(n)	USLNTN

* * *

25. unless, without, lessen, thout(n)	UWOLTN

***
32. other   OTHER

To avoid repetition, the sequences indicated by the asterisks have
been skipped.

The problem of readability is obvious. An item with four or
fewer variants is somewhat easier to handle. For this reason, I
have tried to limit each range of variants to four related variants.
This sometimes results in an artificiality, as the following example
will reveal, but it makes for a more readable printout.

The frame Quarter — four contains six significant known responses: of, to, till, before, until, and unto. If these six variants
were to be listed with all combinatorial possibilities, the result
would be a very complex and unmanageable code. In order to preserve my format and limit the coding to 16 possibilities, I broke
the item into two parts as follows:

quarter — four

1. of	9. to, before
2. to	10. till, before
3. till	11. of, to, till
4. before	12. of, to, before
5. of, to	13. of, till, before
6. of, till	14. to, till, before
7. of, before	15. all four responses
8. to, till	16. other responses

quarter un — four

1. until
2. unto
3. until, unto
4. other responses

Economically, it would be better to split the six-response item
into two three-item units, but this conflicts with the logic of the
data. Hence the split between responses containing the un-
prefix and other responses was chosen. The real danger of this
technique is not how the item is split but that it is split at all.
Special instruction must be given the analyst to avoid coding
quarter unto four both as other responses (16) to item quarter —
four and as unto (2) to item quarter un — four.

6.0 DEFINING THE FIELDS

6.1 <u>The Define Field Statement</u>. All of the variant responses
in a particular answer set constitute an individual field, a set of
one to three contiguous columns of the punched card which, for the
sake of clarity, may be given a name. This name will appear in
the printout as the label for the classification variables in each
distribution. After my data were coded and my cards keypunched,
I proceeded to give names to my fields. This naming procedure,
which also provides specifications for locating the cards of the
data to be processed, is called a Define Field Statement.[5] A
sample Define Field Statement follows:

DEFINE FIELD   2POUNDX= 91 (0-2)   (O=POUND, 1=POUNDS,
                          2=BOTH)

That is, the field is the set of columns used for the response frame
<u>This weighs two</u> ——. This is column 91 (that is, it appears in
column 11 of card number two). It has three possible responses
(0-2) which are <u>pound</u>, <u>pounds</u>, and both <u>pound</u> and <u>pounds</u>.

6.2 <u>The group mode</u>. In cases where it seemed useful to
combine responses within a given frame, I used the 'group
mode'. This makes it possible, in the Define Field Statement,
to combine punches within a given field. As the following example demonstrates, instead of the exact age of my informants
I can specify some grouping of age, in this case, decade grouping:

DEFINE FIELD AGE=9-10 (20-29, 30-39, 40-49, 50-59,
                          60-69, 70-79, 80-89, 90-99)(TWENTY,
                          THIRTY, FORTY, FIFTY, SIXTY,
                          SEVNTY, EIGHTY, NINETY)

That is, the field of the informant's age appears in columns 9 and
10. Although the exact ages of the informants were processed
initially, I am only interested in retrieving decade groupings.
Thus, I let the computer do the grouping for me. This way I still
have the exact ages in the data in case I should desire to use them.
To get at them, all I have to do is write a different Define Field
Statement which specifies exact ages.

The Define Field Statement need not utilize all the input data.
For example, in the program run on Maine nonverb grammatical
items, there was no need to define the field of 'field worker' even
though it appears in the data in columns 14 and 15. It was not
necessary, in this particular program, because one man did all
the field work in that State. If the program were to involve a
comparison of several States (thus probably comparing the work

of several field workers also), it would be necessary to define
that field.

    In all, 81 fields, including informant background data, were
defined in this program. The responses of each informant were
coded from the Atlas files to the list manuscript (which was simply
a matrix of columns of responses and rows of informants).

7.0 DISTRIBUTING THE DATA

    After the data were coded and the fields defined, it was
necessary to decide which particular relationships I wanted to dis-
play. As mentioned earlier, one of the goals of this research was
to get at significant sociolinguistic relationships which had been
hitherto ignored or which had been discovered only through hours
of laborious hand-sorting. The computer classifies and counts
according to the combinations of categories of several fields
simultaneously. In order to produce such frequency distributions,
it is necessary to write a Distribute Statement as part of the program. This statement specifies a matrix in which the categories
of one field are printed across the top of the page and those of
another down the left side of the page. The counts of the responses
in each category of the cross tabulation are listed. The Distribute
Statement gives the number and dimension of the frequency distributions and ultimately produces a count of their variants. Some
sample Distribute Statements follow:

    DISTRIBUTE (HALFX2* SEX)
    DISTRIBUTE (2POUNDX* AGE)
    DISTRIBUTE (TROUGHX* OCCUPAT)
    DISTRIBUTE (9FXHIGH* TYPE)

That is, I was able to determine quickly and accurately the relationship of an informant's sex to his use of the variant responses
to <u>half — two</u> (<u>past</u>, <u>after</u>, etc.). I was also able to see what
effect age has on the use of the inflectional form of <u>pound</u>, what
part occupation plays in the distribution of inflected and uninflected
<u>trough</u> and what type of person (cultivated, semicultivated, or
uncultivated) is more apt to inflect <u>foot</u> in response to the frame,
<u>nine — tall</u>.

8.0 RESULTS OF THE PROGRAM

    8.1 <u>Distributions</u>. This program, of course, is only sugges-
tive of what can be done with the Atlas materials once the data are
submitted to automation. These materials will be more accessible

and reproducible than ever before. More significant, the dialec-
tologist will be able to broaden his investigation of the sociological
implications of American speech through improved handling of
data. As indicated previously, one of the benefits of our program
is in the area of distributions by occupation, sex, age, and type.
Sample matrixes are illustrated below (reject signifies that there
was no response by an informant for that item):

Matrix 1:

TYPE NAMEDX	UNCULT	SEMICT	CULT	REJECT
AFTER	18	10	2	0
FOR	9	19	0	0
AFTRFR	6	6	2	0
REJECT	1	1	1	0

Matrix 2:

AGE XTELLME	20	30	40	50	60	70	80	90
TO	1	0	4	6	14	18	6	4
FORTO	0	0	2	2	2	4	2	1
BOTH	0	0	0	0	0	1	0	0
REJECT	0	0	0	0	2	3	1	1

Matrix 3:

XTELLME NAMEDX	TO	FORTO	BOTH	REJECT
AFTER	21	7	0	2
FOR	24	4	0	0
BOTH	9	1	0	4
REJECT	1	0	0	2

It is not my purpose in this paper to comment on the sociological significance of the preceding distribution displays. Rather,
they are presented as examples of the kinds of frequency distributions which may be obtained easily by using this program.
Further distributions may be tabulated to discover whatever relationships the investigator is interested in. Matrixes 1 and 2 dis-
play the grammatical items in relationship to background data of
the informants. Matrix 3 displays the relationship of the responses
of two grammatical items to each other and clearly demonstrates
how easily this interesting phase of dialect study may be handled

by computer processing. Moreover, once Atlas programs become standardized, it should be relatively easy to crosstabulate grammatical and vocabulary items and find distributions across lexical and structural boundaries in which the number of speakers, for example, who use nine foot high can be correlated with those who say bucket instead of pail.

8.2 Cartography. Cartography, including the preparation of isoglosses, is another aspect of dialectology in which automation can be useful. The machine can be directed to print out the numbers of all communities in which a particular response appears. Charting responses onto maps can be greatly simplified by this procedure.

8.3 Methods of data collection. One last use of an automatic retrieval system for the Atlas materials involves the method of data collection. It is undoubtedly true that the well-trained field workers are the best persons to gather data about language. But it is also true that few well-trained field workers are available for the collection of data and only limited financial support is accessible to them. The Atlas interview has been criticized for being both too long and too incomplete. If there is some way to shorten the interview and yet maintain completeness while, at the same time, increasing the number of field workers, the progress of the Atlas will be insured.

Perhaps the compartmentalized analysis of Atlas materials suggested here is a step toward the solution of the problem. The fact that we have not dealt with phonetic transcription in this program shows that this compartment can be left out. Since phonetic transcription is not required, one major hurdle to competent data gathering may be overcome. It seems probable that a short questionnaire dealing with nonverb grammatical items might be administered by a college student in an advanced course in the English language. If he were given useful suggestions for eliciting responses naturally and effectively, his nonphonetic field work might be used to broaden the coverage of the Atlas nonverb grammatical items just as various multiple choice checklists of vocabulary items have broadened Atlas coverage of lexical materials. The data could be coded as the field work is being done — possibly on a machine-graded answer sheet similar to the multiple choice answer sheets used in some large college courses. If so, the step of transforming raw data to coded data will be eliminated at the field work stage.

8.4 <u>Summary</u>. The advantages of such an approach are
numerous. The data already gathered by field workers for the
Atlas can be utilized for, as I have already indicated, this material
serves as a basis for future collecting. Secondly, the amount of
data will multiply tremendously, for it will be limited only by our
own energy. Our files can be updated yearly and, as long as
students and informants are honest, we can get a more accurate
picture of current American grammatical practice.

NOTES

1. See for example Glenna Ruth Pickford, 'American Linguistic Geography: A Sociological Appraisal', <u>Word</u> 12.211-33
(1956).

2. See E. Bagby Atwood, <u>The Regional Vocabulary of Texas</u>
(Austin, 1962), and Gordon R. Wood, 'Dialect Contours in the
Southern States', <u>American Speech</u> (December, 1963), in which
electronic data processing was utilized.

3. William Card and Virginia McDavid, 'Paper for private
circulation' (Chicago Teachers College South, November, 1963).

4. Since this was written the matter of informant identification
has been considered at a conference involving Raven I. McDavid,
Jr., editor of <u>The Linguistic Atlas of the Middle and South Atlantic</u>
<u>States</u>; Virginia McDavid, associate editor; William Card, member
of the Local Policy Committee of the Atlas; and Frederic Cassidy,
director of a five-year data-gathering project for a dictionary of
American Regional English. It was agreed that the county was
the appropriate geographical subunit. Mr. McDavid suggested a
numbering system incorporating a feature devised by Hans Kurath,
as follows:

Columns	Field
1-2	State
3-5	County
6	Type
7-8	Informant by type
9-10	Age
11	Sex
12-13	Ethnic

It was agreed that this system was compatible both with computer-
izing DARE materials and with the projected publication in list
manuscript form of the Atlas records of MSAS.   McDavid and
Cassidy agreed to a division of the labor necessary to produce
standard county numbers compatible with the filing order of all
existing Atlas projects.

     5.   For further details, see A 709-1401 Program for 101
Simulation 12-19 (Bloomington, 1963).

FORMAL PROBLEMS

Chapter 4

Some Studies in Syntax-Directed Parsing

Ranan B. Banerji

0. INTRODUCTION

0. 0 In recent years considerable interest has been manifest, both among linguists[1] and among computer scientists,[2] in developing methods for mechanical parsing of sentences in a language. In the early phases of this work, the parsing algorithms developed were strongly grammar dependent, so that the computer program for parsing one given language was completely different from that for parsing a different language. In other words, the program embodied the grammar envisaged for the language. Indeed — this is especially true in the case of computer sciences — in some cases the only concept of the grammar which was discernible was its embodiment in the program.

0. 1 In recent years a lot of interest has been directed toward methods known as syntax-directed parsing.[3] In these methods the computer program may be considered to be an interpreter which parses sentences according to the format supplied by the grammar, which is an entity outside the interpreter, being treated as a piece of data as it were. One may say that while the programs indicated in paragraph 0. 0 answer the question, 'what is the structure of this given sentence?' the ones indicated in this paragraph answer the question 'what is the structure of this given sentence according to this given grammar?'

0. 2 Syntax-directed parsing has the obvious advantage of enabling easy changes in grammar at the experimenter's discretion without involving any change in the program. On the other hand, since it is designed to process any grammar within a given class, its structure cannot be tailored to a specific language so as to make it eminently efficient for quick and efficient parsing of sentences in that language. How efficiently a specific syntax-directed parsing algorithm will process sentences in a specific

language is dependent on the grammar envisaged for that language. The range of efficiency over different grammars, however, may not be the same for different algorithms. A number of syntax-directed parsing algorithms are known at present and already some efforts have been made to study their efficiencies with respect to given grammars.[4] However, the problem of efficiency range will take deeper study.

0. 3 In the present paper we shall study certain aspects of the efficiency of a specific parsing algorithm. Like most of the parsing algorithms at the time of writing of this paper, the algorithm envisages the grammars to be context-free phrase structure grammars. It may be worthwhile to point out here that syntax-directed parsing algorithms, although they do not envisage a specific grammar, have to envisage a specific class of grammars to assure uniformity of operation. This class need not be context free (a few efforts are already under way for syntax-directed parsing in transformational grammars[5]), but they have to be a well-defined class.

0. 4 The algorithm we shall discuss here was suggested in its original form by Alec Glennie.[6] The form in which we shall present it here will differ from his — we believe — only in non-essential features. The method is also essentially similar to the one suggested by Conway.[7]

0.5 The essential point that we want to make at this point about our results here is that although the efficiency of an algorithm is grammar dependent, this may not mean that in general the efficiency is as strongly language dependent. In case an algorithm is not efficient for a certain grammar, it may often be possible to suitably modify the grammar to an equivalent form (without changing the language) for which the same algorithm is more efficient. As a matter of fact, the Rhodes-Kuno-Oettinger predictive analysis method is essentially the result of modifying an arbitrary grammar to the so-called standard form.[8] Such a change of grammar may not always be acceptable to the linguist or the machine translator, since the parsing (i. e. the structural description or P-marker[9]) is changed entirely, unless the originally envisaged parsing can be recovered unequivocally from the obtained one. When this recovery is possible one says that the new grammar is 'strongly equivalent' to the old one. Unfortunately, in what follows we shall not be able to demonstrate

that the changes suggested by us for the grammars result in
strongly equivalent grammars. We shall only assure ourselves
of equivalence, that is, that the language will remain unchanged
on introducing the suggested changes in the grammar. At the
time of writing, very little is known about tests for strong equivalence.[10]

0. 6 What has been said above essentially sets out the background of the present paper. In the rest of this section we shall
summarize the content of the remaining sections for the benefit
of readers who may want to read only parts of the paper.

0. 7 In section 1 of this article we shall introduce the concept
of a context-free grammar in a precise way. This is somewhat
redundant to the mathematical linguist — however, for the other
readers of this paper it may be worthwhile to restate it and to
bring out the fact that we are dealing with an axiomatically defined
mathematical structure, and very little else. To some, this
structure is evidently adequate for describing certain aspects of
natural languages. To others it is clearly inadequate for dealing
with any aspect of language since language is an entity from which
no aspect can be abstracted. We shall flatly refuse to enter the
controversy here, since we consider it to be outside our pale of
competence. We shall then define what we mean by structural descriptions, derivations, sentences, languages, and parsing; and
we shall exhibit the basic philosophy of the Glennie parsing algorithm. A recursive flowchart for carrying out the Glennie algorithm
will then be exhibited, and certain computer tricks for realization
of recursion pointed out. The operation of the flowchart will be
exemplified.

0. 8 In sections 2 and 3 we shall point out two difficulties
associated with the Glennie algorithm. One, which we shall call
the 'Loop', occurs in certain grammars and renders the Glennie
algorithm completely powerless to work with them. However,
it will also be pointed out that such a grammar can always be
modified to an equivalent grammar on which the Glennie algorithm
can operate. The method of modification will be exemplified and
a flowchart for the method exhibited.

0. 9 The other difficulty, called by us 'back-up',[11] renders
the Glennie algorithm inefficient on certain grammars. We shall
exemplify a technique whereby one can change such grammars to
equivalent grammars where the inefficiency is prevented. A

flowchart for the technique will be exhibited and the technique exemplified.

0.10 Unfortunately the technique, unlike the technique discussed in paragraph 0.8 above, is not universally applicable and in the case of grammars where the technique is not applicable, the flowchart leads to a nonterminating program. What is worse, there is no method available whereby one can decide for a grammar whether the back-up-preventing technique will terminate or not. This fact will be discussed in detail.

0.11 After a few concluding remarks in section 4, we shall include in the appendices some detailed examples of the mode of operation of the loop-preventing and back-up-preventing flow-charts, as well as a failure of the latter. We shall also include clear proofs of some of the statements made in the body of the paper — endeavoring to exhibit the proofs in such a manner as to be intelligible to the nonmathematician.

1. CONTEXT-FREE GRAMMARS AND THE GLENNIE ALGORITHM

1.1 A context-free grammar is defined by exhibiting three finite sets of objects. The objects in one set are called the terminal symbols or words. These are the symbols that occur in the sentences of the language being described by the grammar. One may think of these terminal symbols as the words[12] of the language. The objects in the second set are called nonterminals or phrase names. These never occur in the sentences of the language. This set has a prespecified member, called the sentence symbol. Terminal symbols will generally be represented by strings of Latin letters or by single lower-case Latin letters, depending on the language being exemplified. The nonterminals will be represented either by single capital Latin letters or by strings of Latin letters enclosed in angular brackets. The sentence symbol will generally be represented as 'S'.

1.2 The objects in the third set are called productions, each of which takes the form of a string of symbols, consisting of a phrase name (nonterminal), followed by an arrow pointing to the right ($\longrightarrow$), followed by a string of terminal symbols and non-terminals.

1.3 Each grammar has its own sets of terminal symbols, nonterminals, and productions. These describe a language by the following uniform definition, which is the same for all grammars. We introduce this definition through the following steps.

1.4 A derivation in a context-free grammar is a progression of strings, obtained as follows. The first element of the progression is S. At every step of the progression, one locates the left-most nonterminal in the string comprising the last element in the progression, chooses any production which has this nonterminal at the left of the arrow and replaces the nonterminal in the string by the string on the right-hand side of the arrow in this production. If at some step of the derivation the resulting string consists of all terminal symbols, then such a string of terminal symbols ending a derivation is called a 'sentence of the language described by the grammar'. Any language which can be described by a context-free grammar is a context-free language.

1.5 The following examples may clarify the definition and some of the definitions to follow. We shall take a grammar which will generate a set of strings, some of which will look like English sentences. It is by no means construed that the grammar is even a part of the grammar of English. We shall later on have to exemplify languages which have no connection with natural languages at all. However, the example does bring out the intuitive contents of our definitions and points out what sort of formal operations could parse English sentences if English were a context-free language.

1.6 In our example, the set of terminal symbols will contain the following strings or words:

old	ate	malt
gray	dog	the
killed	cat	
worried	mouse	

The set of nonterminals will contain the following phrase names:

<NP>	S
<VP>	A
N''	V
N'	
S '	

The productions will be the ones shown in Table 4.1. The productions actually comprise the three columns named jointly as productions. The columns 'Phrase name', 'Position 1', and 'Position
2' are of no importance at present. Nor is the column headed
'Definition number'. The column headed 'Production number' is
for identification purposes only.

Let us now look at a derivation.

1	S
2	<NP><VP>
3	the N'' <VP>
4	the N' S' <VP>
5	the dog S' <VP>
6	the dog <NP> V <VP>
7	the dog the N'' V <VP>
8	the dog the A N'' V <VP>
9	the dog the old N'' V <VP>
10	the dog the old N' V <VP>
11	the dog the old cat V <VP>
12	the dog the old cat killed <VP>
13	the dog the old cat killed V <NP>
14	the dog the old cat killed worried <NP>
15	the dog the old cat killed worried the N''
16	the dog the old cat killed worried the A N''
17	the dog the old cat killed worried the grey N''
18	the dog the old cat killed worried the grey N' S'
19	the dog the old cat killed worried the grey malt S'
20	the dog the old cat killed worried the grey malt <NP> V
21	the dog the old cat killed worried the grey malt the N'' V
22	the dog the old cat killed worried the grey malt the N' V
23	the dog the old cat killed worried the grey malt the mouse V
24	the dog the old cat killed worried the grey malt the mouse ate

At each step of the derivation, the left-most nonterminal is
replaced. For instance, in step 6 the left-most nonterminal, <NP>,
is replaced. It is replaced by means of production number 2, which
has <NP> on the left-hand side of the arrow: the resulting next step
7 of the derivation has <NP> replaced by the string the N'' which
occurs to the right of the arrow in production 2.

Step 24 of the derivation contains no phrase name and hence no
further progression is possible. This string, then, is a sentence
of the language described by the grammar.

Table 4. 1

Production Number	Definition Number	Phrase Name	Production	$_1$Position$_2$	
1	1	S	$\longrightarrow$	\<NP\>	\<VP\>
2	1	\<NP\>	$\longrightarrow$	the	N''
3	1	N''	$\longrightarrow$	N'	S'
4	2	N''	$\longrightarrow$	A	N''
5	3	N''	$\longrightarrow$	N'	
6	1	A	$\longrightarrow$	old	
7	2	A	$\longrightarrow$	grey	
8	1	S'	$\longrightarrow$	\<NP\>	V
9	1	V	$\longrightarrow$	killed	
10	2	V	$\longrightarrow$	worried	
11	3	V	$\longrightarrow$	ate	
12	1	\<VP\>	$\longrightarrow$	V	\<NP\>
13	1	N'	$\longrightarrow$	dog	
14	2	N'	$\longrightarrow$	cat	
15	3	N'	$\longrightarrow$	mouse	
16	4	N'	$\longrightarrow$	maït	

1.7 Let us now define <u>parsing</u> and <u>structural description</u>. One says that a certain string y is derived from another given string x if y is a step in a derivation starting at x. It is not hard to see that if x be broken up into two arbitrary parts x_1 and x_2, that is if x_1 and x_2 are two strings and x is obtained by writing x_1 and x_2 side by side (a fact we shall often express in concise notation by writing $x = x_1 x_2$), then y can be broken into two parts y_1 and y_2 such that y_1 can be derived from x_1 and y_2 can be derived from x_2. (A rigorous proof of this fact can be given.[13] However, since the fact is so easily acceptable to common sense and is also true, we need not go into this.)

1.8 Let us now look at the derivation exemplified above. The entire sentence, of course, is derived from the second step, that is from $\langle NP \rangle \langle VP \rangle$, hence the sentence can be broken up into two parts, one derived from $\langle NP \rangle$ and the other from $\langle VP \rangle$. A perusal of step 12 will indicate that <u>the dog the old cat killed</u> is derived from $\langle NP \rangle$ and hence <u>worried the grey malt the mouse ate</u> is derived from $\langle VP \rangle$. However, <u>the dog the old cat killed</u> is derived also from <u>the N'S'</u> in step 4; <u>dog</u> is derived from N' and <u>the old cat killed</u> is derived from S'.

1.9 Proceeding in this manner we can identify certain terminal symbols and strings of terminal symbols as being derived from a nonterminal. This identification can be effected by enclosing each string derived from a nonterminal in a pair of brackets and attaching the phrase name (nonterminal) to the right-hand bracket. Since one can readily identify the left bracket corresponding to a right bracket, one can, from such a notation, readily identify the phrase name corresponding to the strings which are derived from phrase names. The sentence in the above example will have its substrings identified as follows:

$$((the((dog)_{N'}((the((old)_{A}((cat)_{N'})_{N''})_{N''})_{\langle NP \rangle}(killed)_{V})_{S'})_{N''})_{\langle NP \rangle}$$

$$((worried)_{V}(the((grey)_{A}((malt)_{N'}((the((mouse)_{N'})_{N''})_{\langle NP \rangle}$$

$$(ate)_{V})_{S'})_{N''})_{N''})_{\langle NP \rangle})_{\langle VP \rangle})_{S}$$

1.10 Such an identification of what may be called the <u>structure</u> of a sentence is called parsing. To those used to thinking of a parsing as the exhibition of a tree-like structure we could say that the two methods are essentially identical. If one identifies each bracket pair as coming from a node and envisions that the inner pairs correspond to lower nodes than the outer pairs, one would obtain, for this above sentence, the tree found in Figure 4. 1. We shall not indicate here a formal procedure for conversion of the bracketed string to the tree and vice versa; it is probably intuitively clear and the purpose of the present paper is to exhibit some other mechanical procedures.

1. 11 The mechanical procedure or program we want to discuss first in detail is one which, given a grammar and a string, will determine if the string belongs to the language described by the grammar and, if it does, will indicate its structure by parsing it. The overall mode of operation of the program can best be exemplified in terms of the above example again. The program essentially scans the string from left to right. Starting at the extreme left it first assumes that the string to its right is derived from S. If this assumption is to be true, then, according to production number 1, it must be divisible into two parts, the first part derived from <NP> and the latter part derived from <VP>. However, if the first part is derived from <NP> then it must consist of the followed by a string derived from N''. Since the left-hand word of the string is indeed the, the program shifts attention to the right of this word and assumes that the string to its right is derived from N''. To test for this, one has to test for three possibilities, that this string be divisible into strings derived from N' and S', from A and N'', or that the string be simply derived from N'. These are checked as above, yielding the fact that dog the old cat killed is indeed derived from N'', and hence the dog the old cat killed is derived from <NP>. Thus the program shifts attention to the part worried the grey malt the mouse ate and, according to the direction of production number 1, assumes it is derived from <VP>. It is to be borne in mind that all this time, while the program was checking for <NP>, V, N'', etc., through the application of many of the productions, after the success of these, the rest of production number 1 has still to be checked and this has to be kept 'in the back of the program's mind' so to speak.

1. 12 Instead of giving another rough sketch of how <VP> is checked for in the second part of the sentence (we shall consider the program in great detail in what follows), it may be worthwhile to point out another basic fact. It will be noticed that although the operation of the program is quite complicated, it consists basically of the repeated application of a single program — one which, on being given a phrase name and a string, determines whether the string can be derived from the phrase name. The successive

questions are in this case: First, 'Is the dog the old cat ... ate
derived from S?'; 'Is the dog the old cat killed derived from
<NP>?'; 'Is the first word the?'. Since it is, the next questions
are: 'Is dog the old cat killed derived from N''?';'Is dog derived
from N'?'. Since it is, the next questions are: 'Is the old cat
killed derived from S'?'; 'Is the old cat derived from <NP>?', etc.
At this last point the program is checking for <NP> and the affirmative answer to this check would provide only a partial answer to
another check for <NP> on another string — a check started earlier
but so far incomplete; only if the old cat be derived from N'' and
killed be derived from V will the dog the old cat killed be checked
as derived from <NP> and, after this, not until worried the grey
malt the mouse ate is checked as derived from <VP> is the check
for S complete. The questions, then, follow not in sequence, in
the sense that the second question is asked after the answer to
the first is received, but as a part of the first question. The program, as it were, used itself as its own subprogram.

1. 13 Since the number of occurrences of the same program
in the overall operation is rather large (as the example above no
doubt bears out), it is not advantageous to have the same program
repeat itself in the larger program. Also, the total number of
occurrences of the program cannot be ascertained initially. Hence
the only way one can realize an operation such as the above in an
actual computer is through the use of subroutines. When a subroutine has to be used, the main program which uses the subroutine communicates to the subroutine (by storing it in some area
available to the subroutine)where the operation of the main program is to be resumed after the subroutine has completed its
operation. This imposes no difficulty as long as a subroutine is
not used until all of its previous uses have been completed. In the
present case, however, it is precisely this condition which is not
fulfilled, and on completion of the subroutine, control may have
to be transferred to various places depending on which use of the
subroutine has been completed.

1. 14 Another problem involved in this situation deals with
data. While the subroutine is working on one set of data, it may
use itself as a subroutine with a different set of data. This makes
it necessary to make data available to the subroutine according to
which use of the subroutine is under way.

1. 15 These two problems are solved in a computer by storing
both the data and the transfer-of-control address, not in specific

memory cells, but in what are known as <u>push-down stacks</u>.[14] The
exact procedure for the realization of a push-down stack in a
computer is strongly dependent on the available technology and
need not concern us here. For our purposes, it will suffice to
think of these as being similar to a stack of cards on which data
may be recorded. As a card bearing a new piece of data is placed
on the top of the stack, the cards below are hidden by the data at
the top. Any time the card at the top is destroyed, the data on the
card immediately below is made available.

1. 16 The mode of use of the push-down stack for programming
purposes will become clear as we peruse the flowcharts that
follow. In the first flowchart (Figure 4. 2), embodying the Glennie
parsing algorithm, the stack will be used only for the storage of
data and not for specifying the point of return from the subroutine
to the parent routine. In the exemplification of the procedure, we
shall exhibit stacks by writing the successive entries on the stack
in a vertical column. The bottom entry of a column will be considered to be the datum on the top card of the stack.

1. 17 Before coming to the detailed discussion of the flowchart,
it may be worthwhile to explain in detail the conventions used there
and to discuss the five push-down stacks used in the program. It
should also be pointed out that because of the difference in philosophy
between the conventional computer memory structures and a structure
involving stacks, our notational conventions may be slightly different
from those in the rest of this volume.

1. 18 The Glennie algorithm, when considered as an interpreter
(in the original paper, as well as in the Conway algorithm, the
analyzer embodies the grammar, i. e. acts as a compiled program),
uses five push-down stacks which we shall call here A, B, C, D,
and E. A contains the location of a marker which moves along the
words (terminal symbols) of the sentence to be analyzed. As this
marker moves along the sentence, its words, as well as the brackets
needed for parsing the sentence (see below), are put down in an
output string. The position of the output string at which the next
symbol is to be written at any stage of the program is marked by
another marker whose location is stored in push-down stack B.
Stack C contains the phrase name (nonterminal) which is being tested
for. Generally, when the subroutine starts with a phrase name in
C and a specific position of the input marker in A, the test being
conducted is for checking the assumption that some string starting
at the position marker is derived from the specific phrase name.

The program conducts this test by assuming that the derivation of the string from the phrase name starts with a specific production which has the phrase name on its left. In Table 4. 1 of paragraph 1. 6, the different productions having the same phrase name on the left are numbered consecutively. These numbers are called the definition numbers. When the program checks for a certain string being derived from a phrase name, it may find that the starting production needed is not the one having the specific definition number assumed initially, but one having a different definition number. The definition number being tried is stored in a push-down stack D. Again, as a specific definition is tried, it is assumed that the string being tested can be broken up into parts, each separately derived from the symbols in the string in the right-hand side of the production under consideration. The testing for these symbols has to be done consecutively and hence a record has to be kept at running time of the program about which symbol in the right-hand side of the definition is being tested for. This information, designated here 'the position number in the phrase', is recorded in stack E.

1. 19   A few other explanations are needed before the working of the flowchart shown in Figure 4. 2 can be clearly understood. One is that the parsed sentence, as envisaged in the output of this program, does not include the left parenthesis. Also, instead of the right parenthesis, it has the phrase name itself, which was placed as a subscript of the right parenthesis in our previous example in paragraph 1.9. This phrase name in the output string is followed by an integral number which indicates the position of the corresponding left parenthesis that was omitted. The method for restoring this parenthesis can be best brought out by first indicating what the parsing output would look like for the sentence shown in paragraph 1. 6 and comparing it with the parsing shown in paragraph 1.9. The output appears as follows;

the dog N' 1 the old A 1 cat N' 1 N'' 1 N'' 2 $<$NP$>$ 2 killed V

1 S' 2 N'' 2 $<$NP$>$ 2 worried V 1 the grey A 1 malt N' 1 the mouse

N' 1 N'' 1 $<$NP$>$ 2 ate V 1 S' 2 N'' 2 N'' 2 $<$NP$>$ 2 $<$VP$>$ 2 S 2

To restore the parenthesis, one goes from left to right until the first phrase name is encountered, which is replaced by the right parenthesis with the phrase name as a subscript. Then one counts as many words to the left as is indicated by the following integer and inserts a left parenthesis at the end of the count. The integer

is removed. This process is repeated until all the phrase names
and integers are removed. When during the counting to the left
a right parenthesis is encountered, the entire string between the
right parenthesis and the corresponding left parenthesis is counted
as a single word. It can be seen that the parsing in paragraph 1.9
can be obtained from the string exemplified above by this procedure.

    1.20 A few words used in the flowchart need explanation also.
When a stack is said to be pushed[15] by the program, it means that
a new card is placed on the top of the stack and the content of the
previous top card is copied into it. Hence, if the stack before
push looked as follows:

<S>
<VP>
<NP>

then after push it looks as follows:

<S>
<VP>
<NP>
<NP>

Again, when the stack is said to be popped it means that the top
card of the stack is removed without any change in the content
of the other cards. The card immediately below the top card becomes the top card. When a symbol is put on a stack, it is written
on the top card of the stack, destroying the previous content of
the top card. When a symbol is to be placed in a stack without
destroying the previous content, the stack must be pushed before
putting the symbol. Each card on a stack will be called a level
of the stack. Thus pushing increases the levels of a stack,
popping decreases it. When the subroutine is running with a
certain number 'x' of cards in the stack, we will say the program
is 'at level x'. All stacks start with one card in it.

    1.21 One more convention needs to be established. When in
the flowchart we use an expression like 'phrase name A' or 'position C', we shall mean the phrase name or position written on the
top card of stack A or C. When we want to refer to a symbol by

referring to itself rather than by the stack it is contained in, we shall enclose the symbol in quotes. Thus, 'A' will refer to the letter Aye, and A will refer to the content of the top card of stack A.

1.22 The reader will do well to verify that the operations indicated in the flowchart do parse sentences. To aid in this we are appending below a table (Table 4.2) indicating the successive situations of the stacks. Instead of indicating each situation by a separate table, we have included certain integers on the extreme left of the table which indicate the same thing. To find a specific situation, one fixes on an integer and considers only those rows which are numbered by integers smaller than or equal to this integer. All the rows above the row numbered by this integer are to be considered as existing on the stack. The rows below are to be considered as having been popped on return to the row numbered by the integer.

1.23 Before ending this section it ought to be pointed out that the Glennie algorithm was designed specifically for unambiguous languages, that is, languages wherein each sentence had only one possible parsing. It is not too difficult to modify the algorithm to exhibit all the parsings of a sentence in ambiguous languages. Indeed, the Rhodes-Kuno-Oettinger algorithm, which is closely analogous to the one under discussion, is capable of exhibiting all the parsings. The present algorithm, when faced with a number of definitions, tries them in sequence until one of them yields an effective analysis. Any later definitions are ignored. One can make a modification wherein all the definitions would be tried, irrespective of their successes; however, only the successful definitions would give rise to output tapes. In this case, the output tapes would have to be put on stacks also. We shall make no attempt to do this here. As the flowchart stands at present, it will get only one parsing for any sentence, ignoring any other parsings that may exist.

2.0 PREVENTION OF LOOP

2.1 The grammar we discussed in Table 4.1 was free from a characteristic which mathematical linguists call 'left-recursiveness', that is, occurrences of productions where the first position (or 'handle'[16]) of a production coincides with the phrase name. One could quote for example the production which might occur in

Table 4.2

Serial Number	A	B	C	D	E	Output
1, 62	~~1~~ ~~7~~ 14	~~1~~ ~~27~~ ~~56~~ ~~59~~ 60	S	1	~~1~~ 2	S 2
2, 29	~~1~~ ~~7~~ 7	~~1~~ ~~2~~ ~~25~~ ~~26~~ 27	<NP>	1	~~1~~ 2	the <NP> 2
3, 5, 28	~~2~~ ~~7~~ 7	~~2~~ ~~3~~ ~~25~~ 24 25	N''	1	~~1~~ 2	N'' 2
4	~~2~~ 3	~~2~~ ~~3~~ #5	N'	1	1	dog N' 1
6, 26	~~3~~ ~~6~~ 7	~~3~~ ~~18~~ ~~21~~ ~~22~~ 23	S'	1	~~1~~ 2	S' 2
7, 25	~~3~~ ~~4~~ 6	~~3~~ ~~6~~ ~~16~~ ~~17~~ 18	<NP>	~~1~~ 2	~~1~~ 2	the <NP> 2
8, 10, 12, 24	~~4~~ ~~5~~ 6	~~6~~ ~~9~~ ~~14~~ ~~15~~ 16	N''	~~1~~ 2	~~1~~ 2	N'' 2
9	4	6	N'	~~1~~ ~~2~~ ~~3~~ 4	1	
11	~~4~~ 5	~~6~~ ~~7~~ 8 9	A	1	1	old A 1
13, 15, 19, 21, 23	~~8~~ ~~6~~ ~~5~~ 6	~~9~~ ~~12~~ ~~9~~ ~~12~~ ~~13~~ 14	N''	~~1~~ ~~2~~ 3	~~1~~ ~~2~~ 1	N'' 1
14	~~5~~ 6	~~9~~ ~~10~~ ~~11~~ 12	N'	~~1~~ 2	1	cat N' 1
16, 18	6	12	S'	1	1	
17	6	12	<NP>	1	1	
20	5	9	A	1	1	
22	~~5~~ 6	~~9~~ ~~10~~ ~~11~~ 12	N'	~~1~~ 2	1	cat N'1
27	~~6~~ 7	~~18~~ ~~19~~ ~~20~~ 21	V	1	1	killed V 1
30, 32, 61	~~7~~ ~~8~~ 14	~~27~~ ~~30~~ ~~56~~ ~~57~~ 58	<VP>	1	~~1~~ 2	<VP> 2
31	~~7~~ 8	~~27~~ ~~28~~ ~~29~~ 30	V	~~1~~ 2	1	worried V 1
33, 60	~~8~~ ~~9~~ 14	~~30~~ ~~31~~ ~~54~~ ~~55~~ 56	<NP>	1	~~1~~ 2	the <NP> 2
34, 36, 38	~~9~~ ~~10~~ 14	~~31~~ ~~34~~ ~~52~~ ~~53~~ 54	N''	~~1~~ 2	~~1~~ 2	N'' 2
35	9	31	N'	~~1~~ ~~2~~ ~~3~~ 4	1	
37	~~9~~ 10	~~31~~ ~~32~~ ~~33~~ 34	A	~~1~~ 2	1	grey A 1
39, 41, 59	~~10~~ ~~11~~ 14	~~34~~ ~~37~~ ~~50~~ ~~51~~ 52	N''	1	1	N'' 2
40	~~10~~ 11	~~34~~ ~~35~~ ~~36~~ 37	N'	~~1~~ ~~2~~ ~~3~~ 4	1	malt N'' 1
42, 56, 58	~~11~~ ~~13~~ 14	~~37~~ ~~45~~ ~~48~~ ~~49~~ 50	S'	1	~~1~~ 2	S' 2
43, 55	~~11~~ ~~12~~ 13	~~37~~ ~~38~~ ~~43~~ ~~44~~ 45	<NP>	1	~~1~~ 2	the <NP> 2
44, 46, 50, 52, 54	~~12~~ ~~13~~ ~~12~~ 13	~~38~~ ~~41~~ ~~38~~ ~~41~~ ~~42~~ 43	N''	~~1~~ ~~2~~ 3	~~1~~ ~~2~~ 1	N'' 1
45	~~12~~ 13	~~38~~ ~~39~~ ~~40~~ 41	N'	~~1~~ ~~2~~ 3	1	mouse N' 1
47, 49	13	41	S'	1	1	
48	13	41	<NP>	1	1	
51	12	38	A	~~1~~ 2	1	
53	~~12~~ 13	~~38~~ ~~39~~ ~~40~~ 41	N'	~~1~~ ~~2~~ 3	1	mouse N' 1
57	~~13~~ 14	~~45~~ ~~46~~ ~~47~~ 48	V	~~1~~ ~~2~~ 3	1	ate V 1

French, say, to replace definition 2 for N'' in Table 4. 1. Since
the adjective follows the noun we would need a production like

$$N'' \longrightarrow N'' \ A$$

2.2 A left-recursive grammar would be completely unsuitable
for the application of the Glennie algorithm discussed in section 1
above. To see why this is so, let us see what would happen if we
entered box 2 of the flowchart with the top level push-down stacks
looking as follows:

7	8	N''	2	1

So, position 1 of definition 2 of N'' being N'', the next level of
the stacks would have the appearance:

7	8	N''	2	1

which is identical to the previous level, and box 2 would be entered
over and over again without any movement of the input and output
tapes.

2.3 We propose to get around this difficulty, not by modifying
the Glennie algorithm but by modifying the grammar itself to one
describing the same language but free from left-recursiveness.

2.4 The method for doing this will be explained by introducing
several examples. Intuitive arguments will be given to show that
the method achieves what it is expected to achieve without attempting
in any way to prove the fact, except in the appendix, since the
proofs are somewhat involved mathematically. Moreover, the
intuitive arguments will seem sufficient to all but the mathematician.
What will be unsatisfying to the nonmathematician in the following
sections will be the fact that our examples will be artificially constructed and the sentences described by the grammar will have
nothing to do with natural languages. But this dissatisfaction has
no real cause, since even the language discussed in the examples so
far has had only deceptively superficial similarity to natural languages.

2.5 As an initial example, let us take a language having the
following grammar:

$$S \longrightarrow Sb$$
$$S \longrightarrow a$$

which is clearly left-recursive. It describes a language whose
sentences consist of a single a followed t / an indefinite number
of b's. Now the same language could be described by the grammar:

$$S \longrightarrow aX$$
$$S \longrightarrow a$$
$$X \longrightarrow bX$$
$$X \longrightarrow b$$

This grammar is not hard to construct from the previous one, as
a little thought will show. We shall set out below a general method
for effecting this change when more than two productions are involved.

  2.6 However, one other thing needs to be pointed out before
going into details. It is the fact that, although it may not be evident on looking at a grammar, when position 1 of a production
coincides with its phrase name, the phenomenon of looping can
again take place. Consider the following grammar:

$$S \longrightarrow Ab$$
$$A \longrightarrow SA$$
$$A \longrightarrow b$$

With this grammar, if one enters box 2 of the flowchart with the
top of the stacks looking as follows:

| 1 | 1 | S | 1 | 1 |

the next following position would be:

| 1 | 1 | A | 1 | 1 |

and then once more:

| 1 | 1 | S | 1 | 1 |

the cycle repeating itself indefinitely.

  2.7 Before any modification like the ones in paragraph 2.5
above can be applied, a preliminary modification must be made
on the grammar so as to make all the hidden loops explicit. This
can be done easily also, without modifying the language. The
method can probably be explained best in terms of the example
above. Let us consider the first production $S \longrightarrow Ab$. Here,
though position 1 of the definition does not coincide with the phrase
name in the definition, this position is a nonterminal and there
may be a definition of it which has S in position 1. In the case of

this example this is indeed true, since we have the definition:

$$A \longrightarrow SA$$

To make this phenomenon 'come out into the open', we write the grammar by replacing the occurrence of A in position '1' of the first production by the right-hand sides of the productions having A as the phrase name, obtaining the grammar:

$$S \longrightarrow SAb$$
$$S \longrightarrow bb$$
$$A \longrightarrow SA$$
$$A \longrightarrow b$$

which has no more hidden loops and describes the same language. That it describes the same language can be seen with a little intro-spection, or by trying to generate identical sentences from the two grammars. A proof of the equivalence of grammars obtained from one another by the above procedure (replacing a nonterminal on the right of a production by the right side of all definitions of the nonterminal) will be given in the appendix.

2.8 The flowchart shown in Figure 4.3 carries out the opera-tion outlined in the example in paragraph 2.7 above. The only thing to be pointed out here is that this program also uses itself as its own subprogram, the reason being that one does not know how deep one may have to 'chain' on the nonterminal in position 1. It may be that A has B at position 1 of a definition, B has C at position 1 of a definition, C in its turn has D in position 1 and finally D has A in position 1 of a definition. In the grammar in our example, we were just lucky to find the loop merely by des-cending two levels.

2.9 We have introduced a new innovation in this flowchart over the previous one by having introduced two push-down stacks involving the exit address. This program has two possible exits, one when its operation is found unnecessary, and another when it exits after carrying out the operation. When a program (either itself or another program — see below) uses this program as a subroutine, the subsequent operation of the user program depends on the exit taken by the used program. In the present situation the only program which uses this program is itself and so we could have found out from the number of levels left in the push-down stack whether an exit is a termination exit or an exit to the user program. However, since our job does not end with making the loops explicit but also must lead to a program which modifies it,

we felt it safer to put the exit addresses in push-down stacks.
Moreover, since we shall soon be using this program as a subprogram of another program for preventing back-up, we will not
be able to take recourse to the level-counting procedure of section
1 at all.

2. 10 The subroutine of Figure 4. 3 can only be entered after
another program has placed in stack A a phrase name and in B a
symbol (phrase name or otherwise — see below) whose occurrence (in position 1 of any definition of the phrase name in A) is to
be made explicit. Initially, A and B will contain the same phrase
name, but at higher levels this may not remain true. The user
program also has to enter in stacks D and E the points of exit of
this program for the 'unnecessary' and 'completed' cases. The
program itself uses stack C for holding the current definition
number at any level of recursion and stack F to keep track of which
of the two exits to use at this level. The actual use of this program will occur in later flowcharts.

2. 11 We shall make use of the flowchart of Figure 4. 3 in the
flowchart of Figure 4. 4, which actually modifies a grammar to
prevent loops. In the appendix we have included the first few steps
of a table similar to Table 4. 2 in section 1 to indicate the operation
of the flowcharts. However, we want to include in the body of this
section the example for which this table is given and indicate the
results of the operations on this grammar. The grammar we
start with is as follows:

$$S \longrightarrow Bc$$
$$S \longrightarrow SbB$$
$$B \longrightarrow Cd$$
$$B \longrightarrow Dx$$
$$C \longrightarrow m$$
$$C \longrightarrow n$$
$$D \longrightarrow Sy$$
$$D \longrightarrow 1$$

The program first makes all loops explicit. It does so by starting
to make occurrence of S in position 1 of the definitions of S explicit.
In the definition $S \longrightarrow SbB$ it is already explicit, but the production
$S \longrightarrow Bc$ may or may not lead to a loop. To check this, the program makes the occurrence of S in position 1 of definitions of B
explicit. To do this, it has to make occurrence of S in position 1
of the definition of C explicit. There being no such occurrence

(all definitions of C leading to terminal symbols), it tries to make
the occurrence of S in position 1 of the definitions of D explicit.
When this is done, one uses these explicit definitions to modify
the definition of S. The grammar looks as follows at this stage:

$$S \longrightarrow Cdc$$
$$S \longrightarrow SbB$$
$$S \longrightarrow lxc$$
$$S \longrightarrow Syxc$$
$$B \longrightarrow Cd$$
$$B \longrightarrow Dx$$
$$C \longrightarrow m$$
$$C \longrightarrow n$$
$$D \longrightarrow Sy$$
$$D \longrightarrow l$$

No further modification is necessary to make the loops explicit.
At this point control is returned from the program in Figure 4.3
to the program in Figure 4.4, which proceeds to modify the grammar to prevent loops. This process, though essentially similar in
principle to the one exemplified in section 2.5 above, may not
always be as simple. In our present example, for instance, there
are two definitions of S which lead to loops. Also, there are two
definitions of S additional to this. We can first transform the two
definitions of S by introducing two more auxiliary variables, N
and M, and rewriting the grammar thus:

$S \longrightarrow SN$	$B \longrightarrow Cd$
$S \longrightarrow M$	$B \longrightarrow Syx$
$M \longrightarrow Cdc$	$B \longrightarrow lx$
$M \longrightarrow lxc$	$C \longrightarrow m$
$N \longrightarrow yxc$	$C \longrightarrow n$
$N \longrightarrow bB$	$D \longrightarrow Sy$
	$D \longrightarrow l$

and then modify it to:

$S \longrightarrow MP$	$B \longrightarrow Cd$
$S \longrightarrow M$	$B \longrightarrow Syx$
$P \longrightarrow NP$	$B \longrightarrow lx$
$P \longrightarrow N$	$C \longrightarrow m$
$M \longrightarrow Cdc$	$C \longrightarrow n$
$M \longrightarrow lxc$	$D \longrightarrow Sy$
$N \longrightarrow yxc$	$D \longrightarrow l$
$N \longrightarrow bB$	

It may be remarked in passing that in the two last stages of modification the phrase name D does not appear on any string derived from S. The D, so to speak, has been 'rendered useless'. This does not occur in every case of such modification however. See, for instance, the example in section 2. 7 above. Hence, after these algorithms are used to modify a grammar, it may be worthwhile to remove the useless phrase names. An algorithm for doing this is already known.[17]

3. PREVENTION OF BACK-UP

3. 1 In this section we shall take up the study of another phenomenon which renders the Glennie algorithm, if not powerless (as does a loop), at least somewhat inefficient. The phenomenon can best be understood by referring to Table 4. 2 in paragraph 1. 22 above, with special reference to serial numbers 13 to 22. We note in number 13 that the input tape is in position 5 (cat) and the program is trying to recognize an N'' phrase starting here. The first definition of N'' being N' S', the program goes down to the next level (serial number 14), testing for an N' phrase. The second definition of N' being cat, the tape moves one step to the right, and since no more words need be looked up to test for N', it goes up to the previous level (serial number 15) with input tape in position 6. It then checks for the next phrase name, S', in the definition on N'', going down one level (serial number 16) and, by the definition of S', goes down another level (serial number 17) to check for $<$NP$>$, with the input tape still in position 6. The word in position 6 (killed) does not agree with the; no other definition of $<$NP$>$ being available, the program exits from this level (serial number 18) and, no more definitions of S' being available either, exits to the next previous level (serial number 19). Here, a new definition being available, the program 'starts afresh', backing up the tape to position 5 (see box 7 in Figure 4. 2). Then, after descending one level and conducting a futile search for an A according to definition 2 of N', it returns (serial number 20, 21) and starts on the third definition (serial number 22), looking at the same word (cat) and recognizing it to be an N' as the sole element of N'', this time correctly. This backing up of the tape should not be necessary, however, since even after back-up the program looks at the same word (cat), changing only its interpretation. The question one is tempted to ask is, 'could this reinterpretation be done in retrospect, rather than by actual reexamination of the words. ' The question

is especially important in view of the possibility that the length of
the back-up need not always be restricted to one word but can be
quite long. To convince oneself that this may be the case, one
may consider the grammar:

$$S \longrightarrow M\alpha$$
$$S \longrightarrow N\beta$$
$$M \longrightarrow TM$$
$$M \longrightarrow x$$
$$N \longrightarrow LN$$
$$N \longrightarrow y$$
$$L \longrightarrow TM$$
$$T \longrightarrow m$$

and try to parse the sentence:

$$mmmxmmxy\beta$$

3.2 Before considering this last grammar, let us once more
go back to the grammar in Table 4.1 and ask ourselves what the
effect would be if production numbers 3 and 5 were modified to
appear thus:

$$N'' \longrightarrow N'X$$
$$X \longrightarrow S'$$
$$X \longrightarrow$$

A new phrase name, X, has been introduced, and takes on two
possible definitions, one for each of the two definitions on N'' with
an identical handle. The definitions have on their right hand the
strings on the original definitions of N'', with the common handle
deleted. In this special case, one such string is nonexistent
(nothing remains in the right-hand side of definition 3 of N'' after
removing the common handle N'). This leads to a rather unusual
kind of production which we have not encountered before. However,
it does not do the parsing algorithm any harm. In fact, box 2 in
Figure 4.2 is for taking care of precisely this exigency.

3.3 The rule for modification for preventing back-up, then,
is simply: if two or more definitions of a phrase name have the
same handle, replace them with one definition with the handle
followed by a new phrase name whose right-hand sides are obtained
from those of the old definitions by removing the common handle.
This works all right if the common handles can be seen explicitly.
But here also the same problem can arise that arose in connection
with removing infinite loops. The grammar indicated in paragraph

3. 1 is a case in point, where the common handles have to be
made explicit. A program for doing this is shown in Figures 4. 5
and 4. 6, which uses Figure 4. 3 as a subroutine. The working of
the entire program can be gleaned by looking at its working on
the grammar above. A table has been given in the appendix to
indicate the appearance of the stacks as the program runs. In
addition we give below a rough description of its working.

3. 4 The program checks for common handles for all nonterminals, one at a time. Hence it tries to find any common
handle of S; it finds M and N as handles of the two definitions of
S. These are not identical; however, they are both nonterminals
(M and N), so the program successively checks to see if N occurs
as the handle of M or vice versa. For this purpose it uses the
program in Figure 4. 3. In this case M has T as its handle and T
has a terminal symbol as its handle — so N never appears as a
hidden handle of M. Similarly, N has L as a handle and L has T
as a handle — so M never occurs as a handle of N either. At this
point the program looks for a common handle for M and N, starting
over at the beginning of the program (taking care of the push-down
stacks, of course). Then it tests for the occurrence of T as a
handle for L, using the program in Figure 4. 3. Since T is a
handle for L, and since M and N have a common handle (at the next
higher level), the definitions of N involving L in the handle are
changed yielding a grammar:

$$S \longrightarrow M\alpha$$
$$S \longrightarrow N\beta$$
$$M \longrightarrow TM$$
$$M \longrightarrow x$$
$$N \longrightarrow TMN$$
$$N \longrightarrow y$$
$$L \longrightarrow TM$$
$$T \longrightarrow m$$

This exit from the level for testing the common handle of M and N
starts a redefinition of S, yielding a grammar:

$$S \longrightarrow TM\alpha$$
$$S \longrightarrow x\alpha$$
$$S \longrightarrow TMN\beta$$
$$S \longrightarrow y\beta$$
$$M \longrightarrow TM$$
$$M \longrightarrow x$$

$$N \longrightarrow TMN$$
$$N \longrightarrow y$$
$$L \longrightarrow TM$$
$$T \longrightarrow m$$

which can now be changed in several steps of application, to the grammar:

$$S \longrightarrow TX$$
$$S \longrightarrow x\alpha$$
$$S \longrightarrow y\beta$$
$$X \longrightarrow MY$$
$$Y \longrightarrow \alpha$$
$$Y \longrightarrow N\beta$$
$$M \longrightarrow TM$$
$$M \longrightarrow x$$
$$N \longrightarrow TMN$$
$$N \longrightarrow y$$
$$L \longrightarrow TM$$
$$T \longrightarrow m$$

which is free of all back-up.

3.5 The reader must be warned at this point that, unlike the loop-prevention program which is an effective procedure in all cases, the back-up-prevention program is not guaranteed for success. To see this, one may consider as an example the following grammar:

$$S \longrightarrow aSc$$
$$S \longrightarrow B$$
$$B \longrightarrow aBb$$
$$B \longrightarrow ab$$

If we apply the procedure of the above paragraphs to this grammar we shall initially get the modified grammar:

$$S \longrightarrow aX$$
$$B \longrightarrow aY$$
$$X \longrightarrow Sc$$
$$X \longrightarrow Bb$$
$$X \longrightarrow b$$
$$Y \longrightarrow Bb$$
$$Y \longrightarrow b$$

which, on reapplication of the method, yields:

$$S \longrightarrow aX$$
$$B \longrightarrow aY$$
$$X \longrightarrow aZ$$
$$X \longrightarrow b$$
$$Y \longrightarrow Bb$$
$$Y \longrightarrow b$$
$$Z \longrightarrow Sc$$
$$Z \longrightarrow Bb$$

It will be noticed that the two definitions of Z behave exactly like two definitions of X in the grammar in which X appeared for the first time. The back-up-prevention routine, then, would be effective again and another phrase name would be produced with identical definitions. This process would continue indefinitely.

3.6 All grammars, then, cannot be rendered free of back-up by this procedure. In the example cited in the previous paragraph, we have demonstrated one way in which this procedure may fail to terminate on some grammars. In this case and similar cases we can study the grammar beforehand to decide that it would be a waste of time to free it from back-up. Unfortunately, this may not always be possible. We have not been able to derive any essentially finite method which, applied to a grammar, can tell us whether it can be made free of back-up. There is a possibility that such a method may be impossible to construct, just as a method for testing the ambiguity of a grammar is impossible to construct.[18] Unfortunately we have not been able to formally establish the impossibility either. While no grammar with an infinite number of ambiguous sentences can be made back-up-free, it is not true (as our example above shows) that a grammar which cannot be made back-up-free is necessarily ambiguous. Thus the impossibility for a test for ambiguity (as well as for certain similar phenomena such as infinite intersection)[19] does not necessarily imply the impossibility of testing for back-up. Meanwhile the procedure roughly described above and made precise in the flowcharts of Figures 4.5 and 4.6 does provide what is called a semidecision procedure for back-up prevention. If the described method, applied to a grammar, terminates, then the modified grammar resulting from the application would be free of back-up. However, if the method does not terminate after some prespecified time, one has at present no way of knowing whether the grammar can be freed from back-up or not — a few more cycles might have completed the process, or they might not. It is unfortunate that the state of the art has to be left at this rather unsatisfactory stage.

4. CONCLUDING REMARKS

4. 1 We have seen in recent years an increase of interest in
syntax-directed parsing both among linguists and computer specialists. For reasons of efficiency as well as applicability of
some generalized algorithm, it is often found necessary to use
special 'tricks' in the algorithm, as has been suggested by Conway[20]
in his discussion of the syntax-directed parsing of Cobol. Very
often, such tricks need not be incorporated separately in the parsing
algorithm, but can be made to take the form of a special change
of the grammar to an equivalent form. Since linguistic structures
are presently somewhat better understood than the theory of
computing algorithms, it is much easier to study effects of changes
in grammatical forms than changes in algorithms.

4. 2 Any change in a grammar with the aim of increasing the
efficiency of parsing algorithms naturally has to keep the language
unchanged. This invariance over language can generally be
achieved without too much difficulty, although a lot still remains
to be understood about language-preserving transformations on
grammars. The few modifications of grammars that have been
considered for their usefulness have been simple enough so that
their language-preserving nature can be understood easily. However, techniques for investigating equivalence (albeit no uniformly
applicable technique can be developed) are highly necessary. This
is one reason why we have included in the appendix some proofs
of the equivalence-preserving nature of the class of transformations
on grammars that we have discussed here. These transformations
are of such a simple nature that such proofs are almost unnecessary.
However, the technique of proof may be of interest for future applications.

4. 3 However, it must be remembered that mere maintenance
of equivalence is not sufficient when transforming grammars. One
has to maintain what Greibach refers to as strong equivalence[21] so
that the phrase marker of a sentence according to one grammar is
derivable from the phrase marker of the same sentence according
to the other grammar. Very little is known about strong equivalences between grammars[22] at present.

4. 4 The Glennie algorithm (which has been discussed here
in the interpretive mode) is a representative of the class of
algorithms termed 'top-to-bottom' by Petrick.[23] The Rhodes-
Kuno-Oettinger predictive analysis falls in this category. The

'bottom-to-top' algorithms of Robinson[24] form another class of
algorithms for syntax-directed parsing. A comparison of the
different classes of algorithms and the effectiveness of the variants within a class has been investigated only to a very small
extent. Further efforts in this direction ought to prove extremely
fruitful.

APPENDICES

1. The appearance of the push-down stacks at the first ten stages of the operation of the program in Figures 4.4 and 4.3 on the grammar shown in section 2.11 is as follows: (The format of the representation is identical with that of Table 4.2, section 1.22.)

Serial No.	A	B	C	D	E	F		Remarks
0, 10								Entering Fig. 4.4 return to Fig. 4.4 at 10. Final form of grammar.
1, 7, 9	S	S	~~1~~ ~~0~~ ~~1~~ ~~2~~ ~~3~~ 4	1	2	~~0~~	1	Entered Fig. 4.3 Second modified grammar.
2, 4, 6	B	B	~~1~~ ~~2~~ ~~1~~ ~~2~~ 3	4	5	~~0~~	1	first modified grammar.
3	C	S	~~1~~ 2	4	5	0		
5	D	S	~~1~~ 2	4	5	~~0~~	1	
8	C	S	~~1~~ 2	4	5	0		

The next few steps of the program result in no further modification of the grammar and are left as an exercise for the reader. The first modified grammar, obtained on return from serial number 5 to serial number 6, is as follows:

S ⟶ Bc   B ⟶ mlx   D ⟶ Sy
S ⟶ SbB   C ⟶ m   D ⟶ 1
B ⟶ Cd   C ⟶ n
B ⟶ Syx

The second and final forms of the grammar have been displayed in section 2.11.

2. The appearance of the push-down stacks at the first 19 stages of operation of the programs shown in Figures 4.5 and 4.6 (including Figure 4.3 as a subroutine) on the grammar exemplified in section 3.1 is as follows:

Serial No.	A	B	C	D	E	F	G	Remarks
0								Enter Fig. 4.6
1, 7, 11, 19	A	A	1	13	14	∅ 1	1 2	Enter Fig. 4.5 Second modification of grammar
2, 6	N	M	1 2	7	8	0		Enter Fig. 4.3
3, 5	L	M	1	4	5	0		
4	T	M	1	4	5	0		
8, 10	M	N	1 2	10	11	0		Enter Fig. 4.3
9	T	N	1	4	5	0		
							1 ∅ 1 2 3	Re-enter Fig. 4.5
12, 14, 16, 18	M	N	1 2 3	20	6	∅ 1	1 2 3 1	first modified grammar
13	L	T	1	7	8	∅ 1		Enter Fig. 4.3
15	T	y	1	10	11	0		
17	T	x	1	7	8	0		

The rest of the operation which culminates in the final production of the grammar shown at the end of section 3.4, produced
by box 13 in Figure 4.6, is left to the reader. The modified
grammars have already been shown in section 3.4.

3. Some proofs regarding transformations preserving weak
equivalences: an introduction to the Ginsburg[25] formalism. The
reason this appendix is included is to point out that a certain
approach to context-free grammars is useful in the study of equivalence. The reasons it is not included in the text are twofold:
first, the kind of grammatical changes we have introduced in the
paper are so simple that a rigorous proof of equivalence preser-
vation in their case may seem out of place to many. Second, the
concepts and techniques involved herein are so different from
those used in the body of the text as to make it uninteresting to
anyone but mathematicians and those linguists who really want to
know about the formal aspects of the subject. However, we have
endeavored for the benefit of the latter to make the exposition ab
initio and explain the concepts carefully.

The major innovation in the point of view we shall adopt here
lies in thinking of the phrase names as representing sets of strings
of terminal symbols. That is, we can say about a language that
there is a set of strings called sentences, another set called noun
phrases, another set called nominals, and so on. Each terminal
symbol also represents a set of strings, i.e. the one consisting
of that terminal symbol alone.

On such sets we define two operations, union and concatenation.
If A and B are two sets of strings, we shall mean by A + B (read:
'A union B') those strings which appear in at least one of the two
sets, A or B. By AB we will mean the set of all those strings
which can be obtained by taking any string from A and adjoining
or concatenating to it some string taken from B.

The grammar of a language expresses certain phrase types
as derived from other phrase types by means of these operations.
To see this, let us take as an example the grammar:

$$S \longrightarrow Bc$$
$$S \longrightarrow SbB$$
$$B \longrightarrow Cd$$
$$B \longrightarrow Dx$$
$$C \longrightarrow m$$
$$C \longrightarrow n$$
$$D \longrightarrow Sy$$
$$D \longrightarrow l$$

discussed in section 3 and rewrite it in a slightly different form:

$$S = Bc + SbB$$
$$B = Cd + Dx$$
$$C = m + n$$
$$D = Sy + l$$

which to the naked eye looks almost like a set of simultaneous
algebraic equations. But it must be remembered that the interpretation is quite different. What the set of equations above says,
is: 'There is a set C of strings whose only members are the
string "m" and the string "n". There is also a set D of strings
which has the string "l" as one member and whose other members
are obtained by taking any member of the set S (defined later)
and adjoining the terminal symbol y to it. There is a set B whose
members are obtained either by taking an element of C and
adjoining the terminal symbol d to it or taking an element of D
and adjoining the terminal symbol x to it. The set S of strings

is obtained either by adjoining the terminal symbol C to some
member of B or by taking a member of S, adjoining the terminal
symbol b to it and adjoining to the resulting string any member
of "B". '

It is clear that the above set of sentences say exactly what
is said (under interpretation) by the four equations above. There
is, therefore, partial justification in the linguist's contention that
mathematics does not tell us anything more than what the linguist already knows. However, the use of mathematical notations
is just a little bit more than a matter of 'prestige'. For one thing,
it is evident that once the interpretation of the symbolism is firmly
ensconced in the reader's mind, there is a certain advantage to
being able to say in four lines what would otherwise take a full
paragraph to say. The avantages do not stop here, however, as
we shall show in what follows.

Given a set of equations of the form above one can, in a step-
by-step manner, build up the sets of strings denoted by the phrase
names. We shall exemplify this method in terms of the grammar
above and then proceed to formulate the discussion in general
terms.

We first define a sequence of sets of strings for each phrase
name, calling them S^0, S^1, S^2, S^3..., B^0, B^1, B^2, B^3..., C^0,
C^1, C^2, C^3..., D^0, D^1, D^2, D^3... . The sets are constructed
as follows: A^0, B^0, C^0 and D^0 are empty sets. Then for any
value of i,

$$S^{i+1} = B^i C + S^i b \ B^i$$
$$B^{i+1} = C^i d + D^i x$$
$$C^{i+1} = m + n$$
$$C^{i+1} = S^i y + 1$$

To exemplify this process, let us put i=o. Then $S^1 = B^0 c +$
$S^0 b \ B^0 =$ the empty set again (B^0 is empty and anything concate-
nated with an empty set still yields an empty set. Notice the
difference between an empty string and the empty set of strings).
Similarly,

$$B^1 = \text{the empty set}$$
$$C^1 = (m, n)$$
$$D^1 = 1$$

Now putting i=1 we obtain:

$$S^2 = \text{empty}$$
$$B^2 = (md, \ nd, \ 1x)$$

$$C^2 = (m, n)$$
$$D^2 = 1$$

Again:

$$S^3 = (mdc, \ ndc, \ lxc)$$
$$B^3 = (md, \ nd, \ lx)$$
$$C^3 = (m, n)$$
$$D^3 = 1$$

and so on.

It can be seen that for all i, S^i is contained in S^{i+1}, that is, every element of S^i is an element of S^{i+1}. It is not hard to believe (though the proof may be hard to read) that, if S, B, C, D are the smallest set of strings that satisfy the original polynomial equations, then each element of S is an element of some S^i for some i and every element of S^i for every i is an element of S. We shall use this fact to prove our equivalence theorems by invoking the following tricks over and over. If S and S_1 are the set of sentences of the two grammars, we shall show that every element of S^i is an element of S_1^j for some j and vice versa. However, since we are interested in proving these theorems for context-free grammars in general, let us introduce a symbolism which avoids giving specific names to nonterminals and specific forms to the polynomial equations. To this end we shall denote the nonterminals by A_1, A_2, $A_3 \ldots$, A_n, and the corresponding sequence of sets by A_i^j in general, i.e. by

$$A_1^o, \ A_1^1, \ A_1^2 \ldots, \ A_2^o, \ A_2^1 \ldots, \ \ldots, \ A_n^o, \ A_n^1 \ldots$$

We shall denote arbitrary polynomial forms by $f_1(A_1, \ A_2 \ldots A_n)$, $f_2(A_1, \ A_2 \ldots A_n)$ etc., f's with different subscripts denoting different polynomials. A general grammar then would look as follows:

$$A_1 = f_1(A_1, \ A_2 \ldots A_n)$$
$$A_2 = f_2(A_1, \ A_2 \ldots A_n)$$

$$A_n = f_n(A_1, \ A_2 \ldots A_n)$$

and the equations for the A_i^j take the form:

$$A_i^o = \text{the empty set for all i}$$

and;

$$A_i^{j+1} = f_i(A_1^j, \ A_2^j \ldots A_n^j)$$

We are now ready to tackle the various equivalence proofs

a) The changes in the grammar we made to make either the loops or the common handles explicit depended on one (so far unproved) fact, namely that if an occurrence of a nonterminal (A_2, say) in the definition of another nonterminal (A_1, say) be replaced by the definitions of the former nonterminal, the language defined by the modified grammar is identical to that defined by the unmodified grammar. In symbols, if

$$A_1 = f_1(A_1, A_2 \ldots A_n) \qquad B_1 = f_1(B_1, f_2(B_1, B_2 \ldots B_n), B_3 \ldots B_n$$
$$A_2 = f_2(A_1, A_2 \ldots A_n) \qquad B_2 = f_2(B_1 \ldots \ldots B_n)$$

and

$$A_n = f_n(A_1, A_2 \ldots A_n) \qquad B_n = f_n(B_1 \ldots \ldots B_n)$$

be two grammars, then for each i, A_i and B_i are identical.

To prove this we shall first set up the sets A_i^j and B_i^j by setting up $A_1^0 = A_2^0 \ldots A_n^0 = B_1^0 \ldots B_n^0 = \phi$, the empty set, and for each j

$$A_i^{j+1} = f_i(A_1^j A_2^j \ldots A_n^j)$$
$$B_1^{j+1} = f_1(B_1^j, f_2(B_1^j, B_2^j \ldots B_n^j), B_3^j, \ldots B_n^j)$$

and for all i greater than 1 and all j

$$B_i^{j+1} = f_i(B_1^j, B_2^j, \ldots B_n^j)$$

We shall now proceed to show that for all i and j, any string in A_i^j is also in B_i^j (i.e. A_i^j is a subset of B_i^j, or in symbols: $A_i^j \subseteq B_i^j$)

This statment is trivially true for j=0, since both A_i^0 and B_i^0 are empty sets. We shall now show that if for any j, $A_i^j \subseteq B_i^j$, then it follows that $A_i^{j+1} \subseteq B_i^{j+1}$. This is seen as follows. We have for all i greater than 1

$$A_i^{j+1} = f_i(A_1^j, A_2^j \ldots A_n^j)$$

however, since $A_i^j \subseteq B_i^j$ for each i,

$$f_i(A_1^j,\ A_2^j\ \ldots A_n^j)\ \subseteq\ f_i(B_1^j,\ B_2^j\ \ldots B_n^j)$$
$$=\ B_i^{j+1}$$

proving the assertion when i is greater than 1. For the one other remaining case,

$$A_1^{j+1}\ =\ f_1(A_1^j,\ A_2^j,\ \ldots A_n^j)\ \subseteq\ f_1(B_1^j,\ B_2^j,\ \ldots B_n^j)$$

but since

$$B_2^j\ \subseteq\ B_2^{j+1},$$

$$f_1(B_1^j,\ B_2^j,\ \ldots B_n^j)\ \subseteq\ f_1(B_1^j,\ B_2^{j+1},\ B_3^j \ldots B_n^j)$$

$$=\ f_1(B_1^j,\ f_2(B_1^j,\ B_2^j,\ \ldots B_n^j),\ B_3^j,\ \ldots B_n^j)$$

$$=\ B_1^{j+1}$$

So, since $A_i^o \subseteq B_i^o$ for all i, we have $A_i^1 \subseteq B_i^1$ for all i, and so $A_i^2 \subseteq B_i^2$ for all i, and so on. Hence, a member of A_i, being a member of some A_i^j, is a member of B_i^j and hence of B. This shows that the language described by the first grammar is a subset of the language described by the second grammar. But this is not enough to show that the grammars are equivalent. Hence we shall now show that for all i and j,

$$B_i^j \subseteq A_i^{2j}$$

Once more, this is clear for j=0, since B_i^o and A_i^o are empty sets; it is also quite easily seen to be true that for all i greater than 1, if $B_i^j \subseteq A_i^{2j}$, then $B_i^{j+1} \subseteq A_i^{2j+2}$. For i=1, we have

$$B_1^{j+1}\ =\ f_1(B_1^j,\ f_2(B_1^j,\ B_2^j\ \ldots B_n^j),\ B_3^j,\ \ldots B_n^j)$$

$$\subseteq\ f_1(A_1^{2j},\ f_2(A_1^{2j},\ A_2^{2j},\ \ldots A_n^{2j}),\ A_3^{2j}\ \ldots A_n^{2j})$$

$$=\ f_1(A_1^{2j},\ A_2^{2j+1},\ A_3^{2j}\ \ldots A_n^{2j})$$

$$\subseteq\ f_1(A_1^{2j+1},\ A_2^{2j+1},\ \ldots A_n^{2j+1})\ =\ A_1^{2j+2}$$

So that for all i, $B_i^o \subseteq A_i^o$, whence $B_i^1 \subseteq A_i^2$, $B_i^2 \subseteq A_i^4$, and so on. Thus any member of B_i is an element of some B_i^j and hence a member of A_i^{2j} and hence a member of A_i. Hence, B_i is a subset of A_i; and since we have already seen that A_i is a subset of B_i, the two languages are identical.

b) The method by which an explicitly common handle was made to 'merge' into a single definition through the introduction of a new phrase name can be similarly shown to leave the language unchanged. The method effectively is based on the following proposition. If

$$A_1 = f(A_1, A_2 \ldots A_n) \; g(A_1, A_2 \ldots A_n) + h(A_1, A_2 \ldots A_n)$$
$$A_2 = f_2(A_1, A_2 \ldots A_n)$$
$$A_3 = f_3(A_1, A_2 \ldots A_n)$$
$$\cdot$$
$$\cdot$$
$$\cdot$$
$$A_n = f_n(A_1, A_2 \ldots A_n)$$

and

$$B_1 = f(B_1, \ldots B_n) \; C + h(A_1, A_2 \ldots A_n)$$
$$B_2 = f_2(B_1 \ldots B_n)$$
$$\cdot$$
$$\cdot$$
$$\cdot$$
$$B_n = f_n(B_1 \ldots B_n)$$
$$C = g(B_1 \ldots B_n)$$

are two grammars, then for all i, $A_i = B_i$ (note that nothing is said about C).

We shall first show that for all i and j, $B_i^j \subseteq A_i^j$. This is evidently true for $j = 0$. Also, for all i greater than 1, it can be easily seen that if $B_i^j \subseteq A_i^j$, then $B_i^{j+1} \subseteq A_i^{j+1}$. For $i = 1$ we note:

$$A_1^{j+1} = f(A_1^j, \ldots A_n^j) \; g(A_1^j \ldots A_n^j) + h(A_1^j \ldots A_n^j)$$
$$\supseteq f(B_1^j, \ldots B_n^j) \; g(B_1^j \ldots B_n^j) + h(B_1^j \ldots B_n^j)$$
$$= f(B_1^j, \ldots B_n^j) \; C^{j+1} + h(B_1^j, \ldots B_n^j)$$

$$\supseteq f(B_1^j \ldots B_n^j) \ c^j + h(B_1^j, \ldots B_n^j)$$

$$= B_i^{j+1}$$

This would immediately lead, as in the case (a) above, to the conclusion that $B_i \subseteq A_i$ for all i. We now proceed to show that $A_i^j \subseteq B_i^{2j}$. Again this is trivially true for $j = 0$ and it also follows easily that for all i greater than 1, if $A_i^j \subseteq B_i^{2j}$, then $A_i^{j+1} \subseteq B_i^{2j+2}$. For $i = 1$ we have:

$$A_1^{j+1} = f(A_1^j, A_2^j \ldots A_n^j) \ g(A_1^j, A_2^j \ldots A_n^j) + h(A_1^j \ldots A_n^j)$$

$$\subseteq f(B_1^{2j}, \ldots B_n^{2j}) \ g(B_1^{2j} \ldots B_n^{2j}) + h(B_1^{2j} \ldots B_n^{2j})$$

$$\subseteq f(B_1^{2j+1}, \ldots B_n^{2j+1}) \ c^{2j+1} + h(B_1^{2j+1}, \ldots B_n^{2j+1})$$

$$= B_1^{2j+2}$$

The rest of the argument is similar to case (a).

c) We are now left with showing that the method employed for removing loops leaves the language unchanged. One can express this statement in symbols as follows:
If

$$A_1 = f_1(A_1, \ldots A_n)$$

$$A_2 = f_2(A_1, \ldots A_n)$$

.

.

.

$$A_{n-1} = f_{n-1}(A_1, \ldots A_n)$$

$$A_n = A_n f(A_1, \ldots A_n) + g(A_1, \ldots A_n)$$

and

$$B_1 = f_1(B_1, \ldots B_n)$$

$$B_2 = f_2(B_1, \ldots B_n)$$

.

.

.

$$B_{n-1} = f_{n-1}(B_1, \ldots B_n)$$

$$B_n = g(B_1, \ldots B_n) \; C + g(B_1, \ldots B_n)$$

$$C = f(B_1 \ldots B_n) \; C + f(B_1 \ldots B_n)$$

be two grammars, then the languages described by the two are identical.

To show this, we shall first show that $A_i^j \subseteq B_i^{j^2}$ for all i. Once again, this is true for j = 0. Also for all i less than n, if $A_i^j \subseteq B_i^{j^2}$, then

$$A_i^{j+1} = f_i(A_1^j, \ldots A_n^j) \subseteq f_i(B_1^{j^2}, B_2^{j^2}, \ldots B_n^{j^2})$$

$$= B_i^{j^2+1} \subseteq B_i^{(j+1)^2}$$

for i = n,

$$A_n^{j+1} = A_n^j \; f(A_1^j, \ldots A_n^j) + g(A_1^j, \ldots A_n^j)$$

$$= [A_n^{j-1} \; f(A_1^{j-1}, \ldots A_n^{j-1}) + g(A_1^{j-1}, \ldots A_n^{j-1})]$$

$$f(A_1^j, \ldots A_n^j) + g(A_1^j, \ldots A_n^j)$$

$$= A_n^{j-1} \; f(A_1^{j-1}, \ldots A_n^{j-1}) \; f(A_1^j, \ldots A_n^j) + g(A_1^{j-1}, \ldots A_n^{j-1})$$

$$f(A_1^j, \ldots A_n^j) + g(A_1^j, \ldots A_n^j)$$

$$= A_n^{j-2} \; f(A_1^{j-2}, \ldots A_n^{j-2}) \; f(A_1^{j-1}, \ldots A_n^{j-1}) \; f(A_1^j, \ldots A_n^j)$$

$$+ g(A_1^{j-2}, \ldots A_n^{j-2}) \; f(A_1^{j-1}, \ldots A_n^{j-1}) \; f(A_1^j, \ldots A_n^j)$$

$$+ g(A_1^{j-1}, \ldots A_n^{j-1}) \; f(A_1^j, \ldots A_n^j)$$

and so on, yielding finally

$$A_n^{j+1} = g(A_1^o \ldots A_n^o) \; f(A_1^1 \ldots A_n^1) \ldots \ldots f(A_1^j, \ldots A_n^j)$$

$$+ g(A_1^1, \ldots A_n^1) \; f(A_1^2 \ldots A_n^2) \ldots f(A_1^j \ldots A_n^j)$$

$$+ g(A_1^2 \ldots A_n^2) \; f(A_1^3, \ldots A_n^3) \ldots f(A_1^j \ldots A_n^j)$$

$$+ \ldots + g(A_1^{j-1}, \ldots A_n^{j-1}) \; f(A_1^j, \ldots A_n^j)$$

$$+ \; g(A_1^j, \ldots A_n^j)$$

Similarly,

$$C^{j+1} = f(B_1^j, \ldots B_n^j) \; C^j + f(B_1^j, \ldots B_n^j)$$

$$= f(B_1^j, \ldots B_n^j) \, [f(B_1^{j-1}, \ldots B_n^{j-1}) \, C^{j-1} + f(B_1^{j-1}, \ldots B_n^{j-1})]$$

$$+ \; f(B_1^j, \ldots B_n^j)$$

$$= f(B_1^j \ldots B_n^j) \, f(B_1^{j-1}, \ldots B_n^{j-1}) \, C^{j-1} + f(B_1^j, \ldots B_n^j) \, f(B_1^{j-1}, \ldots B_n^{j-1})$$

$$+ \; f(B_1^j, \ldots B_n^j)$$

and continuing,

$$C^{j+1} = f(B_1^j, \ldots B_n^j) \, f(B_1^{j-1}, \ldots B_n^{j-1}) \ldots f(B_1^o, \ldots B_n^o)$$

$$+ \; f(B_1^j, \ldots B_n^j) \, f(B_1^{j-1}, \ldots B_n^{j-1}) \ldots f(B_1^1, \ldots B_n^1)$$

$$+ \; \ldots .$$

$$+ \; f(B_1^j, \ldots B_n^j) \, f(B_1^{j-1}, \ldots B_n^{j-1})$$

$$+ \; f(B_1^j, \ldots B_n^j)$$

whence

$$B^{j+1} = g(B^j, \ldots B^j) \, C^j + g(B^j, \ldots B^j)$$

$$= g(B_1^j \ldots B_n^j) \, f(B_1^{j-1}, \ldots B_n^{j-1}) \ldots f(B_1^o \ldots B_n^o)$$

$$+ \; g(B_1^j \ldots B_n^j) \, f(B_1^{j-1}, \ldots B_n^{j-1}) \ldots f(B_1^1 \ldots B_n^1)$$

$$+ \; \ldots .$$

$$+ \; g(B_1^j \ldots B_n^j) \, f(B_1^{j-1}, \ldots B_n^{j-1})$$

$$+ \; g(B_1^j, \ldots B_n^j)$$

and hence, if $A_i^t \subseteq B_i^{t^2}$ for all t less than j

$$B_n^{j+j^2+1} = g(B_1^{j+j^2}, \ldots B_n^{j+j^2}) f(B_1^{j+j^2-1}, \ldots B_n^{j+j^2-1}) \ldots f(B_1^o \ldots B_n^o)$$

$$+ \ldots$$

$$+ g(B_1^{j+j^2}, \ldots B_n^{j+j^2}) \ldots f(B_1^{j^2}, \ldots B_n^{j^2})$$

$$+ g(B_1^{j+j^2}, \ldots B_n^{j+j^2}) \ldots f(B_1^{j^2+1}, \ldots B_n^{j^2+1})$$

$$\vdots$$

$$+ g(B_1^{j+j^2}, \ldots B_n^{j+j^2})$$

$$\supseteq g(B_1^{j+j^2}, \ldots B_n^{j+j^2}) f(B_1^{j+j^2-1}, \ldots B_n^{j+j^2-1}) \ldots f(B_1^{j^2} \ldots B_n^{j^2})$$

$$+ g(B_1^{j+j^2}, \ldots B_n^{j+j^2}) \ldots \ldots \ldots \ldots \ldots \ldots \ldots f(B_1^{j^2+1}, \ldots B_n^{j^2+1})$$

$$+ \ldots$$

$$+ g(B_1^{j+j^2}, \ldots B_n^{j+j^2})$$

$$\supseteq g(B_1^o \ldots B_n^o) + (B_1^1, \ldots B_n^1) f(B_1^4 \ldots B_n^4) \ldots f(B_1^{j^2}, \ldots B_n^{j^2})$$

$$+ g(B_1^1, \ldots B_n^1) f(B_1^4 \ldots B_n^4) \ldots \ldots f(B_1^{j^2}, \ldots B_n^{j^2})$$

$$+ \ldots$$

$$+ g(B_1^{j^2}, \ldots B_n^{j^2})$$

$$\supseteq g(A_1^o \ldots A_n^o) f(A_1^1, \ldots A_n^1) f(A_1^2, \ldots A_n^2) \ldots f(A_1^j, \ldots A_n^j)$$

$$+ g(A_1^1, \ldots A_n^1) f(A_1^2, \ldots A_n^2) \ldots f(A_1^j, \ldots A_n^j)$$

$$+ \ldots$$

$$+ g(A_1^j \ldots A_n^j) = A_n^{j+1}$$

whence $B_n^{(j+1)^2} \supseteq B_n^{j^2+j+1} \supseteq A_n^{j+1}$,

showing that $A_i \subseteq B_i$ for all i. To show $B_i \supseteq A_i$, we proceed to show that $B_i^s \subseteq A_i^{s^2}$ in a similar manner.

NOTES

1. Susumu Kuno and Anthony G. Oettinger, 'Multiple Path Syntactic Analyzer', Mathematical Linguistics and Automatic Translation Report NSF-8, Sec. I (Computation Laboratory of Harvard University, 1963). C. Douglas Johnson, 'The Berkeley Parser', 1964 Annual Meeting of the Association for Machine Translation and Computational Linguistic (Bloomington, Indiana). Jane J. Robinson, 'An Automated Phrase Structure Grammar of English', 1964 Annual Meeting of the Association for Machine Translation and Computation Linguistics (Bloomington, Indiana).

2. K. Samelson and F. L. Bauer, 'Sequential Formula Translation', Communications of the Association for Computing Machinery 3.76 (1960).

3. E. Irons, 'A Syntax Directed Compiler for Algol 60', Communications of the Association for Computing Machinery 4.51 (1961).

4. Stanley Petrick and Thomas Griffiths, 'On Relative Efficiencies of Context Free Grammar Recognizers' AFCRL-TM-64-2 (January, 1964).

5. Stanley Petrick, 'A Recognition Procedure for Transformational Grammars', Second Congress on the Information System Sciences (Hot Springs, Virginia, 1964).

6. Alec E. Glennie, 'On the Syntax Machine and the Construction of an Universal Compiler', Technical Report No. 2, Computation Center, Carnegie Institute of Technology (Pittsburgh, Pa., 1960).

7. Melvin Conway, 'Design of a Separable Transition Diagram Compiler', Communications of the Association for Computing Machinery 6.396 (1963).

8. Sheila Greibach, 'Inverse of Phrase Structure Generators', Mathematical Linguistics and Automatic Translation, Report NSF-11 (Computation Laboratory of Harvard University, 1963).

9. Noam Chomsky, 'On the Notion, "Rule of Grammar" ', Structure of Language and its Mathematical Aspects: Proceedings of the 12th Symposium in Applied Mathematics, American Mathematical Society (1961).

10. See, however, William Lynch, 'Ambiguity in Backus Normal Form Languages', Ph.D. Thesis (University of Wisconsin, 1963). Also, Sheila Greibach, 'A New Normal Form Theorem for Context-Free Phrase Structure Grammars', Journal of the Association for Computing Machinery 12.42 (1965).

11.   We shall use the words 'Loop' and 'Back-up' as technical
terms in the future with the precise meaning defined in appropriate
places.   The reader is warned against interpreting them with any
colloquial English meaning.

12.   This use of the word <u>word</u> is nontechnical, as opposed to
its use as a technical synonym for 'terminal symbol'.

13.   Yehoshua Bar-Hillel, Y. Perles and E. Shamir, 'On Formal Properties of Simple Phrase Structure Grammars', <u>Zeitschrift
für Phonetik, Sprachwissenschaft und Kommunikationsforschung</u>
14.143 (1961).

14.   The words 'push-down stack' form a technical term defined
in what follows.   It is not to be construed to be a colloquialism with
a colloquial meaning.

15.   The terms, 'push', 'pop', and 'put' are technical terms with
meaning as defined in the text.   They are not to be construed to be
colloquialisms with meanings in colloquial English.

16.   The word 'handle' will be used throughout this paper as a
technical term following Greibach (see note 8).   It is not to be construed to have a colloquial meaning.

17.   See op. cit., note 13.

18.   Noam Chomsky, 'Formal Properties of Grammars', <u>Hand-
book of Mathematical Psychology</u> 2.323 (New York, 1963).

19.   See note 13.

20.   See op. cit. in note 7.

21.   See op. cit. in note 8.

22.   See, however, Lynch, op. cit., in note 10.

23.   See op. cit. in note 4.

24.   See Robinson, note 1.

25.   Seymour Ginsburg, 'Two Families of Language Related to
Algol', <u>Journal of the Association for Computing Machinery</u> 9.350
(1962).

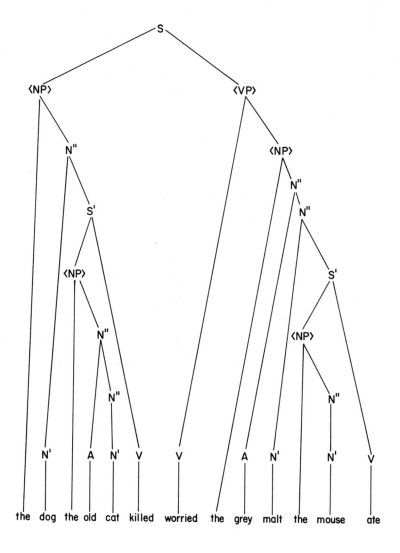

Figure 4.1

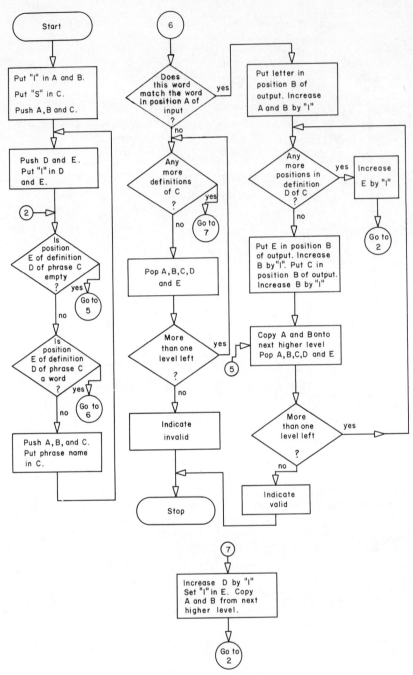

Figure 4.2   The Glennie Algorithm as an Interpreter

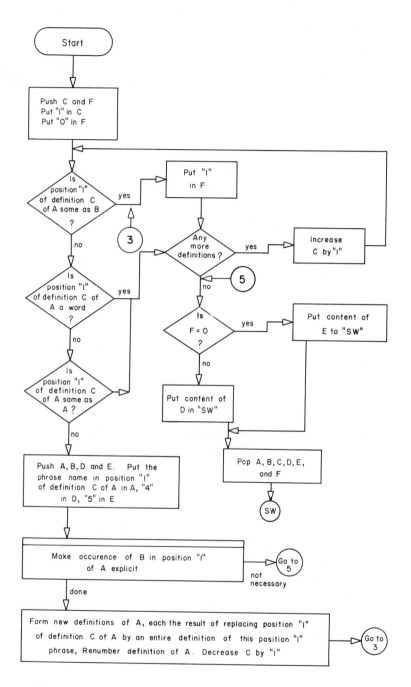

Figure 4.3   Flowchart for making occurence of B
in position "I" of A explicit.

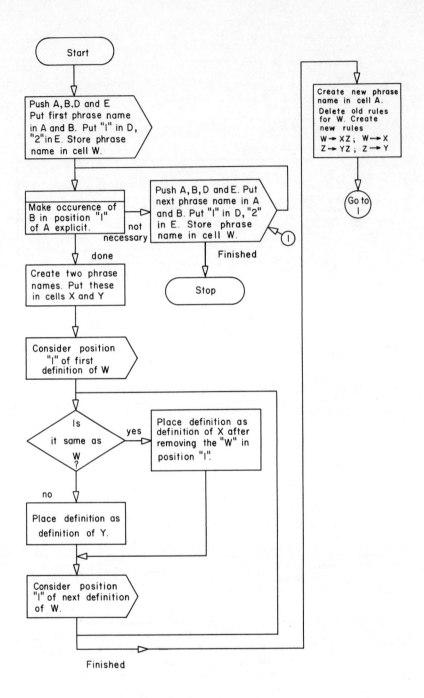

Figure 4.4   Flowchart for preventing loops

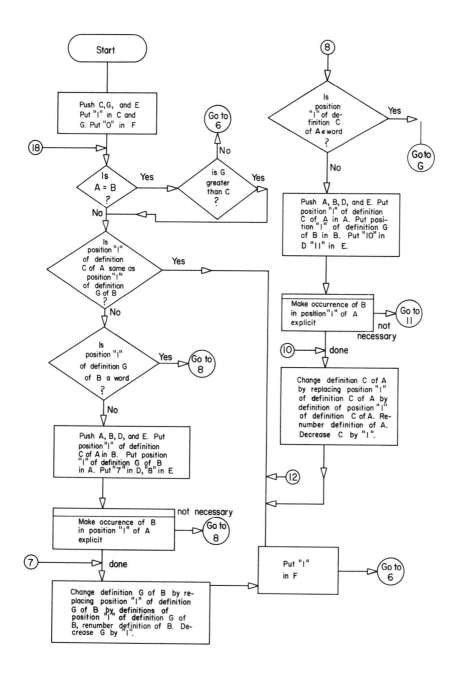

Figure 4.5   Flowchart for making common handle of A and B explicit.

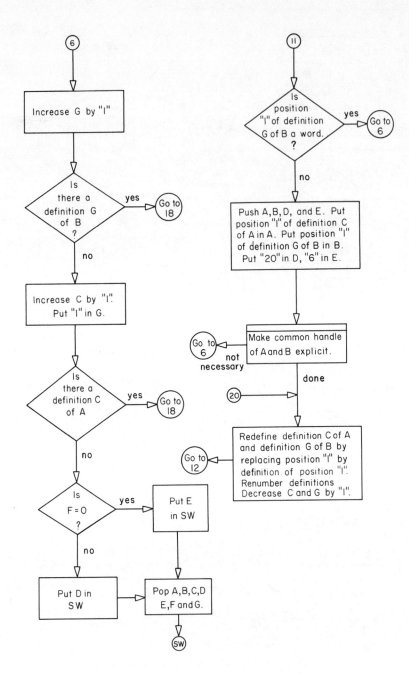

Figure 4.5 – Page 2

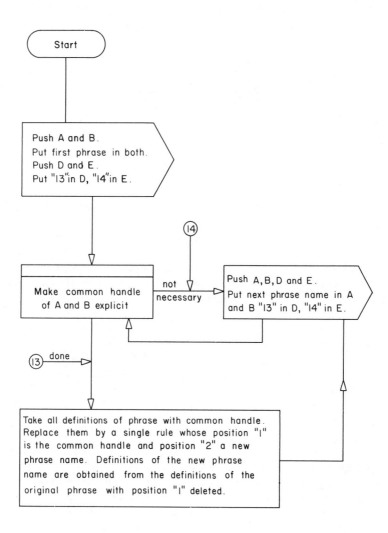

Figure 4.6   Flowchart for preventing backup.

Chapter 5

A Program For the Determination of
Lexical Similarity between Dialects

Albert J. Schütz and Jerome Wenker[1]

1.0 LINGUISTIC BACKGROUND

1.1 Introduction. Since linguists first noticed variation
among speech communities in Fiji, they have used the term 'dialects'
to mark this variation. Its extent, however, has remained loosely
labeled, largely because of a lack of precise interpretation of data.
As missionaries, ethnographers, and linguists moved westward
through the Fiji Group, their estimates of dialect diversity ranged
from 'very similar' to 'great enough to form two distinct groups'.
For either of these extremes, minimum evidence was cited.

The phrase 'Fijian dialects' suggests greater linguistic homo-
geneity within the group than actually exists. The term in fact has
more political and geographical than linguistic significance, since
the diversity among speech patterns on Fiji is greater than that
among some sets in the Malayo-Polynesian Group traditionally
treated as separate languages. But it is customary to speak of a
single Fijian language. In order to make more precise statements
about Fijian dialect diversity, it is necessary to compare not total
systems but more abstractable features. Some of these features
that have been described and discussed elsewhere[2] are: the phonemic
systems, sets of markers, types of morphological constructions,
pronoun systems, and a limited number of syntactic constructions.
Some general statements about lexical relationships have been
made, based on the patterns derived from geographical mapping
and plotting of isoglosses. However, there is a need for a set of
more specific statements about the lexical relationship between
the members of each different pair of villages.

1.2 Collection of data. Bauan, the official dialect, was used
as the eliciting medium. The basis for the lexical sample was
the Swadesh 200-word list, with the following omissions:

geographically unsuitable items like <u>freeze</u>, <u>ice</u>, and <u>snow</u>; items
that for various reasons were difficult to elicit such as <u>warm</u>;
and multimorpheme translations of single English morphemes,
such as <u>ulu-ni-vanua</u> 'head-of-land' for 'mountain'.

The word lists, along with other linguistic data, were tape-
recorded in the field. Some transcription was done at the time,
but most of it was done later with the help of a Bauan speaker. A
phonemic analysis was done for each village, and the regular
consonant correspondences were tabulated as the linguist became
more familiar with the material. An awareness of the occasional
sound correspondences came much later, when the responses for
each item were collated and their distribution shown on a dialect
map.

1.3 <u>Cognate vs. phonetically similar</u>. Even though the lexical
systems of various communities in Fiji are not as divergent as some
early selected word lists have indicated, they are significantly
different. A sample figure of lexical diversity, as measured by the
conventional method of cognate inspection, is about 60 per cent for
villages on the extreme ends of the main island of Viti Levu, 150
miles apart by coastal road. The figure is likely to be even lower
between the outer island groups to the west and to the east. But
because of a history of interaction among the villages, there are
no dialects that have not been influenced by some others. For
example, Bauan, spoken throughout the group, is the official language for all government, religious, and educational transactions.
As a consequence, it is used as the medium of communication for
speakers of dialects with a low degree of mutual intelligibility. It
is difficult to measure the effect that the official dialect has had
on the vocabularies of the other dialects, since there were only a
few glossaries compiled before the time at which Bauan was
adopted. Interest in the non-Bauan dialects (largely from mission-
ary sources) dropped sharply when there was no longer a need to
use them as teaching media. But as early as 1876, the influences
of Bauan on the other dialects was noted. In his introduction to a
collection of texts from different dialects, A. S. Gatschet remarked
that 'probably an excessive Bau element has crept into some of
the specimens, owing to the circumstance that they were obtained
from young men, whose speech approximates more to Bau than
that of the older men.'[3] Today, comparisons between younger
and older speakers show that this trend has continued.[4] Consequently, there are likely to be Bauan borrowings in the word lists

from any of the other dialects, and, with a few exceptions (comparable to the English borrowings maakete 'market' and tii 'tea' in an area in which a /t/ borrowing would normally occur as /ʔ/), they cannot be distinguished from 'true' cognates. Since any count of purported 'cognates' will in fact yield a figure for word pairs that are phonetically similar, forms displaying phonetic similarity have been used to avoid any unwarranted historical conclusions about the data.

1.4 Utility of computer in phonetic comparison. Among various advantages of electronic data processing — accuracy, consistency, speed, ability to handle large amounts of data — the first of these would be least applicable if we desired a measure of cognation. Because we have no standards for accuracy in cognate-counting other than the linguist's decisions, any deviations from his results are, by definition, inaccurate. Although a program can be designed to manipulate the given data in a number of ways, it has no way of drawing on the exterior data that a linguist sometimes uses for his decisions. But no exterior data are required to measure phonetic similarity, and in this measurement, the computer can combine the other advantages listed with as high a degree of accuracy as hand inspection would produce.

The most important use of the computer in this project is the reduction of a large (and generally unmanageable) body of comparative data to more succinct statements. Comparative methodology can be quite cumbersone, particularly when it involves $n(n-1)/2$ comparisons for either the 23 villages used in the trial runs or the 100 in the total collection of data.

1.5 Utilization of results. Although, for the reasons given above, it would be difficult to draw historical conclusions from the project results, they could serve as part of an index to the similarity among dialects at the present time. It may be possible to use the results to tell what kinds of differences — types of regular correspondences, syllable ordering, types of reduplication, etc. — make greater obstacles to intelligibility between dialect pairs.

In addition, in examining the procedures involved in machine-counting and hand-counting, we may be better able to understand what kinds of exterior data or experience the linguist draws on to decide, in less clear-cut cases, the relationship between two forms.

1.6 Methodology

1.610 Types of similarity between forms. Within this group of related dialects, most of the cognates show identity[5] or regular correspondences. For example, in a hand comparison of two lists of 175 items, 40 items were identical, 29 showed regular correspondences, 34 had some degree of similarity, and 72 were not similar. Programming for recognition of identical items or those with regular correspondences seems relatively simple, since the symbols will be either identical or matched from a short list of correspondences. Recognizing those pairs fitting into neither of these categories, but still showing some similarity of form, is more complicated. These remaining forms that are similar have the following characteristics: 1) occasional correspondences, such as /β/ to /ð/; 2) phoneme-to-zero correspondences, particularly for /k/, /β/, and /ð/; 3) metathesis; and 4) an extra sequence, either similar or dissimilar to the rest of the form.

1.620 Possible units for comparison. Although the investigator doing a hand comparison of word lists probably scans whole forms in his first comparison, it seemed more practical to use some smaller unit in the program. Several possibilities follow.

1.621 Phoneme. Using the phoneme as a basic unit, Flowchart 5.1 shows a broad outline for comparison. Boxes 1 and 2 rewrite /ʔ/ for certain villages to avoid equating /ʔ/ corresponding to Bauan /t/ with /ʔ/ corresponding to Bauan /k/.[6] Following the No direction, Box 3 checks for identity of symbols. If the symbols are identical, this is recorded, and a check is made to see that neither of the words has ended. If the symbols are not identical, they are checked to see that two consonants or two vowels are being compared. If a consonant is being matched with a vowel, Box 9 allows certain consonant-to-zero correspondences. Box 7 lists the allowable consonant correspondences, both regular and occasional. If none of these operations checks, a negative answer is recorded, and the next pair of phonemes is checked. The end-of-word subroutine, Flowchart 5.2, divides the words into syllables and reorders the syllables of one form to check for metathesis and reduplication. To note the latter, the extra sequences in forms of unequal length are matched with the rest of the form. For each different reordering and matching, the percentage figures for phoneme correspondences are stored, and the highest used for tabulation.

1.622 Syllable. An alternate to the preceding plan is the use of the syllable (definable, for the purposes of this study, as any CV sequence, or V when preceded by a space or another V) as the basic unit for comparison. It is possible to list all allowable syllable correspondences — for example, /ⁿdi/ — /ti/, etc. Flowchart 5.3 is a broad outline of the initial stages of a syllable-to-syllable comparison routine, using these correspondences.

1.623 Distinctive feature. Another linguistic unit that could possibly be used for comparison is the distinctive feature, which for purposes of the present study is viewed as an articulatory component. Considering the consonant phonemes of the overall pattern to be bundles of articulatory components, it is possible to account for all the contrasts by listing components of three types: position, manner, and cofeature (nasalization and labialization). Thus any consonant can be described by checking the appropriate columns in Table 5.1. Two examples are given.

Table 5.1

	POSITION					MANNER						COFEATURE			
	labial	dental	alveolar	glottal	velar	glide	lateral	trill	stop	spirant	nasal	nasalization	nonnas.	labialization	nonlab.
/p/	X								X				X		X
/ŋgʷ/					X				X			X		X	

/p/, as shown above, is a combination of labial position, stop manner, and absence of nasalization and labialization as cofeatures. /ŋgʷ/ is a combination of velar position, stop manner, and the cofeatures of nasalization and labialization.

If we examine the consonant correspondences (Table 5.2) in terms of articulatory components, we find that the relationships between the corresponding pairs can be described in terms of phonetic distance — there are correspondences between certain

Table 5.2

n_d — t	# — x
ŋ — ŋ^w	# — β
s — h	# — k
r — n_r	# — ð
? — t	+ any two from the following groups:
? — k	$n_g{}^w$, n_g, k, k^w
p — β	k, k^w, x, x^w
p — m_b	

points of articulation, certain manners of articulation, and presence
or absence of cofeatures. In Table 5.1, the arrangement of the
columns and the addition of the logically unnecessary categories of
nonnasalized and nonlabialized are graphic means of illustrating
this pattern: ANY TWO CONSONANTS MATCH OR CORRESPOND
WHEN THEIR COMPONENTS FALL IN THE SAME COLUMN OR
ADJACENT COLUMNS. Blank columns appear on the table to prevent two unrelated columns from being adjacent. For example,
under position, correspondences of /t/ to /?/, /k/ to /?/, or /s/
to /h/ are allowed, but not /k/ to /t/. Under manner, a stop-to-
spirant correspondence such as /p/ to /β/, or /k/ to /x/ is allowed.
An additional set of instructions is needed to account for the
limited number of consonant-to-zero correspondences.

1.63 Choice of unit for comparison. Because of its functioning
in the language, the syllable was used as the unit for comparison
in the present program. The structural reason for its use is that
it operates as a unit for the following processes: 1) Reduplication.
Because of the syllable structure, there is no reordering of elements smaller than a syllable. The pattern $C_1V_1C_2V_2$ cannot become $V_1C_1C_2V_2$. 2) Metathesis. For a similar reason, there
is no metathesis of the patterns $C_1VC_2 \to C_2VC_1$ or $V_1CV_2 \to$
V_2CV_1. 3) Other morphological constructions. Although the
most productive morphological construction — transitive suffixation — has been eliminated from the data, there are examples
that seem to reflect older constructions. These elements, although
unidentifiable, are always at least a syllable in length. The practical reasons for this choice are: 1) the simple structure makes
identification of syllable boundaries easy; 2) the syllable structure
also limits the number of different syllables that can occur[7];
3) the stability of the vowels throughout the dialects limits the
number of corresponding syllables in the overall pattern; and

4) some operations with syllables were already necessary in the
preceding plan.

With the addition of one more feature, vowel quality, the distinctive feature analysis was used as a means for syllable comparison. This eliminated the need for separate correspondence
tables. This approach may produce some undesirable results.
For example, the program is likely to be more complicated, and
some correspondences may be posited that have little validity.
But it is also likely that this procedure will show some relationships that were too obscure or whose occurrences were too infrequent for the linguist to observe. Were there not a series of
irregular sound correspondences scattered throughout the data,
it would have been simpler to check each syllable pair against a
list of regular correspondences. The phonetic-distance method
was used to discover either more examples for, or exceptions to,
the theory of the relationship of Fijian sound correspondences to
distinctive features.

The resultant index of phonetic similarity, having taken into
account the patterning of distinctive features that seems to exist
for both regular and occasional correspondences, should show a
high correlation to counts of related forms.

2.0 THE PROGRAM

2.1 Introduction. A computer program capable of automatically
comparing lexicons from Fijian utilizing only the list of dialect vocabulary entries as input data has been devised. Due to limitations
in time, the full computer program — called the 'Fiji Lexical-
Comparison Program' — has not been completed. However,
enough work has been done to indicate the feasibility and practicality of the computational technique used. This section describes
the data, technique, results achieved, and suggests plans for future
research in computer-aided dialect analysis.

2.2 The input data. The input data for the program consist of
the word lists for each dialect. In each list the entries are numbered and blanks are used for missing entries so that, for example,
entry five on the first list is to be compared with entry five on
every other list that contains a word at this location.

For the computer this input data must be keypunched onto IBM
cards. Each word list is given in one deck of cards, with each card
containing four consecutive dialect entries. The first 72 columns
of each card contain these four words, with the first word starting

in column 1, the second word starting in column 19, the third
word starting in column 37, and the fourth word starting in column
55. Thus each word is limited to a maximum of 18 characters and
if this vocabulary is missing a word, all 18 characters at the position on the card of this word are blank. Columns 75-77 contain
the number of the last word on the card. Thus a card containing
words five through eight of the dialect would contain 008 in columns
75-77. Finally, all dialects which are to be compared are assigned
unique arbitrary numbers and columns 78-80 contain the number of
the dialect which uses the words given in columns 1-72. All cards
containing data on a single dialect must be kept together for the
computer.

The words of the various Fiji dialects are keypunched using the
letters A, E, I, O, and U for the vowels and B for $/^mb/$, C for
$/\delta/$, D for $/^nd/$, G for $/\eta/$, H for $/h/$, K for $/k/$, L for $/l/$, M
for $/m/$, N for $/n/$, P for $/p/$, Q for $/^\eta g/$, R for $/\check{r}/$, S for $/s/$,
T for $/t/$, V for $/\beta/$, W for $/w/$, X for $/x/$, Y for $/y/$, DR for
$/^nr/$, GW for $/\eta^w/$, KW for $/k^w/$, QW for $/\eta g^w/$, XW for $/x^w/$,
and ' for $/?/$ for consonants. All other characters are assumed
to be typing mistakes.

The syllables of each word consist of # V or CV, where #
represents a blank, V represents any vowel given on the above
vowel list and C represents any consonant given on the above
consonant list. Thus V always represents a single character
while C represents either one or two characters. Limiting syllable
forms greatly simplifies the computations of the program.

2.3 The Fiji Lexical-Comparison Program. The Fiji Lexical
Comparison Program must prepare all dialect pairs for comparison
and then calculate the phonetic relationship between the members
of each pair. For simplification, the discussion of the program
will be divided into two segments. The first segment, called the
control program, includes all operations required to prepare
each dialect pair for comparison. The second segment, called
the comparison program, uses the data pertaining to each of the
two given dialects as input data and produces the numbers indicating
the relationship of these two dialects as output.

The control program uses the dialect vocabularies, prepared
according to the card format described above, as input data. As
each dialect vocabulary is read, it is converted into the numerical
format, described below, required by the comparison program
and assigned an input sequence number.

   The basic sequence of operations used by the control program
is outlined in this and the following three paragraphs. The first
dialect is read, converted into the required format, and stored
as one of the two dialects to be compared. The second dialect is
read, converted into the required format, written on magnetic
tape (thus saving the converted data for future reference), [8] and
stored as the second of the two dialects to be compared. Then the
first two dialects are compared by use of the comparison program.
The results of the comparison are then printed as the output of
this first dialect-pair comparison.

   The third dialect is then read, converted into the required
format, written on magnetic tape, and stored as the second of
the two dialects to be compared. Then the first and third dialects
are compared and the results of the comparison are printed. This
process of reading, converting, writing, storing, and comparing
dialect pairs is continued until every remaining dialect has been
converted, written on magnetic tape, compared with the first dialect
read, and all of the results have been printed. At this point the
first dialect has been compared with all remaining dialects so it
can be set aside, and all remaining dialects have been converted
and stored on magnetic tape ready for comparison.

   The magnetic tape containing the converted dialects is re-
wound and the second dialect is read and stored as the first of the
two dialects to be compared. The third dialect is then read, stored
as the second of the two dialects to be compared, and compared
with the second dialect. This process of reading, storing, and
comparing dialect pairs is continued until every remaining dialect
has been compared with the second dialect read, and all of the
results have been printed. At this point the second dialect has
been compared with all remaining dialects so it too can be set
aside.

   The magnetic tape containing the converted dialects is reposi-
tioned and the third dialect is read and stored as the first of the two
dialects to be compared. The remaining dialects are then read,
stored, and compared with the third dialect. This process of
reading and storing one dialect followed by reading, storing, and
comparing every remaining dialect with this dialect is continued
until each dialect has been compared with every remaining dialect.
When this has been completed, every dialect has been compared
once, and only once, with every other dialect and the Fiji Lexical-
Comparison Program has completed the processing of all of the
dialects.

The preceding four paragraphs have outlined the major parts of the control program and have given sufficient information on all parts of this control program except for the description of the conversion of the input dialect vocabularies into the numerical values required by the comparison program.[9] The conversion program requires that each dialect word be subdivided into its syllables and that each syllable be replaced by a number identifying the distinctive features of that syllable. As mentioned previously, the syllables of Fiji dialects have the form # V or CV which, as keypunched, appear as v, cv, or ccv. Thus the program has no problems in subdividing the dialect word into syllables. The distinctive feature values for each vowel and consonant are stored in tables and, by reference to these tables, the characters given in the dialect word are replaced by the desired numbers. These numbers are stored in consecutive machine-word locations and, after the word has been completed, additional zeroes are stored to complete a block of nine[10] machine words for each dialect word. Thus the complete conversion program consists of subdividing each dialect word into its syllables, replacing each syllable by the numeric value of its distinctive features, and adding additional zero numbers to complete a block of nine machine words for each dialect word.

The segment of the Fiji Lexical-Comparison Program remaining to be discussed is the comparison program. This program compares the two dialects that have been selected by the control program and converted into numbers by the conversion part of the control program. The input to the comparison program consists of two lists of numbers, one list from each dialect to be compared. Each list consists of 200 blocks of nine numbers, since the dialect vocabulary is defined to be 200 words long[11] and each dialect word is set to be nine machine words long.

The comparison program uses the first block of nine numbers in the first list and the first block of nine numbers in the second list to compare the first word on the first list with the first word on the second list. The result of this word-pair comparison, to be discussed later, is a number called the word-pair-comparison value, which indicates the phonetic relationship of these two words. The value of this number, to be discussed later, ranges from zero, indicating no relationship, to $1-2^{-35}$, indicating identity. (In the following discussion, 'identity' will refer to identity of symbols.) The second block of nine numbers from the first list is then compared with the second block of nine numbers from the second list. This process is continued until each word on the first list has been

compared with the equivalent word on the second list. If a dialect
word is missing from one or both lists, one or both blocks will
consist of zeroes, no word-pair comparison is made, and a zero
is used to indicate that no comparison is possible.

When all word-pair comparisons have been made, the computer is ready to combine the results of these word-pair comparisons
and obtain the numbers used to indicate the relationships of the two
dialects. The number of words present in both vocabularies, and
hence the number of comparisons possible, is calculated. The
number of word pairs deemed to be related is counted and the percentage is calculated by dividing this number of word pairs by the
total number of word pairs compared. The average of the word-
pair-comparison values for all word pairs, and for all word pairs
deemed related is then calculated. These two averages, the percentage of word pairs deemed to be related, and the number of
possible word-pair comparisons are the final results of the comparison program.

The most important part of the program is the calculation of
the word-pair-comparison value, since the results of the dialect-
pair comparison depend on how accurately the word-pair-comparison
routine calculates this value. Based on the results obtained with
this preliminary program, it can be said that the current program
is reasonably accurate, and with some revisions can be expected
to be more so. However, before discussing the weaknesses of the
program and how technically feasible revisions can improve the
results, a description of the technique used for word-pair comparisons is necessary.

The word-pair-comparison technique is divided into three parts.
The first calculates the relationships between syllables, the second
selects syllable pairs for analysis, and the third uses these selected
syllable pairs to obtain the word-pair-comparison value.

The first part of the comparison of the two words is to compare
each syllable of the first word with each syllable of the second word.
This comparison is done by use of a syllable-pair-comparison program which computes a syllable-pair-comparison value for each
syllable pair. This syllable-pair-comparison value is a number
which indicates the degree of similarity of the two syllables such
that the number is small if the two syllables are identical and large
if they are not.[12] The distinctive features of the syllables are
divided into four groups — one group consists of the distinctive
features of vowel quality and the other three groups subdivide the
distinctive features of the consonant into 'position', 'manner', and

'cofeature'. The number of differences in distinctive features is counted for each group and the sum of: 1) the number of differences in 'vowel quality' distinctive features multiplied by 23; 2) the number of differences in 'position' distinctive features multiplied by 22; 3) the number of differences in 'manner' distinctive features multiplied by 21; and 4) the number of differences in 'cofeatures' multiplied by 4 is then formed. To this value 8192 is added if the two syllables are not identical.

These syllable-pair-comparison values are then used in the following manner to select the syllable pairs which indicate the maximum amount of similarity.

The syllable in the first word which shows the maximum similarity to a syllable in the second word is identified by selecting the smallest syllable-pair-comparison value.[13] This syllable-pair-comparison value is stored at the head of a list, the number supplying the location of the syllable selected from the first word is stored as the second number on the list, and the number supplying the location of the syllable selected from the second word is stored as the third number on the list. Then all syllable-pair-comparison values using either of the two syllables selected are set aside. This last step has the effect of deleting one syllable from each word with the two syllables 'deleted' forming the syllable pair with the maximum degree of similarity.

The next calculation consists of using the remaining syllables in each word to select the syllable in the shortened first word which shows the maximum degree of similarity to a syllable in the shortened second word. This second syllable pair is identified by selecting the smallest number among the remaining syllable-pair-comparison values.[14] This new syllable-pair-comparison value is stored on the same list as the syllable-pair-comparison value first selected and this new value is followed by the number supplying the location of the syllable selected from the first word and the number supplying the location of the syllable selected from the second word.[15] Then all syllable-pair-comparison values using either of these two syllables selected are set aside. This has the effect of deleting a second syllable from each word with the two syllables 'deleted' having a degree of similarity second only to that of the first syllable pair deleted.

Again the remaining syllables of each word are used to find the syllable in the twice-shortened first word which shows the maximum degree of similarity to a syllable in the twice-shortened second word. The syllable-pair-comparison value found and the numbers

of the syllables selected are added to the list. This process is
continued until every syllable of the shorter word has been paired
off with some syllable of the longer word.

If the two words have the same number of syllables, this
second part of the word-pair-comparison program is completed.
If not, each remaining syllable of the longer word is compared
with every syllable of the shorter word and the syllable pair showing
the maximum degree of similarity is added to the list.[16] Thus
each excess syllable of the longer word is paired with the syllable
of the shorter word which it must nearly resembles in value and
position.

When the above calculations have been completed, the results
consist of a list of numbers with three numbers for each syllable
of the longer word. The first of these three numbers is the number
indicating the relationship between one specific syllable of the first
word and one specific syllable of the second word, the second of
these three numbers is the number supplying the location of that
specific syllable in the first word, and the third of these three
numbers is the number supplying the location of that specific syllable
in the second word. Thus each syllable of the longer word is paired
with one syllable of the shorter word and each syllable of the shorter
word is paired with at least one syllable of the longer word. This
list of syllable numbers and syllable-pair-comparison values is the
input data to the third and final section of the word-pair-comparison
technique.

Because the current syllable-pair-comparison program cannot
produce a range of values usable for accurately identifying the degree
of similarity of syllable pairs which are not identical, the third
segment of the word-pair-comparison technique is limited to identifying syllable pairs as being identical or not identical. Thus this
word-pair-evaluation routine is limited to the use of the number of
syllables in the shorter of the two words (called SYLMIN), the
number of syllables in the longer of the two words (called SYLMAX),
the number of syllables in the longer of the two words which are
identical with syllables in the shorter of the two words (called
MATCH), and the relative positions of the syllables in each syllable
pair. At present the ordering of syllables in each word pair is
ignored because the syllable-pair-comparison values are not accurate
enough to warrant the use of the syllable ordering. Thus only
SYLMIN, SYLMAX, and MATCH are used in obtaining the word-
pair-comparison value.

The word-pair-evaluation routine, which produces the word-pair-comparison value, uses a series of calculations depending upon the values of SYLMIN, SYLMAX, and MATCH to calculate the desired value. Thus if MATCH is zero, indicating that there are no identical syllables, the word-pair-comparison value is set to zero. If MATCH is not zero, but the longer of the two words has at least two more than twice as many syllables as the shorter of the two words, then the word-pair-comparison value is arbitrarily set to .000002, since it is assumed that the difference in word length precludes any possibility of the two words being cognates.

Next, if the number of identical syllable pairs (MATCH) is less than the number of syllables in the longer of the two words (SYLMAX), the word-pair-comparison value is set to be $\dfrac{\text{MATCH}}{\text{SYLMAX} + 1}$. If the number of identical syllable pairs (MATCH) is equal to the number of syllables in the longer of the two words (SYLMAX) and both words have the same number of syllables (SYLMAX equals SYLMIN), then the two words are identical (except for a possible reordering of the syllables), and the word-pair-comparison value is set to be $1-2^{-35}$.

Finally, if the number of identical syllables (MATCH) is equal to the number of syllables in the longer of the two words (SYLMAX), but the two words do not have the same number of syllables, then the longer of the two words contains all of the syllables of the shorter word and at least one syllable of the shorter word appears twice in the longer word. When this occurs, the word-pair-comparison value is set to be $.5 + \dfrac{\text{MATCH}}{2(\text{SYLMAX} + 1)}$, which is an average of the two previous equations for calculating the word-pair-comparison value.

The net result of this word-pair-evaluation routine is to produce a number indicating the relationship of the two words with zero indicating no relationship and $1-2^{-35}$ indicating that the two words are identical. The word-pair-comparison values produced by this routine are then used to calculate the relationship of the vocabulary pair as described above.

2.4 Current limitations. While the program discussed above is capable of recognizing items with either a very high or a very low degree of phonetic similarity, it does not identify all phonetically similar (hence, related[17]) items. The basic problem is, as mentioned above, the limitations in the syllable-pair-comparison program.

Since the syllables of the Fiji dialects have the form $\#V$ or CV, it would be easy to have the computer first identify the syllable pair as being one of the following eight combinations : 1) CV-CV; 2) CV-CV_1; 3) CV-C_1V; 4) CV-C_1V_1; 5) CV-$\#V$; 6) CV-$\#V_1$; 7) $\#V$-$\#V$; or 8) $\#V$-$\#V_1$. After eliminating combinations 1) and 7), since these are the cases where the syllable pairs are identical, a fairly simple computation involving the syllable-pair combination, the number of distinctive features which appear in both syllables, the number of distinctive features which appear in only one of the syllables, shifts of distinctive features as described in section 2. 3 above, and the types ('position', 'manner', 'cofeature', and 'vowel quality') of distinctive features which are in both syllables or in only one of the syllables can be devised. This computation need produce only a syllable-pair-comparison value capable of differentiating syllable pairs into three groups: 1) identical; 2) related; and 3) unrelated.

Using these three groupings, it will be relatively simple to design a word-pair evaluation routine which can accurately assess the relationship of the two words. This in turn will automatically improve the accuracy of the numbers used to evaluate the relationship of each dialect pair.

3. 0 EVALUATION

3. 1 Comparison with existing programs. Although the computer is a valuable tool for lexicostatistical research, this portion of the field of language data processing has received less attention than it deserves. One use of the computer in lexicostatistics so far is to do the numerical computations after the linguist has assigned the cognate identifications by hand.[18] To use this program, the linguist must take the equivalent words in each language, identify the words which appear in only one language and, for the remaining words, assign identification numbers to each group of cognates. Once the linguist has made the cognate classifications for every word in every language, then the cards containing these data are prepared and read into the computer. The computer takes each pair of languages and counts the number of words available for comparison and the number of these word pairs which the linguist has said are cognate.

Programs that make more of the decisions include those for phonostatistical analysis,[19] comparative reconstruction,[20] and cognate and correspondence recognition[21] .Undoubtedly, a more thorough search of the literature would reveal additional related projects.

In terms of the number of decisions required for the linguist, the present program seems to stand midway between the program described below and some of those that search for cognates and correspondences. The Fiji Lexical-Comparison Program requires the linguist to have done phonemic analyses of all the input dialects and to have discovered the sound correspondences, since they are at present an integral part of the program.

It is expected that when the proposed alterations of the program are completed, it will have a fairly high degree of accuracy. Aside from those items that will be affected by the improved syllable-comparison routine, 9 out of 182 were found in one printout to register low relation, while the linguist, on the basis of general comparative information, would possibly consider them related. But even for hand-counting, most of these examples were of the coin-tossing variety.

3.2 _Future plans._ The immediate plans for the Fiji Lexical-Comparison Program are, as indicated previously, first to complete the segments of the program necessary for handling all dialect-pair comparisons, and second to improve the syllable-pair-comparison program and the word-pair-evaluation routine. Once these alterations have been completed, the program will be completed and the problem of analyzing Fiji dialect lexicons will be reduced to that of adding to the input data and analyzing the computed dialect-pair relationships.

However, it may be possible to input lexical data from other related languages by alterations of the program that converts each syllable into distinctive features. For instance, some of the consonant correspondences shown by Tongan, one of the closest languages to Fijian, fit well into the phonetic distance scheme: F. /^{m}b/ —T. /p/, F. /s/ —T. /h/, F. /^{g}g/ —T. /k/, F. /k/ —T. /$^?$/. Other correspondences such as F. /β/ —T. /f/ would require minor changes; still others such as F. /#/ —T. /$^?$/, F. /y/ —T. /#/, and F. /r/ —T. /#/ would require major changes, since they involve multiple correspondences and several phoneme-to-zero correspondences. Vowel correspondences are even more complex, involving some assimilation in the Tongan forms. Another related language, Rotuman, has /f/ corresponding to Fijian /t/, illustrating the nonuniversality of the phonetic distance theory.

Using the present program for other languages or dialects with similar syllable structure will, of course, give an indication of phonetic similarity. But unless the syllable-comparison routine

and the program that converts syllables into distinctive features
are altered to fit each group, the results will be of little linguistic
interest.

NOTES

1. The first-named author is primarily responsible for part 1
of this paper, the second-named author for parts 2 and 3.

2. Albert J. Schütz, 'A Phonemic Typology of Fijian Dialects',
Oceanic Linguistics 2. 62-79 (1963); Albert J. Schütz, A Dialect
Survey of Viti Levu, Fiji (in preparation).

3. A. S. Gatschet, 'Specimens of Fijian Dialects', ed. from
manuscript of the Rev. Lorimer Fison, Int. Z. allg. SprW. 2. 194
(1885).

4. Albert J. Schütz, 'Lexical Differences between Generations
in Fiji', Te Reo 6. 28-29 (1963).

5. Since identity between phonemes of different systems is
theoretically impossible, 'identity' here refers to identity of symbols. Since the phonological systems are generally similar, each
symbol represents approximately the same distinctive features in
all dialects for which it is used.

6. This is an inconsistency in the present design, a departure
from phonetic similarity to an existing phonemic correspondence.
A program for measuring only phonetic similarity would have to
equate all glottal stops, whether they corresponded to /t/ or /k/.

7. In the overall pattern — all 'nonidentical' syllables from
all dialects — there are 102 different syllables: 23 consonants
combining with five vowels, plus individual occurrences of the
vowels, minus certain sequences that do not occur.

8. Due to limitations in time, the sections of the program
that write, read, and process this intermediate magnetic tape have
not been completely coded. The only instructions which are missing
are the specific input and output commands. Because this section
of the program has been extensively checked by hand simulation,
no major computational problems are anticipated when this section
is completed.

9. Any further discussion of the control program — except
for the conversion program — would consist of computational

conventions and details which are not pertinent to the linguistic discussion of the program.

10. Thus, at the present time the program is limited to words of no more than nine syllables. However, the program has been designed so that this number can be changed by altering only one card in the symbolic deck of the Fiji Lexical-Comparison Program.

11. Because of the omissions listed in Section 1, the total of 200 is never used in the present program. The number may be changed by altering only one card in the symbolic deck of the Fiji Lexical-Comparison Program.

12. The major weakness of the current program is, as will be discussed later, the syllable-pair-comparison program. The present program does not yet account for the 'adjacent' and 'non-adjacent' columns described in part 1.

13. If two syllable pairs show the same degree of similarity by having the same syllable-pair-comparison value, the syllable pair with the greater similarity in syllable position is chosen. Thus, for example, in comparing two words with syllables WXYZ and VZYU, the syllable pairs Y-Y and Z-Z will have the same small syllable-pair-comparison value, but since Y is the third syllable in each word and Z is the second syllable in one word and the fourth syllable in the other, the syllable pair Y-Y will be chosen. Similarly, in comparing QRST and RTP the syllable pair R-R (first syllable in one word and second syllable in the other) would be chosen in place of the syllable pair T-T (second syllable in one word and fourth syllable in the other).
  If two syllable pairs have the same syllable-pair-comparison value and the same degree of similarity in syllable position, the first syllable pair found is chosen since it will be closer to the beginning of the words. Thus, for example, in comparing two words with syllables KLMN and OKNJ, the syllable pair K-K (first syllable in one word and second syllable in the other word) will be chosen before the syllable pair N-N (third syllable in one word and fourth syllable in the other word).

14. The calculation used to select the second, the subsequent, syllable pairs is exactly the same as the calculation used to select the first syllable pair. If consideration of the position of the syllables is required by this calculation, the syllable position in the full word is used and <u>not</u> the position in the shortened word.

15. At this point in the computation the list which is being built contains six numbers. For the purpose of summarizing this much of the calculation, the values of these six numbers are:

1) the number supplying the location of the syllable in the first word which shows the maximum degree of similarity to a syllable in the second word; 2) the number supplying the location of that syllable in the second word; and 3) the value of the comparison of these two syllables, followed by: 4) the number supplying the location of the syllable in the first word (other than the syllable given in 1) above) which shows the maximum degree of similarity to a syllable in the second word (other than the syllable given in 2) above); 5) the number supplying the location of this newly chosen syllable in the second word; and 6) the value of the comparison of these two syllables. On the list itself these numbers appear in the sequence 3, 1, 2, 6, 4, and 5.

16.   The syllable-pair-comparison values set aside during the first part of this computation are used for this calculation. If the syllable in the longer word has the same degree of similarity with two syllables in the shorter word, the syllable positions are used to select which syllable is to be chosen.

17.   The current computation essentially considers that two words are related if: 1) more than half of the syllables of the longer word are identical with syllables in the shorter word; and 2) the longer of the two words has fewer syllables than two plus twice the number of syllables in the shorter of the two words. A more restrictive criterion for relation (a definition of cognate for purposes of glottochronology) is that regular phonemic correspondence is required, at least to the extent of 75 per cent of the phonemes in each member of the pair. Fred W. Householder, Jr., 'Validity of Glottochronology', Current Anthropology 5.326 (1964).

18.   See John B. Carroll and Isidore Dyen, 'High-speed computation of lexico-statistical indices', Lg.38.274-8 (1962) for a discussion of the computational technique used, and Isidore Dyen, 'The Lexicostatistical classification of the Malayopolynexian languages', Lg. 38.38-46 (1962) for a discussion of the results obtained by this program.

19.   Howard P. McKaughan, 'A Study of Divergence in Four New Guinea Languages', American Anthropologist 66.98-120 (1964).

20.   Martin Kay, The Logic of Cognate Recognition in Historical Linguistics, Rand Memorandum RM-4224-PR (Sept., 1964). C. M. Naim, 'A Program for Partial Automation of Comparative Reconstruction', Anthropological Linguistics 4:9.1-10 (Dec. 1962).

21.   H. A. Gleason, Jr., 'Genetic Relationship among Languages', Structure of Language and its Mathematical Aspects 179-89 (1961).

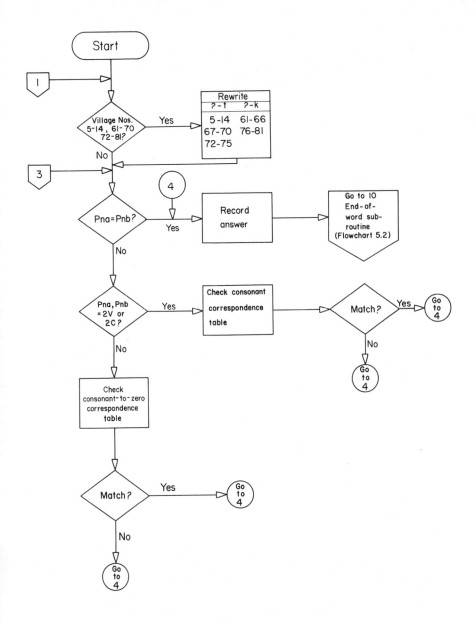

Flowchart 5.1

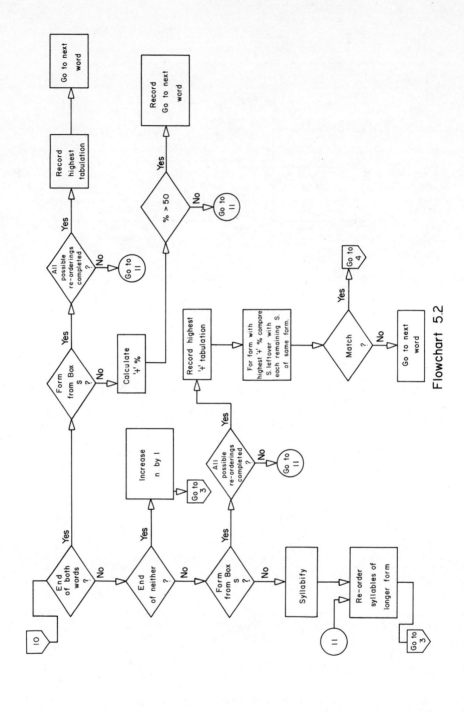

Flowchart 5.2

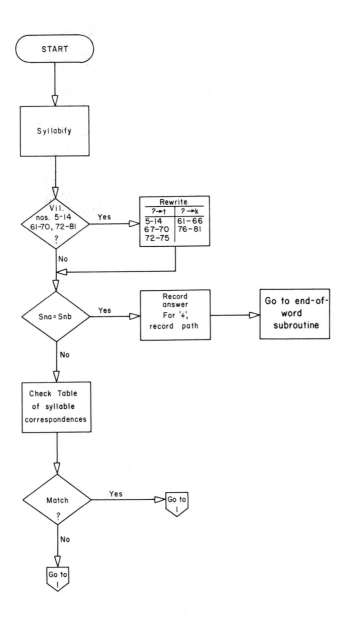

Flowchart 5.3

Chapter 6

Automatic Spelling-to-Sound Conversion

Richard L. Venezky

1.0 INTRODUCTION

The analysis of English spelling-to-sound relationships has recently become an interest of several disciplines. Educators, after years of debate over the relative merits of phonics, the whole-word method, and the various combinations of these two extremes, are attempting to make a thorough analysis of spelling-to-sound correspondences as a prelude to the improvement of reading instruction.[1] Engineers, with the advent of marketable (but limited) optical scanners and speech synthesis devices, have turned their attention in the design of a reading machine for the blind toward the network which would translate between the spelling detected by the optical scanner[2] and the sound stream produced by the synthesis system.[3] Linguists, viewing the widespread use of digital computers in other areas of language analysis, are attempting to convert lengthy printed texts to phonetic form for various linguistic studies.[4]

1.1 <u>Problem.</u> While the ultimate goals of these three groups are quite different, one basic problem is the same — to ascertain the factors which control the conversion of spelling into sound. The purpose of this paper is to examine the practicality of automatic spelling-to-sound conversion for English, taking into account the factors which must be considered in predicting sound from spelling and the methods of implementing these factors on a general purpose digital computer. While much of the information used in this study was derived from studies for the improvement of reading instruction,[5] only the problems of automatic conversion will be considered here.

1.2 <u>Scope.</u> To avoid lengthy definitions and extensive qualifying verbiage, I will limit this discussion to the consideration of a program for a general purpose digital computer that receives distinct input signals for each of the 26 letters of the Roman alphabet and for the blank space, and produces distinct output signals in turn for members of a set of phonemes. Modifications for hyphenated words, apostrophes, and other punctuation marks would be minor and have little bearing upon the basic conversion problem. Attention will be placed upon spelling-to-sound relationships in isolated words, without considering interword alternations and intonation contours. While the phonetically pleasing reading machine must handle these problems, the basic problems are met in dealing with isolated words and must be attended to first. The conversion from phonemic to phonetic output poses no theoretical problems. Assuming that we have a complete description of the allophones of some widely spoken English dialect, then the selection of the proper phonetic form for any phonemic word could be done on the basis of relatively simple decision rules. This is not to say that the design of the synthesis unit is simple — it obviously is not — but such considerations are beyond the scope of this paper.

2.0 PROPOSED SOLUTIONS

Three conversion schemes will be considered: straight dictionary look-up, dictionary look-up with preliminary segmentation, and the algorithm system. To aid in the comparison of these schemes, I will set an acceptability criterion of 96 per cent recognition of the graphemic words in common texts.[6] This means that each scheme must be accurate enough to correctly pronounce at least 96 per cent of the graphemic words it encounters. According to the Thorndike-Lorge word counts,[7] the most common 20,000 English words (words in the common sense — see note 8) would account for this level. Statistics are not available on the number of different words this would be, since the Thorndike counts include common derivatives under the same base form.[8] An estimate of 50,000-60,000 different graphemic words, based upon an examination of the Thorndike-Lorge list, will be assumed for this report.[9]

In considering the three schemes, the most important questions to be answered are the following:

1) Can the scheme be used to reach the acceptability level?
2) Is the scheme practical in terms of equipment and programming costs?
3) How easily can the scheme handle special vocabularies?

If the answer to question 1 is not affirmative, then the other two questions need not be asked — the scheme is totally unacceptable. Question 2 concerns practicality: a theoretically sound idea

that is too expensive to implement has little use. Practicality,
for the most part, will be defined relatively, by comparing the
equipment needed and programming effort required to implement
each scheme. Whether or not the most practical of the schemes
considered here will be practical enough to attract an investor is
not discussed here.

The third question is a corollary of the second. Given that
we have a working, practical scheme, how easily can it be adapted
to the vocabulary requirements of law, or metallurgy, or embryology,
or of any other discipline? Dendrite, acetylcholine, and nucleolus
are not members of the select 20,000, but an automatic converter
used for reading neurological literature would bump into them with
alarming frequency. A conversion system that could not be altered
to handle special vocabularies would have a restricted use.

3.0 STRAIGHT DICTIONARY LOOK-UP

The simplest, surest scheme is straight dictionary look-up.
Input words are matched against dictionary entries until a match is
found. The code for the corresponding phonemic form, stored in
the dictionary in some location relative to the graphemic form, is
then transmitted to the synthesis section. If a match is not found, a
null signal indicating 'no match' is transmitted.[10] There is no doubt
that such a scheme will work. All we need is a standard digital
computer with an auxiliary random access storage device (drum,
disk, auxiliary core storage, etc.).[11] Through trial and error we
could establish what words to include in the dictionary to reach
the criterion level.

Programming such a system would be relatively simple, but
the hardware cost seems excessive when we consider the items in
the auxiliary dictionary storage unit. Besides containing a word
like love and its corresponding phonemic code, the dictionary must
also contain loved, lover, lovers, loving, lovingly, lovelorn and
their corresponding phonemic codes (to say nothing of unloved,
loveless, and lovable). The question now becomes, is it possible
to reduce the size of the dictionary by segmenting the input words
before the look-up process? This possibility will be considered
in section 5.

As a final note, this scheme is easy to modify; a dictionary
update routine would add the new entries in appropriate places in
the dictionary and make necessary address modifications in the
look-up program. While this may involve several hours running
time for merging the new entries with the dictionary, computing

new locations, and modifying the look-up program, no reprogramming would be necessary.

4.0 ALGORITHM SYSTEM

4.1 General evaluation. The opposite extreme from the
straight look-up system is the algorithm system, wherein phonemic
output is computed from the graphemic input. Such a system would
presumably scan the input words[12] and decide, on the basis of
programmed decision criteria, what output to generate for each
grapheme or grapheme cluster it encountered. Rules like 'final
ue after g, except in argue, is silent' and 'gh in word initial position
becomes the phoneme g' would be built into the program along with
rules for segmenting polymorphemic input forms into smaller units.
From an overhead standpoint, such a system would be preferable
to the dictionary look-up system since an auxiliary random access
storage would not be needed, assuming that the conversion program
did not exceed the limits of a standard storage unit. Modifications
would be less necessary than under the look-up schemes, but where
necessary would require reprogramming. (Results of recent
research indicate that rules which would predict the pronunciations
of the most common 20,000 words would equally well predict the
pronunciations of the next 20,000 most common words.[13])

The drawback to this scheme is, however, that it cannot reach
our criterion level and still be practical. The factors which figure
into spelling-to-sound relationships cannot be programmed efficiently.
In many cases we would need to know stress placement, form class,
functor-contentive membership, and even etymology. In addition,
thousands of exceptions to regular patterns would have to be listed
as whole words along with at least part of their pronunciations.
These factors are explained in the examples that follow. I will
forego a discussion of the segmentation process for the present
since that topic will be covered in the discussion of the next scheme
(section 5). In the examples below I am assuming that some type
of segmentation has already taken place.

4.2 Stress placement. Stress placement is important not only
for predicting vowel quality, but also for predicting voicing or non-
voicing of particular consonants and for determining whether or
not the clusters [tj], [dj], [sj], and [zj] are palatalized to [č], [ǰ], [š],
and [ž] before a vowel. Stress also plays a part in the backing of
[n] to [ŋ] before velar stops, but this problem can be handled by
segmenting.[14]

Vowel neutralization in English has been discussed elsewhere
and needs little comment here.[15] Some examples borrowed from
C. F. Thomas[16] and elsewhere to illustrate this problem are
shown below.

Stressed vowel	Unstressed vowel
today [tədé]	Monday [mɔ́ndɪ]
man [mæn]	woman [wʊ́mən]
ask [æsk]	askance [əskǽns]
coral [kɔ́rəl]	corral [kərǽl]
matinee [mætɪné]	coffee [kɔ́fɪ]
surface [sɝ́fɪs]	face [fés]
advice [ædvaɪ́s]	crevice [krɛ́vɪs]

Knowing the stress pattern does not guarantee correct conversion
of vowel graphemes to phonemes, since various other factors
enter into this relationship, but without considering stress, little
regularity can be found in the vowel grapheme-to-phoneme relationships.

The grapheme <x> has two basic pronunciations: viz. [ks] as
in exit, exercise and [gz] as in exert, examine.[17] Whether the voiced
or unvoiced cluster occurs is generally determined by stress placement. If the primary stress occurs on the vowel preceding < x>,
the corresponding phoneme cluster is unvoiced; otherwise it is
voiced. (Preconsonantal and final <x> are always unvoiced. Initial
<x> , pronounced [z], can be handled like intervocalic <x> ,
giving first the cluster [gz]. Then, by the same phonotactical
rules which level initial [kn] (knee, know) and [gn] (gnat, gnaw) to
[n], [gz] would be leveled to [z].)

Evidence from the early Modern English period indicates that
the clusters [tj], [dj], [sj], and [zj] before an unstressed vowel
became [č], [ǰ], [š], and [ž] as in fortune, arduous, cynosure, and
treasure.[18] Since the spellings of the earlier forms have survived,
we must, in order to predict the correct pronunciation, duplicate,
in a sense, the palatalization process. Thus, in fortune and importune we would convert first to [fortjun] and [ɪmpɔrtjun] and then,
knowing that fortune is stressed on the first syllable and importune
on the last, convert to the forms [fɔ́rčən] and [ɪmpɝtjún]. Without
knowing the stress patterns we could not produce the correct
phonemic forms in these cases.

As further examples of the palatalized-unpalatalized cases,
compare the stress placements in the following lists:

Palatalized	Unpalatalized
closure	assume
leisure	gratuity
capitulate	institute
congratulate	assiduity
creature	seduce
credulous	credulity

Stress prediction based upon the graphemic shape of a word only cannot be accomplished with any high degree of accuracy. Consider, as an example, one of the best known and supposedly exceptionless rules for stress prediction — the requirement of penult stress before the adjectival ending <-ic>. First, there is a short list of exceptions: Arabic, catholic, choleric, lunatic, and politic. Secondly, we must distinguish between noun and adjectives with <-ic> endings, and this is impossible on the graphemic level. Therefore, forms like arsenic, arithmetic, heretic and rhetoric would also have to be included in the dictionary and marked as exceptions to the <-ic> stress rule.

The following passage from C. K. Thomas is offered as a final discouraging note on automatic stress prediction:

What determines syllable stress? No completely satisfactory answer can be given, but two historical tendencies may be noted. In native English words, such as the series love, lovely, lovable, loveliness, lovableness, the stress remains on the root syllable. But in words of Greek or Latin origin, such as the series photograph, photography, photographic, or the series equal, equality, equalization, equalitarian, the stress shifts from one syllable to another as the word is lengthened. Words like love illustrate the so called fixed or recessive stress of the native English and Germanic tradition. Words like equal and photograph illustrate the so called free or variable stress of the Greco-Latin tradition.[19]

4.3 Other conditioning factors. The two lists shown below illustrate another conditioning factor.

[ð]	[θ]
the	thaw
them	theft
then	theme
there	thermal
these	thick
they	thin
thither	thistle
thou	thong
though	thug
thy	thigh

In words beginning with the cluster <th> (there is a total of 170 such words in the Thorndike-Lorge 20,000 word list), the corresponding pronunciations [θ] and [ð] are obtained by knowing whether the word is a functor or contentive.[20] Thus, functors have the voiced interdental spirant and contentives have the unvoiced. Without including such information in the algorithms, the correct pronunciation for these words could not be obtained. But the only way to build such information into a system is to list all words beginning with <th>, and code each one with its functor-contentive class membership. If these were the only words that required this process, we might tolerate the listing, but they are not. Compare the pronunciation of the last <a> in these words:

[ej]	[ɪ]
abate	celibate
placate	affricate
vacate	frigate
deprecate	intermediate
dedicate	collegiate
duplicate	duplicate
communicate	novitiate
fabricate	prelate

To determine the correct pronunciation for these forms we must know their form classes. Verbs have the [ej] pronunciation and nouns and adjectives have [ɪ]. Once again, we must include a dictionary in the system — only now we are concerned with over 500 words that have this ending.

The correct pronunciation of <-ng-> also depends upon form class. Compare the following:

[ŋ]	[ŋg]
longer (n)	longer (adj.)
singer	stronger
swinger (one who swings)	younger

The <g> in <ng>, followed by the agentive <er> is silent, but before the comparative <er> becomes [g].

4.4 <u>Further drawbacks</u>. All of these problems could probably be tolerated if algorithms existed for predicting pronunciations in all other cases, but unfortunately this is not the situation. In numerous cases, rules cannot be formulated for predicting the various pronunciations of the same grapheme or grapheme cluster. <ch>, for example, has three different pronunciations, depending mostly upon the etymology of the word. In words derived from Old English, Old French, and early Middle French, the pronunciation is [č] as in church <OE circe and chief <OF chef. Words borrowed from French after the early Middle French period are pronounced with [š] as chef <F. chef, and those borrowed ultimately from Greek generally have [k] as in chord. Since there are few reliable clues to etymology in the graphemic patterns, [21] most words containing <ch> would have to be contained in a dictionary along with the proper pronunciation for that cluster. [22]   This includes about 500 words.

Words ending in <-ine> have no regular pronunciation either, as shown below, and would also have to be included in a dictionary (approximately 150 words):

[aɪ]	[i]	[ɪ]
alkaline	vaseline	crystalline
valentine	libertine	destine
divine	gasoline	doctrine
genuine	nectarine	engine
cosine	vaccine	famine
turpentine	routine	urine

Similarly, words containing <gh> (30 words), words containing <ou> and <ow> not pronounced [au] (approx. 370 words) and words containing irregular pronunciations for <o> (approx. 300) would have to be included in this list, to name just a few. It appears that from 4,000 to 6,000 words containing irregular grapheme-phoneme correspondences have to be included in a dictionary, assuming that the segmentation and stress prediction routines had no exceptions.

With the large number of words whose pronunciations cannot be predicted from their graphemic shapes alone and the added problems of stress prediction and of segmentation, which will be discussed shortly, the algorithm method holds little promise as a practical spelling-to-sound conversion scheme.

5.0 DICTIONARY LOOK-UP WITH PRELIMINARY SEGMENTATION

Since the algorithm scheme is not practical for automated spelling-to-sound conversion, attention should turn to improving the only workable scheme, dictionary look-up. Of the 50 or 60 thousand words which must be stored to meet the 96 per cent

recognition acceptability criterion, only about 20,000 are basic
words. The remaining are regular inflected compounds of these
words, formed by adding <-ed>, <-ing>, <-ly>, and so on to
the basic words. Since all of these derivatives are regular in
some sense,[23] it would appear that a segmentation scheme would
be easy to specify and would, at a minimum, reduce the dictionary
storage requirements by 50 per cent.

A segmentation program would scan each input word, looking
for designated initial and final grapheme strings like <un->,
<in->, <-ment>, <-ness>, and <-able>. These strings would
then be stripped from the word and the remainder matched against
the dictionary entries. If a match were found, the output would
be the phonemic code found in the dictionary plus a phonemic code
for each segment stripped from the word. These latter phonemic
codes would be stored in a table in the segmentation program.
Thus, an input word like <u>workable</u> would first be split into <u>work</u> +
<u>able</u>. The section <work> would be matched against dictionary
entries until a match were found and the phonemic code for [wȝk]
retrieved. To this would be added the code for [əbəl] and the full
form [wȝ́kəbəl] passed to the synthesis unit. In this way the pronunciation for <-able> and other segmentable strings would be
stored only once and only one dictionary entry would be necessary
for each paradigm (or, occasionally, set of paradigms; for
example, the paradigms for <u>love</u> (v) and <u>love</u> (n) would be accounted
for by a single entry in the dictionary, assuming that all affixes
could be segmented).

Not all segmentation is so simple, however. With words like
<u>blamable</u>, we are left with <blam-> after removing the suffix
(-able), but the base form is <u>blame</u>, which does not match this
form. One solution to this problem is to remove final <e> from
dictionary entries and from input forms, but this would require
some means for recording that a final <e> was once present to
avoid merging forms like <u>bite:</u> <u>bit</u>, <u>paste:</u> <u>past</u>, <u>here:</u> <u>her</u>, <u>spare:</u>
<u>spar</u>. To do this, the dictionary must have not only a phonemic
code for each entry, but also an inflectional code that records
whether or not final <e> must be present in any of its forms. The
allocation of the necessary storage to hold the inflectional
codes may not be so drastic, if by doing so 200,000 to
300,000 characters used to store regular derivatives can
be eliminated.

Suffixes like <-ly>, <-ic>, <-ity> require graphemic and
phonemic changes in the base form and probably can not be segmented

economically. <ly>, for example, after polysyllables ending in
<-y>, requires the base to change <y> to <i>. Thus, <u>angry</u>:
<u>angrily</u>. The <y> to <i> alternation could be handled by adding
an additional bit to the inflectional code, but some notion of
functional load of this suffix has to be computed before
the decrease in storage requirements can be weighted
against the increase in segmenting time.

 <-ic> offers more serious segmentation problems, as does
<-ity> and numerous others. Consider the forms

sýmmetry: symmétric
sáne: sánity

aside from the graphemic alternations <y> → <i> and <e> →
<φ>, there are also phonemic alternations and a stress shift, viz.

/ sɪ́mətrì/∼/ sɪmɛ́trɪk/ and
/ sén/ ∼/ sǽnɪtɪ/

In these cases, to store one form for <u>symmetry/symmetric</u> and one
form for <u>sane/sanity</u> would require not only an inflectional code to
indicate the stress shift, but also, codes for the vowel alternations.
Simple one-bit codes will not be sufficient for the phonemic alternations; in fact, the only recourse is to store all of the forms of
all phonemes involved. This requires that a code word be used to
indicate which phonemes (and stresses) belong with which affixes
— and where to find the alternants for any form. Not only is there
a storage problem here, but also a programming problem, in that
considerable time must be consumed in locating the phoneme and
stress alternation code, and in substituting the proper units for the
affix concerned. Segmentation is obviously beyond its practicable
application at this point.

 In many cases a graphemic string identical to common prefixes
and suffixes may be part of the base form, e. g. <un> in <u>union</u> and
<u>uncle</u>. In these cases we could store <u>ion</u> and <u>cle</u> in the dictionary
and reserve one bit to indicate when the form is not affix plus base.
The full pronunciation of <u>union</u> and <u>uncle</u> would be stored also and
the segmenting routine, once it found from the affix code that <un>
were not a prefix, would output the phonemic form retrieved from
the dictionary without prefixing the phonemic code for /ən-/ to it.
This process depends, of course, upon not having other words
beginning with common prefixes and ending in <cle> or <ion>.
Such cases, however, are rare and can be safely ignored.

The full scope of segmentation will have to be determined by trial and error. Theoretically, the determining
process is simple. Select a common affix, find all of the
base forms to which it can be affixed, and tabulate the graphemic and phonemic alternations between the base forms
and the affixed forms.

If there are no alternations, or if there are alternations
which can be handled easily, then the affix is segmentable.
What 'handled easily' means is difficult to make explicit.
Somehow the system designer must balance storage space
and total look-up time (including segmentation) to meet pre-
scribed specifications. The cost of segmentation consists of
increases in program size, average look-up time, and in
overall system complexity — a factor which may affect both
development cost and adaptability.

6.0 CONCLUSIONS

The most practical spelling-to-sound conversion scheme
is the look-up scheme with limited preliminary segmentation.
Except for the segmentation, this approach is quite inelegant
from both a linguistic and a programming standpoint — in
fact, it smacks of brute force. But the ravages of sound
change, promiscuous borrowing, and scribal dilettantism
leave us with little choice.

Lack of elegance nevertheless should not prevent us from
making the most of this conversion scheme. It will, in spite
of its inadequacies, produce the desired results. Furthermore,
additional research may show how to reduce significantly the
size of the stored dictionary. To this end, the following areas
should be considered.[24]

6.1 Storage by word length. Since an optical scanner could
count, with little additional circuitry, the number of graphemes
in each word it recognized, word length could be used to shorten
search time. Dictionary entries, whatever they turn out to be,
could be separated first into groups according to length and then
organized within each group according to some other feature.
This procedure would eliminate considerable storage space since
the same number of characters would not have to be allotted for
every word, but rather, a different character length could be
assigned to each length group.

A table in the look-up program would contain the first dictionary address for each length group while the character-count used to reach the next item location during searching would be the length of the search item itself (assuming character addressing). This process should reduce the dictionary storage requirements by over 50 per cent.

6.2 Type/token considerations. The 1,000 most common words in the Thorndike-Lorge list account for over 75 per cent of all textual words. If, therefore, the dictionary were organized by length groups, then within each length group the next feature of organization should probably be relative frequency of occurrence. It may, however, be better to divide each length group into two groups — one containing words in the first 1,000 group and the other all the remaining — and then alphabetize each of the two groups. The most frequently occurring group would be searched first, using a binary search. If the word were not found there, then the second group would be searched in the same way. Once a complete dictionary list is obtained, the relative search times for these techniques can be computed and compared.

6.3 Recoding. Only 27 different characters are utilized in storing the graphemic words. Assuming a six-bit character, this leaves 37 unused characters which could be used to recode frequently occurring initial and final grapheme sequences and thus further reduce dictionary storage requirements. Leading candidates for recoding are nonsegmentable affixes, and clusters like $\langle$ch$\rangle$, $\langle$gh$\rangle$, $\langle$ph$\rangle$, $\langle$sh$\rangle$, $\langle$th$\rangle$, and $\langle$qu$\rangle$.

If we record for each length group the address and length of each subgroup beginning with a different grapheme, then the initial grapheme could be omitted from every graphemic word in the dictionary — a saving of from 20,000 to 40,000 character locations. The first letter tables would require, in turn, only about 1,000 character locations in central storage.

These considerations may not eliminate the need for an auxiliary storage unit, but every reduction should help make the conversion scheme more practical. Knowing that automatic spelling-to-sound conversion is possible, practicality is now the factor which will eventually determine whether or not such conversion is ever implemented successfully.

NOTES

1. For a summary of current research, see John B. Carroll, 'The analysis of reading instruction: perspectives from psychology and linguistics', Yearbook of the National Society for the Study of Education 336-53 (1964).

2. A technical survey of optical scanners, including characteristics of commercial devices and an extensive bibliography, can be found in Howard Falk, 'Optical character recognition systems', Electro-Technology 74. 42-52, 160 (1964). J. H. Davis, 'Print recognition apparatus for blind readers', J. British Inst. Radio Engrs. 24:2. 103-10 (Aug., 1962), contains an adequate discussion of the requirements of optical recognition systems for reading machines. F. S. Cooper, 'Speech from stored data', IEEE Int. Convention Rec. 7:7. 137-49 (1963), describes current notions in speech synthesis. Included are some rudimentary comments on spelling-to-sound conversion.
While neither scanners nor speech synthesizers are developed sufficiently for the needs of a marketable reading machine for the blind, the state of the art is such that we could now throw together a working, experimental device with existing hardware, assuming that funds were available.

3. The earliest reading machine on record, demonstrated by its inventor E. E. Fournier d'Albe in 1913, did not produce speech-like signals, but rather converted each distinct letter into a different musical chord. (Cf. E. E. Fournier d'Albe, 'On a direct-reading octophone', Proc. Royal Soc. A. 90. 373 (1914). Tactile output devices have been suggested by numerous writers (Cf. J. H. Davis, note 2) and one was even patented in 1932 in England. For a discussion of more current work on reading machines, see Chapters 17-25 in Human Factors in Technology, edited by E. Bennett, J. Degan, and J. Spiegel, (New York, 1963).

4. For a general survey of computer applications in linguistics, see Paul L. Garvin (ed.), Natural language and the computer, (New York, 1963). For more detailed discussions of specific problems, consult the 'Humanities Applications' section of Computing Reviews, published six times each year by the Association for Computing Machinery.

5. My main source of evidence for spelling-to-sound correspondences has been research done by Professor R. H. Weir and me at Stanford University under United States Office of Education

contract Nos. OE-4-10-213 and OE-4-10-206. Our data consists
of spelling-to-sound tabulations for the most common 20,000
English words, taken from E. L. Thorndike and I. Lorge, The
teachers' word book of 30,000 words, (New York, 1941). These
tabulations were obtained through a computer program written
for the CDC 1604. Cf. R. L. Venezky, 'A computer program for
deriving spelling-to sound correlations', MA thesis (Cornell
University, 1962) published in part in H. Levin, et al., A basic
research program on reading, (Ithaca, New York, 1963).

6. By 'common texts' is intended daily newspapers, popular
(nontechnical) magazines, and most fictional prose. Since the
largest unit to be considered is the word, homograph problems
like read /rid/:/red/ cannot be resolved completely and therefore
are not considered in determining the acceptability of any conversion scheme. One of the variant pronunciations for such forms
will be arbitrarily selected as correct and the others will be
counted as incorrect. The number of such cases will be extremely
small, however.

7. Cf. especially F. W. Harwood and A. M. Wright, 'A
statistical study of English word formation', Lg. 32.260-73(1956).
Type-token relations for the Thorndike-Lorge list are given on
page 261 of Harwood and Wright.

8. 'Regular plurals, comparatives and superlatives, verb
forms in s, d, ed, and ing, past participles formed by adding n,
. . . are ordinarily counted under the main word'. Thorndike-Lorge,
p. ix.

9. F. S. Cooper (see reference 1 above) estimates that a
7,000 word dictionary will account for 95 per cent of all text and
that 20,000 words will account for at least 99 per cent. He does
not, however, cite any evidence for his figures, which contrast
quite radically with the Thorndike-Lorge counts, nor is he clear
on whether or not his 7,000 and 20,000 word figures include
derivatives formed with common suffixes.

10. As an alternative to the 'no match' signal, a phonetic form
of the spelling could be output. For example, if the input word
Peoria were not found in the dictionary, the system would output
/pi+i+o+ar+aɪ+e/ with, possibly, a high frequency tone before the
word to signal a capital letter, assuming that upper-lower case
distinctions were retained in the signal from the optical scanner.

11. Assuming that we need to store approximately 50,000
English words with their phonemic codes, with an average of eight
characters per word (graphemic or phonemic), we would require
an 800,000 character storage. This is far in excess of the standard
storage units on present-day digital computers (200,000-260,000
characters: e. g.   CDC 3600;   IBM   360/50;   Univac   1107/8).
800,000 characters is a minimum figure, however, since for an
efficient look-up system we may have to allocate the same number
of characters for each dictionary entry, regardless of whether we
assume a machine with character addressing, word addressing,
or both. This may raise our storage requirements to over 2 million
characters. Means for reducing this storage requirement are
discussed in the conclusion of this paper.

12. Because of (1) the predominant occurrence of regressive
assimilation over progressive assimilation in English, (2) stress
(and vowel) conditioning by various suffixes, and (3) terminal
graphemic markers like <-e->, scanning from right to left would
be the most economical scanning procedure.

13. See reference 4 above.

14. Cf. C. K. Thomas, Phonetics of American English[2] 82 (New
York, 1958). The transcriptions used in this report follow those
of John S. Kenyon and Thomas A. Knott, A pronouncing dictionary of
American English (Springfield, Mass., 1941).

15. Cf. M. D. Berger, 'Neutralization in American English
vowels', WORD 5. 255-7 (1949) and John S. Kenyon, American pronunciation 101-10 (Ann Arbor, 1943).

16. Op. cit., 153.

17. Through palatalization, [ks] and [gz] become [kš] and [gž] as
in luxury and luxurious. Note also that the [ks] - [gz] distinction is
not a case of stress conditioning alone. Only clusters spelled <x>
behave in this fashion, cf. accede, accept. See E. J. Dobson,
English Pronunciation 1500-1700 2.935 (Oxford, 1957).

18. Cf. Otto Jespersen, A Modern English grammar on historical
principles 1. 341-9 (London, 1961), and H. C. Wyld, A history of
modern colloquial English 293-4 (London, 1920).

19. Op. cit., 148. For some interesting work on stress prediction, see Roger Kingdon, The groundwork of English stress
(London, 1958).

20. For definitions of functors and contentive, see C. F. Hockett, A course in modern linguistics, (New York, 1958).

21. J. Vachek has attempted to utilize the concept of synchronically foreign characteristics to explain certain English sound changes. Cf. J. Vachek, 'On the interplay of external and internal factors in the development of language', Lingua 11. 433-88 (1962). While certain graphemic patterns are obviously foreign, e. g. <mn->, <hypo->, the spelling-to-sound correspondences in such forms have been irregularly assimilated to English patterns, so that few consistent rules can be based upon such a notion. (Cf. for example, the discussion of the pronunciation of the Greek form hypo- in the New English Dictionary, 5. 505.)

22. Some, but not very many <ch> spellings have predictable pronunciations. Initial <ch> before <1> or <r> is [k] — chlorine, chrome, etc. , and final <tch> is always [č], match, latch, etc. These account for less than 10 per cent of all <ch> spellings.

23. Cf. Stanley S. Newman, 'English suffixation: a descriptive approach', WORD 4. 24-36 (1948) for an excellent introduction to the linguistic aspects of English suffixation, and T. L. Thorndike, The teaching of English suffixes,(New York, 1941), for type-token statistics on common English suffixes.

24. Much of the discussion which follows concerns dictionary look-up schemes. I have, at present, no data to support the selection of any one dictionary look-up scheme over another. This choice must be based upon required look-up speed, maximum allotted storage space, and certain characteristics of the entries which are to be stored in the dictionary. Look-up schemes used by machine-translation research groups are described in various research reports from these projects. For a bibliography, consult Charles F. Balz, Literature on information retrieval and machine translation (White Plains, New York: IBM Corp., 1962). See also C. E. Price, 'Table look-up techniques for computer programming; Report Number K-DP-515', (Oak Ridge, Tennessee, Union Carbide Corporation, 1965).

Chapter 7

Towards Automatic Morphemicization of
Verbal Forms in Telugu

Dan M. Matson

1.0 THE MOTIVATION

For the past 25 years or so many American linguists have been faced with the problem of teaching exotic languages for which no suitable teaching materials have existed. The problem of 'what to teach' has been handled — with increasing success over the years — by the application of descriptive techniques which are well known. But the problem of 'what to teach first' has received much less attention. It is to this latter problem that this paper is addressed.

What to teach first, and what to teach after that, is an important consideration in teaching any language, but particularly an exotic one, because the beginning students are adults with little time and many responsibilities, often people who need the language as a tool for research and field work; an efficient set of materials — designed to impart the maximum amount of language skill in the time available — is needed for teaching the language.

It is at least plausible if not obvious that one order of presentation of the material might be less efficient than some other order. From this we may assume that there must be a maximal efficiency of presentation for any given language, achievable through the adoption of one or more particular ways of ordering the material presented.

There are two types of data which the linguist qua linguist can bring to bear on this problem of optimal ordering: structural and statistical. The statistical is the motivation for this paper; the structural can be referred to only briefly in this present context.[1]

2.0 THE PHILOSOPHY

Many agree that for maximal efficiency in language teaching the student should be exposed early to those features (both lexical and structural) of the language which have the highest text frequency in the language.

There are credible reasons for this. In the first place, such
features, because of their naturally higher frequency, should im-
press themselves more readily on the student's mind — he will
learn them faster because he meets and needs to know them more
often (this is called reinforcement). Secondly, once the student
has learned these features he will already know a substantial portion
of any new text (written or spoken), and thus be in a position to make
better guesses about the unfamiliar portions, and to concentrate on
learning the unfamiliar material, because there will be proportionally
less of it.

In the seminar which produced this book this line of reasoning
was objected to as illusory, since the most common words in a language will probably also be the most polysemous; consider for
example the three nouns in

(1)   Plants need light for photosynthesis.

The observation on polysemy may be true, but the objection is false:
most of the words in any natural language are polysemous, and the
sooner the student learns how this fact of life is manifested in language A the sooner he will be adequately equipped to use language
A — a goal which is the very essence of efficient language instruction.

In order to take maximum advantage of the beneficial effects
of high-frequency features, it is desirable to raise their frequency
in texts used for teaching still higher by substituting them for
features of low frequency (this is part of what is called editing).
The result is still more reinforcement of the high-frequency features,
still greater ease in their mastery, and correspondingly less inter-
ference with reading efficiency (roughly, amount of comprehension
per unit of study time) from the low-frequency features.

In (1) above this would amount to replacing photosynthesis with
something like making sugar from air and water, which is the
answer the student would get if he did not know what photosynthesis
was and had to ask. Clearly it would not serve the interests of
efficient teaching to remove the polysemous word light and replace
it by the unambiguous phrase radiation from the ultraviolet portion
of the electromagnetic spectrum.

3. 0 THE GOAL

So the question of what to teach first has given rise to the question of what features of the language have the highest text frequency.

Considerations of cost aside, the best way to count the occurrences of the features is with the aid of a computer, which is able

to handle vast quantities of data in a relatively short time with low
incidence of error. The yield of frequency information is of high
statistical reliability and may be broken down in any way desired.

By features I mean items like morphemes, allomorphs, lexemes,
idioms, constructions, parts of speech, and grammatical categories
(person, number, case, tense, mood, aspect, and the like). What
features will be counted will depend on what features the language
has and on their relative complexity.

In Telugu, for example, most of the complexity seems to be
concentrated in the verbal system, so that one's attention to the
grammatical features of the nouns can be limited to counting the
frequency of the irregular plural forms.

It seems, then, that a realistic goal for an early frequency
count for Telugu would be a computer program to take input text
preparsed into three parts of speech — verbs, nouns, and neither
— and to yield frequency data on all noun and verb bases and all
affixes in the verbal system. [2]

4.0 THE MEANS

A fairly gross flowchart of this program is given in Figures
7. 1 and 7. 2, showing the entire operation from card input to printed
output frequencies. Striped blocks in the flowcharts are discussed
in the indicated sections of this paper; the double-striped blocks,
being the central topic of this paper, are flowcharted in detail later.

4. 10 Preparation of input. The card input to this program is
prepared from published Telugu text. In this process (1) the Telugu
graphemes are transliterated into an I/O alphabet of code groups
of Hollerith characters, (2) word boundaries are indicated by blank,
with external sandhi neutralized, and (3) each word is marked by a
one-digit parsing code.

4. 11 Transliteration. The Telugu script in its contemporary
form has 51 graphemes. Since there are 63 characters available
for machine processing, it is not difficult in theory to transliterate
the Telugu graphemes one-to-one into BCD, but the resultant BCD
orthography is very difficult for humans to work with, having very
little in the way of mnemonic properties.

For the benefit of those who must read the card input and
printed output, the source Telugu text is transliterated into a highly
mnemonic 'alphabet' using code groups of one to three Roman letters
for the Telugu graphemes. Long vowels are written double, retroflex consonants are prefixed by 'X', aspiration is indicated by '*',
etc. See 4. 20 for a description of how this orthography is altered
by the program for internal use.

4. 12 Word boundaries. In Telugu orthography every syllable
boundary is potentially indicated by space;[3] furthermore, due to
the action of external sandhi[4] (optionally reflected in Telugu orthography), certain word boundaries do not coincide with syllable
boundaries. The result is that not all word boundaries are marked
by space in Telugu orthography, and not all spaces mark word
boundaries. To program the computer to resolve these ambiguities
would require going far beyond the scope of this paper toward the
land of machine translation, where angels fear to tread.

Accordingly it is assumed that the preeditors who will prepare
the input to this program will close up spurious spaces and eliminate
external sandhi, so as to place word boundaries in one-to-one correspondence with spaces (blank).

4. 13 Parsing code. The final step in preparing the input is
marking each word with its part of speech. To simplify sight-
reading, digits are used, say 2 for nouns, 3 for verbs (both finite
and nonfinite), and 4 for residue (everything else). The parsing
code is written immediately after the word (not preceded by a blank),
followed by a blank before the next word.

4. 20 Decoding routine. The first action of the program is to
retransliterate the input into BCD characters for internal use, one
character per Telugu grapheme. The first three characters in the
input are taken as argument for a look-up in a table of three-
character transliteration codes, e. g. XT* (voiceless aspirated
retroflex stop). If the argument is not in the table, the program
then does a look-up on the first two characters, in a table of two-
character codes, e. g. UU (long high back vowel); and finally, if
necessary, on just the first character, in a table of single-char-
acter codes. Each code has as its associated function a single BCD
character, such that the alphabetic ranking of each Telugu grapheme
corresponds exactly to the position (collating number) of its corresponding single BCD character in the internal collating sequence (see
sorting, 4. 60).

The decoding routine also counts the number of these BCD
characters in each decoded word, and the number of syllables in
each decoded word (see 4. 30, 5. 12).

4. 30 Tape 1. As each input word is decoded, its successive
BCD functions are written in a record on Tape 1 in a field of which
portions will subsequently be referred to as 'Arg' (for 'argument');
see Figure 7. 3. The record also has fields for: 'SC' (syllable
count, provided by the decoding routine — 1 for monosyllables, 2

for disyllables, 3 for words of more than two syllables); 'CC'
(character count, also provided by the decoding routine); and 'Word',
the original orthography of the input, which is carried along with
Arg for ease of identification in case the fail-safe routine is called
(see 4.40).

4.40 Fail-safe routine. At various points throughout the entire
program there are tests for abnormal conditions such as invalid
parsing codes, utter failure to analyze forms successfully, etc. If
such a condition is detected, the fail-safe routine is called, which
causes the contents of the tape-record currently in process to be
printed out for visual inspection, along with the contents of all filled
'Hypo' locations (see 4.50). The program then proceeds to the next
word.

4.50 Tape 2. The analysis of each verbal form (5.0) proceeds
as a series of look-up operations on portions of it. The look-ups
are directed by a series of hypotheses regarding the morphological
structure of the form. Each such hypothesis is provisionally
written in a hypo area in storage('Figure 7.4), and is subsequently
erased if it does not ultimately lead to a successful look-up.

When the nth look-up is successful, the resulting function, which
is the verb base, is written as 'Hypo (n + 1)', all (n + 1) Hypos are
written on Tape 2, and the program proceeds to the next word.

Each record on Tape 2 has two fields, 'Clear' (for sorting —
see 4.60) and 'Code' (for printout — see 4.70). For Hypo 1 through
n, both fields contain identical information (suffix codes); for Hypo
(n + 1) the 'Clear' field is BCD and the 'Code' field is its equivalent
in the I/O alphabet, both fields being supplied as the function of the
successful look-up.

4.60 Sort Tape 2. At EOF on Tape 1, Tape 2 is sorted on the
'Clear' field. This brings together all occurrences of each word,
(noun or verb) base, and suffix code, ready for counting. Because
of the method of assigning the BCD characters to the Telugu
graphemes, a normal sort results in the arrangement of the records
in accordance with the Telugu alphabet. By using numeric initials
for the suffix codes (i.e. using codes like 25, 3&), the suffixes can
be kept separate from the lexical items in the printout. If desired,
the noun and verb bases can be made to list separately by retaining
on Tape 2 the 'PC' (parsing code) from Tape 1 and using it as the
major sort field, with 'Clear' as the minor.

4.70 Print Tape 4. This tape (Figure 7.5) contains all lexical
items in alphabetical order and all suffixes in numerical order,

each with its frequency in the corpus just analyzed. For the reports the 'Code' and 'Counter' fields are printed out, giving each lexical item in the I/O orthography. If desired, the records can be sorted on 'Counter' into ascending or descending order of frequency before printout.

5.0 <u>Verbal analysis routine</u>. Each verbal form is analyzed into a string of <u>base</u> + <u>suffix(es)</u> by a process of 'cutting off' from the right end of the form (right truncation) one or more portions suspected of being suffixes, and then doing a table look-up on what remains. Figure 7.6 gives an overall view of the method. [5]

5.10 Each suffix in the Telugu verbal system has been assigned an arbitrary two-digit number. When a given substring is tentatively identified as a particular suffix, the number of that suffix is written in a <u>hypo</u> area and the substring is right-truncated from the rest of the form. Several hypos must be used in the analysis of a polymorphemic form; the serial number of the current hypo is given by an index P, which is increased one unit with each truncation, and decreased one unit as the contents of each hypo is written on tape following successful analysis of the form.

5.11 The left-hand character of the form being analyzed is in location 'a' in storage, with successive characters in locations (a + 1), (a + 2), etc. The right-hand character of course changes with each truncation; the address of the current right-hand character is stored in location 'c'. Truncation is thus accomplished by simply decreasing <u>c</u>.

Area 'Arg' comprises locations 'a' through <u>c</u>; it contains the argument for the current look-up.

The initial address of the right-hand character of a given full form is (a + <u>CC</u> - 1), where <u>CC</u> is the number of characters in the full form (4. 30).

5.12 If the form to be analyzed is a monosyllable, it is looked up in Table A, which contains the few monosyllabic verbal forms that can occur, such as[6] rā 'come!'. If the form is disyllabic it is first looked up in Table B, which contains the highly frequent umdi 'she is, it is, there is' and a few other forms. If the monosyllable look-up fails, the fail-safe routine (4. 40) is called; if the disyllable look-up fails, the polysyllable routine (Figure 7.7) is called.

6.0 <u>Polysyllable routine</u>. Figure 7.7 shows how the identity of the contents of <u>c</u> transfers command to the appropriate subroutine

for truncation of the right-most suffix. The two right-hand columns
in the decision table are for the benefit of the reader only.

6. 10 Suppose the form under analysis is tin-ina 'eaten'. In
Figure 7. 8 the three right-most characters of this form are truncated
by first placing the number 3 in location 'b' and then changing c to
(c - b). b is then used to compute the number of characters in the
residue of the form, and that number is stored in location 'r'; the
residue tin is then sought in a table containing only arguments of r
characters. This method of storing the verb bases in several
different tables according to their length results in considerable
savings in look-up time over the use of a single all-inclusive table.

6. 20 Similarly, if c contained /u/ (see table in Figure 7. 7),
Hypo P would become 1S, 2S, etc., according as location (c - 1)
contained /n, w/ etc., and the number 2 would become b.

6. 30 The analysis is more involved if c contains /ā/, because
the possible suffixes are of (effectively) two different lengths. And
in either case there is the further complication that there are either
zero or more-than-zero suffixes between the right-most suffix and
the verb base. Together these two facts give 2 x 2 = 4 as the maximum
number of attempts that can be allowed for the analysis of an /ā/-
final form.[7]
In Figure 7. 9 this number 4 is stored in location 'i'; i will be
decreased by one each time the analysis is unsuccessful, and the
fail-safe routine will be called if i reaches zero.

6. 40 To enable the program to keep track of what suffix-position
it is currently working on, location 's' is provided as a logical
switch. Zero becomes s at the top of Figure 7. 8, and 'i' becomes
s if command transfers to Figure 7. 9. If the look-up operation in
Figure 7. 8 is unsuccessful, command transfers to Figure 7. 10,
where s is tested. If nonzero, s is the address of the location to be
tested to direct further branching of the program; in this paper only
one such location is necessary.

6. 50 The following examples should help the reader to follow
the workings of the program as thus far described. The analysis
of the three forms tinn-ā-nu 'I ate', tiḿ-ṭā-nu 'I will eat', and
tin-inā 'even if one eats' can be traced step by step through the
flowcharts by referring to the rows of Table 7. 1, whose columns
show the contents of the various pertinent storage locations at the
end of each step. Columns not germane to a particular step are left
blank in the corresponding row. In the two right-hand columns of
the table, the expression 'MT' is used to refer to the medial decision table of Figure 7. 10.

Table 7.1 (see 6.50).

Step	Arg	P	Hypo P	Successful look-up in Figure 7.8	s	i	go from	to
1	tinnā	1	1S	no	0	0	7.8	7.10
2		2					7.10	7.9
3	tinn	2	92		i	4	7.9	H1
4	tinn	3		yes	i	4	7.8	F1
5	tinn	3	tin					
1	timṭā	1	1S	no	0	0	7.8	7.10
2		2					7.10	7.9
3	timṭ	2	92		i	4	7.9	H1
4	timṭ	2	92	no	i	4	7.8	7.10
5					i	3	7.10	MT
6	timṭ						MT	J1
7	timṭ				i	2	7.10	7.11
8	tim	2	94				7.12	H1
9	tim	3		yes			7.8	F1
10	tim	3	tin					
1	tinin	1	92		i	4	7.9	H1
2	tinin			no	i	4	7.8	7.10
3					i	3	7.10	MT
4	tinin						MT	J1
5					i	2	7.10	7.11
6	tin	1	86				7.11	H1
7	tin	2		yes			H2	F1
8	tin	2	tin					

Table 7.2 (see 6.70)

Analysis of tin-asāg-utā-nu 'I will continue to eat'

Step	Arg	P	Hypo P	Successful look-up in Figure 7.8	s	i	go from	to
1	tinasāgutā	1	1S	no	0	0	7.8	7.10
2		2			0	0	7.10	MT
3					0	0	MT	7.9
4	tinasāgut	2	92		i	4	7.9	7.8
5				no	i	4	7.8	7.10
6					i	3	7.10	MT
7					i	3	MT	J1
8					i	2	7.10	7.11
9	tinasāg	2	94		i	2	7.11	7.8
10				no	i	2	7.8	7.10
11					i	1	7.10	MT
12					i	1	MT	7.12
13	tin	3	38		i	1	7.12	7.8
14	tin	4		yes	i	1	7.8	F1
15	tin	4	tin					

Incidentally, the three examples just given point up the problem of internal sandhi in Telugu verbal forms. Large numbers of verb bases occur in two or more different shapes, conditioned by the first suffix which follows them; the verb 'to eat' has three, tin, tiṅ, and tinn. It seems more efficient to include in the base tables all variants of each base than to program special rules to undo the workings of internal sandhi.

6.60 Figure 7.12 shows the extra programming necessary to accommodate the additional medial suffix -sāg. Location (c - 3) is tested to see whether the allomorph -asāg is present; if so, four characters instead of three are truncated. A similar test was incorporated in Figure 7.11, to check for the presence of the allomorphs -atā and -utā of the future tense morpheme.

6.70 Table 7.2 traces the analysis of a form with two medial suffixes: tin-asāg-utā-nu 'I will continue to eat'.

7.0 This paper has discussed the need for a recognition routine for Telugu verbal forms and has described the form such a routine might take. In order to design a full-capacity routine we must first have complete statements of verb base graphotactics and of the privileges of occurrence of the verbal suffixes relative to one another. Until this information becomes available, a first-approximation routine such as that described here can still relieve the linguist of a good deal of time-consuming work.

NOTES

1. For example, the seemingly very complex system of internal sandhi in the Telugu verbal will not overwhelm the student if it is understood sufficiently well by those who prepare the teaching materials. It consists of two sets of rules, one optional and one obligatory. The optional rules apply to all verbs; there is a different set of obligatory rules for each class of verbs, but almost all of these classes are defined by the phonological structure of their members. All of this suggests teaching the verbs one class at a time, starting with the class having the fewest obligatory sandhi rules — not unlike the practice of teaching Latin or French verbs one 'conjugation' at a time.

2. The noun analysis is not discussed in this paper, being considered of minor importance for two reasons: first, the verbal forms make up nearly 50 per cent of the average Telugu text; and secondly, the noun analysis is a much simpler job, which can be turned over to persons who are not linguists, while the verbal analysis is (in part — see 7.0) turned over to the computer.

3. The orthographic syllable can be rigorously defined for Telugu by a short list of ordered rules, but orthographic practice is inconsistent.

4. See Gerald Kelly, 'Vowel phonemes and external vocalic sandhi in Telugu', JAOS 83. 67-73 (1963) and references given therein.

5. It must be admitted that the program described in this paper is sharply limited in scope, partly due to the customary considerations of space, but partly because not enough is yet known about the Telugu verbal system to make possible a program capable of handling any arbitrarily chosen form.

6. All Telugu citations in this paper are transliterations of the orthography (sometimes with morpheme boundaries indicated by hyphens), including the symbols between slashes. /ṁ/ represents the Telugu grapheme for the nasal homorganic to the stop which follows it.

7. This statement is true only for the purposes of this paper, which deals with only a very few of the actually possible suffixes and strings thereof.

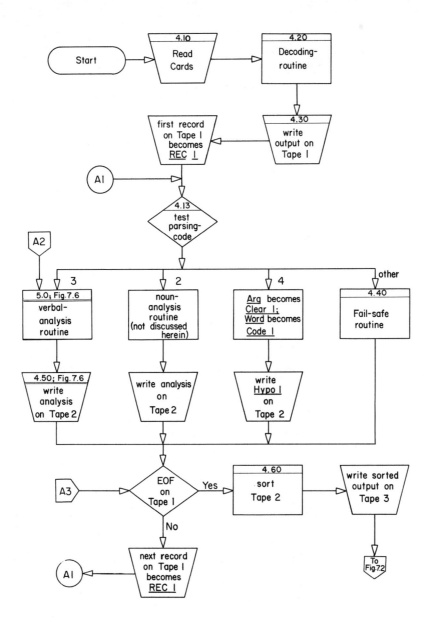

Figure 7.1   Processing of input prior to frequency count.

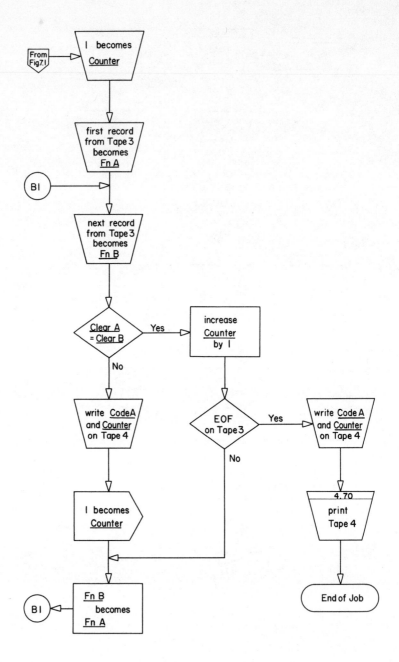

Figure 7.2 Counting and printout of frequencies.

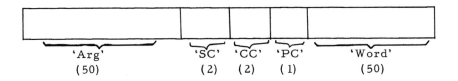

Figure 7. 3.   One record on Tape 1, with names of corresponding
areas in storage, and number of positions in each

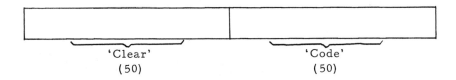

Figure 7. 4.   One record on Tape 2 (Hypo 1, 2, ...) or on
Tape 3 (Fn A, Fn B) (See Figs. 7. 1, 7. 2, respectively.)

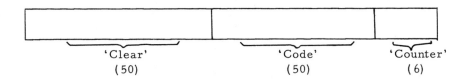

Figure 7. 5.   One record on Tape 4

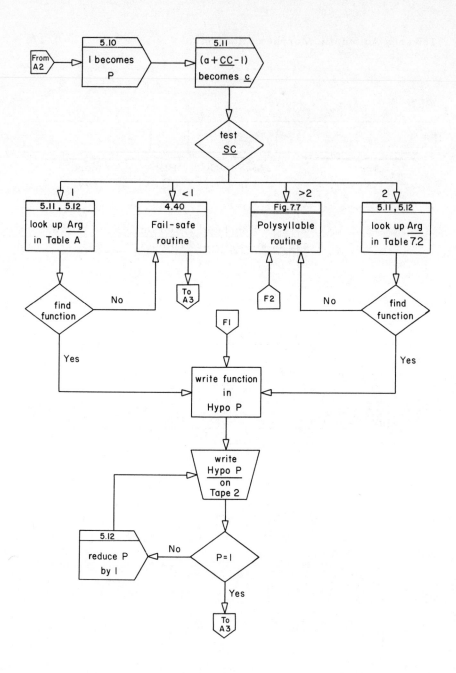

FIGURE 7.6 Verbal analysis routine

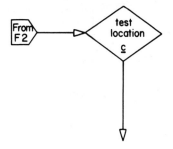

Decision Table, Final

if c̱ contains	then go to	Possible morpheme	Hypo
/a/	Fig. 7.8	a̱ka neg. perf. ppl.	75
		i̱na perf. adj.	79
/u/	6.2	ṉu 1st sg.	1S
		w̱u 2d sg.	2S
		ḏu 3d sg. masc.	3M
		m̱u 1st pl.	1P
		ṟu 2d pl., 3d pl. masc/fem.	2P
/ā/	Fig. 7.9	ā past	92
		ṯā fut.	94
		i̱nā concessive	86
other	Fail-safe		

Figure 7.7   Beginning of polysyllable routine.

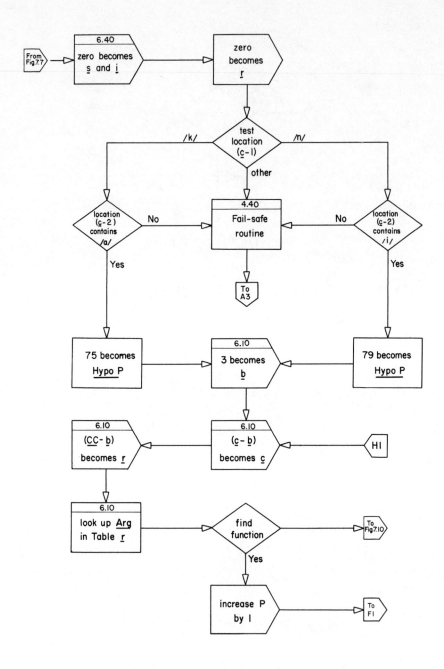

Figure 7.8 Truncation of suffixes with final /a/.

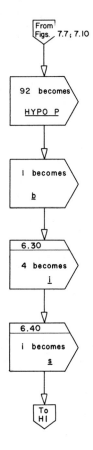

Figure 7.9 First step in identifying /ā/ - final suffix

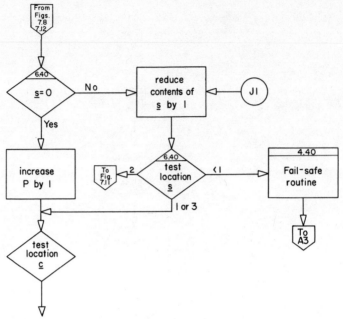

Decision-table, Medial

if c   then
contains go to

		Possible morpheme	Hypo
/ā/	Fig. 7.9	ā past	92
		tā fut.	94
/g/	Fig. 7.12	sāg continuative	38
other	J I		

Figure 7.10   Identification of medial suffix.

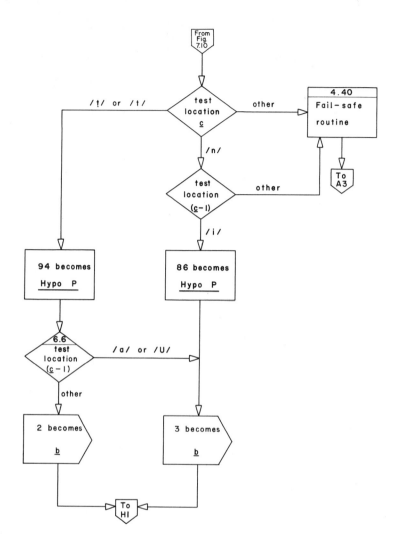

Figure 7.11 Third attempt to identify /ā/ – final suffix

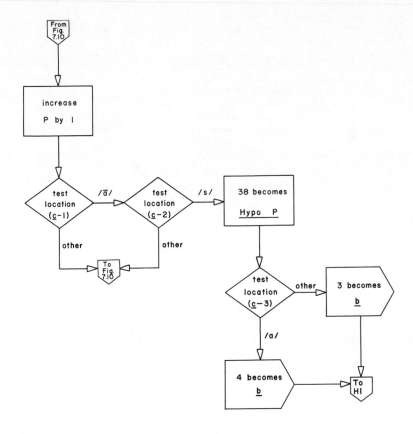

Figure 7.12   Identification of medial suffix — sāg.

Chapter 8

Automatic Verification of Phrase Structure Description

Mary Lu Joynes

0.0 INTRODUCTION

0.1 A generation ago many linguists hoped, and some perhaps
believed, that developments in acoustical engineering would provide
total, unequivocal, and unique solutions to the problems outstanding
in descriptive phonology. While automatic phonological analysis
and the robot secretary are still far from reality today, the use of
such instruments as the sound spectrograph has had some highly
significant results in both practical and theoretical areas. Although
they allow practically as much argument as ever, the phonologies
proposed by linguists from impressionistic work have been sharpened
and occasionally modified by new techniques and more particularly
by a recognition of the differences between the kinds of questions
the linguist may ask the native informant and those he may ask the
machine. In effect, the main value of analytic instruments for the
linguist is as a test, for his impressionistic theory concerning the
data elicited and for his empirical operating procedures.

More recently, with the development of computer technology,
some very ambitious plans and claims have been made for the use
of computers in grammatical analysis. As yet completely automatic grammatical analysis of the so-called neglected languages
seems to be at least as distant a prospect as automatic phonological
analysis. Nevertheless, even at the present stage of computer
technology it is possible to automate some routine stages of linguistic analysis, and in the process perhaps to utilize the by-products
to enrich linguistic theory, just as the information on some aspects
of redundancy, transitional phenomena, discrete and continuous
segments, etc., which emerged from their mechanized investigations, have been used by phonologists.

0.2 The problem presented here is designed to give an extremely simple example of a system for testing an impressionistic

classification frame of two tentative subclasses of prenominal modifiers in English.[1]   Since the problem in question and its proposed approach to solution are to be considered illustrative rather than definitive, the beginning stages of the descriptive process and the formulation of the framework to be tested will be discussed only briefly.   Likewise, the revision of the tentative descriptive framework after the testing process is not given here in any detail.   The computer system is presented only from the standpoint of the role of the linguist, for it is assumed that he will have the help of a competent programmer and will be interested only in the part of the process which involves his own interests and sphere of activity.

The type of grammar represented is basically one of item-and-arrangement.   It is also what is usually called a 'word grammar', although in the early stages of planning it had a phonological component of stress as one of the criteria of classification.[2]   The stress component was of necessity scrapped, along with one of the subclasses based on it, for two practical reasons.   First, while it is possible in theory to construct a computer code which marks stresses, such a code would be extremely complex for a problem which is in other respects a very small-scale operation.   Second, the system presented will begin from a corpus of written English in normal orthography as input.[3]   As yet there is no corpus generally available which marks stresses in a consistent transcription and is of sufficient length to be representative.   Perhaps some significant and useful work can be done on phonologically oriented grammars when such a corpus is made available.

While the system described in some ways resembles the automatic parsing operations detailed elsewhere in this casebook, it is much less sophisticated in that it does not handle every item in the phrase, but only selected items.   After sufficient testing, revision, and additions, it might be rewritten into a full parsing operation, but in the system's use here, as an interim tool for the collection of the specified data about the specified items, those refinements are replaced by a human preeditor.[4]

A collecting and sorting operation of the type presented is a very useful one in testing linguistic classifications made on a distributional basis, but it is done much less frequently than it should be.   If done by hand, such work is extremely tedious and subject to human errors arising from boredom and unconscious revision by the investigator.   Since computers are not subject to boredom and work very rapidly with total consistency, they are much more reliable for tasks of this nature than human investigators.[5]

In addition to its value as a testing device for a descriptive
frame, a system of the type proposed might, after any necessary
revisions, have some utility in other areas of linguistic investigation. A collection of such statistical data on modification patterns
of contemporary American journalistic English might be tested
against a comparable collection based on a corpus of Shakespeare,
respelled Chaucer, or some other variant of English, with interesting
results for the philologist. Similarly, the statistical data on closed-
list modifications and their possible combinations would be extremely
useful for anyone composing graded materials for teaching English
as a foreign language. Comparable studies of French, German, or
other less familiar languages might show that some of the pedagogical
problems which have always been called idiomatic are in fact
patterned. The patterning noted could then be incorporated into con-
trollable drill materials exploiting the systems of both languages.
More extensive and detailed studies of syntactic frequency, when
they are made available, will be at least as useful for teaching
grammar as the familiar word counts have been for the development of lexical fluency.

1.0 REVIEW OF PRELIMINARY PROCEDURES

As background for the framework to be tested, a short survey
of the steps preliminary to the preparation of the classification
system in use at the intermediate stage[6] is necessary. The forms
involved normally occur near the beginning of the noun phrase, are
all of relatively high lexical frequency, are often a cause of difficulty
to students of English as a foreign language, and seem to be members
of a closed list; that is, these classes seem to be relatively free
from borrowings in comparison with the class which includes cerise,
antiphonal, ancient, etc. Many of the handbooks and grammars
simply list them as aberrant forms or place them in similarly vague
lists or categories in opposition to more regular adjectives. A
core of these aberrant or leftover forms was abstracted from several
handbooks and examined for any internal consistencies of any type
that might be found. At this stage some forms were eliminated
from immediate consideration or held for separate study at a later
time. Some of these peripheral forms were the substantive possessives (mine, yours, etc.), own, enough, such, and a few others,
such as the ordinal numbers. The condensed lists were then examined for any other similarities and differences, resulting in the
tentative or intermediate classification framework presented in
Figure 8.1. Up to this point the investigation had proceeded quite

impressionistically, using the native-speaker investigator as informant. In terms of standard procedure, it was time to test the
classification system against some external text as a check on
native-speaker intuition. After the comparison of the text[7] produced nothing that contradicted the previous work, a test on a
larger scale involving other native speakers was begun. Using
grid paper as a primitive generating device, sequences were produced of the items under consideration in all possible combinations
such as what which, what whose, what one's, what my, etc., throughout the chart. Any sequences that had not appeared in the previous
examination of text were submitted to other native speakers in the
form of the question 'Can you think of a sentence in which you
might use /whose our/his five/other this fewest/ etc./?'. Some
of the sequences considered possible were immediately discarded
as segmentable into a substantival followed by a phrase which was
not directly related to it. The informants, as might be expected,
frequently did not agree in their ability to give examples or in
their acceptance of examples given by other informants. In addition
to differences in permissiveness in terms of rhetorical correctness
(since some allowed five less men, while others refused it), the
differences increased with the length of the sequences, allowing a
maximum of three items in sequence, with the exception of sequences
with other, which yielded a very hesitant maximum of four. The
frame of sequences presented in the flowcharts shows the forms
considered to be maximally allowable by even the most permissive
informants. It will not be surprising, therefore, that many of the
sequences leading to OK printout slots will not be used during the
examination of extensive bodies of written text. It is a linguistic
cliché that an informant does not always do what he says he does.
     It is important to call attention to the syntactic context and
boundaries of the phrases which were considered. While the question of segmentation remains one of the most interesting and difficult
in linguistic theory today, cuts must be made and made as consistently as possible, on whatever basis, if any analysis is to be done.
The segment spans dealt with in this study are noun phrases, each
containing one noun head and at least one of the items on the classification frame. In a study in greater depth it might be fruitful to
consider nested phrases, sequences of prepositional phrases, etc.,
but for the purposes of this limited preliminary example nested
phrases (including possessive nouns) are removed in preediting as
if they were open-list modifiers, and the noun head is considered
the end of the construction under consideration. Until preliminary

segmentation can be accomplished reliably by mechanical techniques, the linguist will be forced to make such decisions on an empirical or intuitive basis, for he must have some beginning point, even an arbitrary one.   Perhaps more detailed studies of order restrictions will form a basis, however circular, for more reliable automatic segmentation systems.

2.0 PREPARATION OF DATA FOR INPUT

The flowcharts illustrate a conventionalized format into which the linguist will organize the tentative patternings of the items he has observed, class by class, in preparation for the more technical work of the programmer, and in which he will specify the format of the output he expects.   While the system proposed is said to be a very simple one to program, the detailed steps of an actual working program and coding system are not shown.   It is assumed that the linguist interested in any similar project will not need or want to be his own programmer, but will rather work in cooperation with one who knows the resources of the facilities available to them. In addition to the preliminary data which he plans to test, the questions by which he will test his assumptions, and a suggested format for the output, the linguist is also responsible for the selection and preediting of the corpus to be used as input.

2.1 Figure 8.1 represents the tentative set of classes and subclasses under discussion.   The labels are intended to be mnemonic or loosely descriptive and are only for the convenience of the linguist.   The organization of the chart is binary in form, at least down to the ultimate subclasses which are usually unique forms. Some of the ultimate classes which could not be reduced readily into smaller subclasses include several members, all of which are assumed to have identical intraphrase distribution potential.   For example, the personal pronouns of 1.1.2.1.2.2, the round numbers of 2.2.2.2.1.2.1, and the nonround numbers of 2.2.2.2.1.2.2[8] are assumed to have the same intraphrase distributions respectively, while the nonparadigmatic a, an of 1.2 is considered one form with two spellings.

The binary class divisions are in part a tool of the investigation and in part a result of it.   In setting up the tentative classes, a class frequently appeared to be stable and homogeneous at four or five members, but on further investigation proved to be divisible on the basis of intraphrase distribution of the members with other items under investigation.   Further testing was continued until all the classes had been broken down as far as possible.   It is quite

probable that after statistical tests many of these distinctions can
be ignored as having only marginal utility, but that others will
remain valid. In another sense the binary distinctions made the
formulation of the questions for the processing operation much
easier and possibly more efficient than it would have been with
fewer but larger classes.

2.2 The input for a system which is not equipped for completely
automatic parsing is a problem which can be solved by the use of a
dual input of manually segmented and preedited sequences. While
subsequent work may suggest more useful segmentation principles,
it is reasonable to assume that by the intermediate stage a fairly
valid set of principles for segmentation has emerged. The linguist
then can isolate manually the sequences to be analyzed from the
remainder of the text, which can be filed until it is needed in the
revision stage. The sequences isolated, in the case of this problem
only noun phrases, are then preedited manually. The preediting
process removes everything from the sequence except the forms of
the classes to be tested, substitutes for the noun the cover symbol
N, and if the noun was marked for plurality adds the symbol S. The
cover symbols are of course subject to the discretion of the programmer, who may wish to use some other coding convention. In
the preediting process any spelled numbers will be coded with only
a coding convention to distinguish round and nonround (see Note 8).
Arabic and Roman numerals, although something of a problem, are
best coded as nonround. It is always the first element of a long
number which determines its roundness or nonroundness. The preedited sequence is the working input of the system, while the unedited sequence, the other member of the dual input pair, is stored
for the final printout. Each pair of sequences is assigned a code
number to correspond to its location in the unsegmented corpus in
order to facilitate any later reference to the corpus that might be
needed. An example of one set of a dual input sequence as prepared
by the preeditor before coding would be:

205721   set all the seventy-three fat volumes on all the
         all the nonround NS

The working sequence in the pair is all the nonround NS, while the
final printout sequence is set all the seventy-three fat volumes on.

2.3 The formulation and ordering of the questions for the processing operation is the linguist's chief responsibility in designing
the testing system, and it is here that the most tedious work is done,

and with the greatest possibility of error and of discovery. The principle of the program is a very simple one, based on a series of questions which can be answered affirmatively or negatively. The problem lies in the fact that all the questions must be answerable from data the linguist has already supplied. The questions, in order to be reasonably successful, will start with the largest classes and work downward through the appropriate subclasses to the individual items. If there is a combination of items, the questions will start with the combinations which are shorter and more likely according to the native speaker judgments collected earlier, and will then work to those which are longer and were considered less likely.[9] While theoretically the possibilities of combinations would seem to be extremely large and unwieldy, in actuality they are quite limited and highly restricted in order of combination. Even with an extremely permissive set of allowable sequences there will inevitably be a few combinations which were not provided for in the set of paths leading to OK outlet slots. In order to recover such examples, the RE slots were provided and numbered individually to facilitate revision of the system when it seems desirable to do so.

2.4 The output of the processing operation is fundamentally a sorting and listing, arranged by number, of examples from text of the sequences provided for by the tentative description (the OK slots) and those not provided for (the RE slots). The OK label, therefore, does not in any way mean that the sequence is grammatical or even meaningful. Similarly the RE label does not necessarily indicate that the sequence is ungrammatical or nonsensical, but only that it is for some reason not accounted for by the system. In practical terms the information from the RE slots will be more valuable for the linguist in his evaluation of the description being tested than that obtained from the OK slots. For this reason a great many more RE exits are provided than most systems designers would consider of maximum mechanical efficiency.

From the two basic types of output the programmer can arrange specialized listings for various purposes. If the information seems useful, the printout can tabulate the relative frequency of various types of constructions from the number of times the particular exits are used. On the other hand, a listing of unused OK slots would be very useful information, available with very little effort. Such refinements of the printout are limited only by the data available and the ingenuity of the investigators. While major syntax is of necessity not considered in a limited intermediate stage project of

this nature, it is possible for the linguist to use the revised framework in the preliminaries to such an investigation. By just sorting
the input manually during the preediting process into the major
syntactical categories he wishes to investigate, he can get some rough
information about the patterning of the items and sequences in larger
spans than the intraphrase segments. For example, one run of
input might be presorted into items functioning as the subject of a
finite verb, object of an infinitive phrase, direct object of negative
verb, etc., and the frequency of the items in the separate runs compared with their overall frequency.

3.0 ADVANTAGES OF MACHINE METHOD

In view of the amount of time and effort that the linguist must
spend in setting up the system and in preparing the input, it might
seem that the human operator could perform all the operations
more rapidly and more economically than the machine. Up to a
certain point this assumption is quite correct. In handling extremely
small bodies of data in preliminary stages the tedious process of
manual counting is much more efficient. It also provides the linguist with the opportunity to revise his system while he is working
from it, as he cannot so readily do while the machine is operating.
On the other hand, the blind obedience of the computer follows all
instructions exactly as they are given with a consistency impossible
for a normal human being. This very consistency reveals errors
which the linguist or his assistant working manually might uncon-
sciously overlook or repair by means of an unnoted change in the
system, which might in turn be forgotten before it could be applied
to the entire corpus.

In one sense the use of the machine may seem to eliminate
some of the unexpected discoveries which make linguistic analysis
interesting. In fact, however, the discoveries are simply shifted
from the intermediate or raw counting stage of the process to the
preliminary or planning stage or to the final revision. The process
of preediting the corpus can also expose unexpected problems, which
must be solved before the sequence can be coded as input. In the
system described, the linguist must decide whether a sequence such
as (Did they want) a little cheese(?) is to be edited into a N or a
little N, or whether he wants to include both possibilities. The decisions must be made consistently, if arbitrarily, and with some
control on the criteria by which they are made.

4.0 RESULTS AND USES OF SYSTEM

As was mentioned earlier, the by-products of an investigation can be as interesting and useful as the information which it was planned to uncover. In addition to collecting sequences of forms which were not accounted for in the preliminary framework, the output of the full, unedited sequences gives starting points for further investigation. For example, handbooks have often referred to a particular type of noun, or perhaps noun construction, as a mass-noun or uncountable noun, as illustrated by <u>milk</u>, <u>information</u>, or <u>justice</u>. Certain other nouns, such as <u>fish</u> and <u>species</u>, are what have been called nouns with unmarked plurals. By programming the output slots of the constructions which are expected to produce such nouns into a separate listing, or simply by noting the output numbers of such slots and checking the printouts manually, it is possible to collect extensive lists of nouns with the properties desired. The unedited printout may also be very useful in spotting the distribution of forms not immediately under consideration, but closely related to them. Some of the peripheral forms which were discarded at the beginning of the investigation, such as <u>certain</u>, <u>(a) lot</u>, <u>lots</u>, <u>very</u>, <u>same</u>, <u>only</u>, etc., reappear for reconsideration in the unedited printout. If a similar testing device were set up for verb phrases,[10] information might be made available through the unedited printout about various types of intraphrase adverbial modifiers and their positions in relation to the specified phrase types.

In a very limited sense it is possible to use the processing operation section of the flowchart to generate sequences manually. It would, however, be best to do this after sufficient material had been tested to determine exactly which slots are actually used and which are not. The simulated generation is done by beginning at an OK slot (or a RE slot which has been found acceptable and suitably revised into an OK slot) and tracing backward through its path to the noun, which is then supplied by the investigator, subject to any plurality restrictions applicable at that point. Not surprisingly, however, not all such sequences are equally acceptable to the native-speaker judge. For example, the same slot can produce <u>his every rabbit</u> and <u>her every thought</u>. Thus any generation should be preceded by a collection of nouns or constructions which are semantically as well as formally allowable in that slot. Such a pool can easily be collected for each outlet actually in use, but the result would be possibilities for generation so limited that it would in effect give out as totally acceptable only what had been previously put in from

the corpus. Even without a pool of congruent nouns, however, the
generation and testing of semantic acceptability of modifier sequences
with random nouns might produce interesting lexical information.

The most important product of the investigation remains the
collection and ordering of statistics and examples, from a corpus,
of patterns observed and projected by the linguist from his empirical
work. If the preliminary investigation produced a framework which
was only slightly weak, the intermediate-stage investigation will
show where the defects are. If it was extremely weak, the computer's
work will be virtually useless. If it was adequate, the accumulated
data will point to areas for further investigation along more sophisticated lines, using as reference points the items, classes, and
arrangement patterns already isolated. In any case the linguist is
responsible for the results and the final utility of the description
and for its implications.

NOTES

1. The framework presented in Figure 8.1 was drawn up in
rough outline in connection with an informal workshop on some problems in English syntax during the Linguistic Institute of 1960 in
Austin, Texas. It was revised extensively in 1963-1964. The purpose of the workshop was to subdivide some of the problems, such
as the analysis of verb phrases, noun phrases, pronouns and pro-
nominals, into small units which might be studied formally, distributionally, and semantically, first within the subsections themselves and then ultimately within larger syntactic frames of reference.
Figure 8.1 represents a tentative subsectioning of some of the
modifications within the noun phrase. The terms Primary and
Secondary as used refer only to the first two tentative divisions of
the subsectioning. The names of the divisions of Figure 8.1 are
merely for convenience, and may be replaced if other terms seem
more suitable.

2. All the forms classed as Primaries on Figure 8.1 normally
have minor stress (/ˋ/ˇ/), while those classed as Secondaries typi-
cally have /ˆ/. On the basis of the stress distinction, a second nonparadigmatic subclass, consisting of minor-stressed some and any,
was drawn up, which contrasted with the Secondary pair of the same
spelling. The division, incorporated into drill material, has been
pedagogically useful for students of English as a foreign language,
especially those of Romance backgrounds.

3. An ideal corpus for work of this nature will be that in preparation at Brown University by W. Nelson Francis. It is to consist of 1,000,000 words from randomly chosen sources.

4. It would be possible to use a skipping device in the scanning process which would simply ignore all items but those on the chart. A great deal of waste would result from the process, for the device would also act on listed items found in nested phrases and other modifiers which the preeditor would have rejected.

5. A computer system is by no means infallible. It is subject to both mechanical breakdown and human errors resulting from faulty programming or coding. The explicit nature of mechanical operations, however, usually makes the errors easier to locate and correct than human errors in a manual operation.

6. The term 'intermediate stage' as used throughout the paper refers to the second of three stages of a procedure followed by many linguists in their investigations. The first, or preliminary, stage consists of the gathering of a body of data and formation of tentative hypotheses, classifications, etc., from it. The second, or intermediate, stage consists of the testing of the hypotheses, classifications, etc., against a larger corpus. The third, or revision, stage evaluates the failures of the tentative description to cover the data from the intermediate stage corpus and suggests refinements and changes in the description and directions for further work. In actual practice, of course, the intermediate and revision stages are frequently repeated, using the most recent revisions as the basis for the next intermediate stage investigation.

7. The first corpus was C. E. Ayres, 'The Industrial Way of Life,' Texas Quarterly II, 2. 1-19 (1959). As a more informal balance, the left-most column of the front page of the Dallas Morning News was examined every day for two weeks.

8. The subsectioning of the cardinal numbers in the preliminary stage of the investigation is an example of distributional subsectioning of what at first appeared to be a homogeneous class. The numbers classed as nonround on Figure 8. 1 may appear without a preceding Primary or Secondary in a noun phrase. Those classed as round, however, must be preceded by some such modification. The semantic relation to the decimal counting system is not complete, for ten (and its compounds, such as ten thousand, ten million, etc.) functions as a nonround number, while dozen (and marginally gross) functions as a round number.

9. The question of whether the scanning should be done from left to right or right to left brings up some practical and theoretical points which led to interesting discussions during the summer. For this system, the right-to-left scan was adopted because an earlier trial on the same material using a left-to-right scan had proved more cumbersome. The question that usually arises in connection with scanning is whether the computer does (or should) actually simulate the human process of perception, which is, at least in figurative terms, of the chronologically-based left-to-right type. Aside from the question of whether the computer simulates human speech perception to any degree or not, some linguists would not agree that at the level of the phrase language is necessarily understood in any chronological order. Thus, for such linguists, the whole question is purely rhetorical.

10. A beginning point for such a study is already available in W. F. Twaddell's The English Verb Auxiliaries[2] (Providence, R.I., 1963).

Figure 8. 1

1 Primary
1. 1 Paradigmatic
1. 1. 1 hw-
1. 1. 1. 1 what
1. 1. 1. 2 which
1. 1. 2 Determinatives
1. 1. 2. 1 Possessives
1. 1. 2. 1. 1 Relative-interrogative whose
1. 1. 2. 1. 2 Pronouns
1. 1. 2. 1. 2. 1 Impersonal one's
1. 1. 2. 1. 2. 2 Personal my, thy, our, your, his, her, its, their
1. 1. 2. 2 th-
1. 1. 2. 2. 1 Demonstratives
1. 1. 2. 2. 1. 1 Singular this, that
1. 1. 2. 2. 1. 2 Plural these, those
1. 1. 2. 2. 2 Definite article the
1. 2 Nonparadigmatic a, an

2 Secondary
2. 1 Predeterminatives
2. 1. 1 Restricted both
2. 1. 2 Unrestricted
2. 1. 2. 1 all
2. 1. 2. 2 half
2. 2 Nonpredeterminatives
2. 2. 1 Qualifiers
2. 2. 1. 1 Inclusive of primaries
2. 2. 1. 1. 1 some
2. 2. 1. 1. 2 every
2. 2. 1. 2 Exclusive of primaries
2. 2. 1. 2. 1 Opposition
2. 2. 1. 2. 1. 1 no
2. 2. 1. 2. 1. 2 any
2. 2. 1. 2. 2 Suppletion each
2. 2. 2 Quantifiers
2. 2. 2. 1 Superlative
2. 2. 2. 1. 1 Restricted to NS fewest
2. 2. 2. 1. 2 Unrestricted
2. 2. 2. 1. 2. 1 most
2. 2. 2. 1. 2. 2 least

2.2.2.2   Modification
2.2.2.2.1   Adjectival
2.2.2.2.1.1   Restricted
2.2.2.2.1.1.1   N
2.2.2.2.1.1.1.1   General
2.2.2.2.1.1.1.1.1   <u>much</u>
2.2.2.2.1.1.1.1.2   <u>little</u>
2.2.2.2.1.1.1.2   Specific
2.2.2.2.1.1.1.2.1   <u>one</u>
2.2.2.2.1.1.1.2.2   <u>another</u>
2.2.2.2.1.1.2   NS
2.2.2.2.1.1.2.1   Definite
2.2.2.2.1.1.2.1.1   <u>few</u>
2.2.2.2.1.1.2.1.2   <u>many</u>
2.2.2.2.1.1.2.2   Indefinite <u>several</u>
2.2.2.2.1.2   Numbers
2.2.2.2.1.2.1   Round <u>dozen</u>, <u>hundred</u>, thousand, etc.
2.2.2.2.1.2.2   Nonround <u>three</u>, <u>five</u>, <u>seventy</u>, etc.
2.2.2.2.2   Comparative
2.2.2.2.2.1   Paired
2.2.2.2.2.1.1   <u>fewer</u>
2.2.2.2.2.1.2   <u>less</u>
2.2.2.2.2.2   Unpaired
2.2.2.2.2.2.1   <u>more</u>
2.2.2.2.2.2.2   <u>other</u>

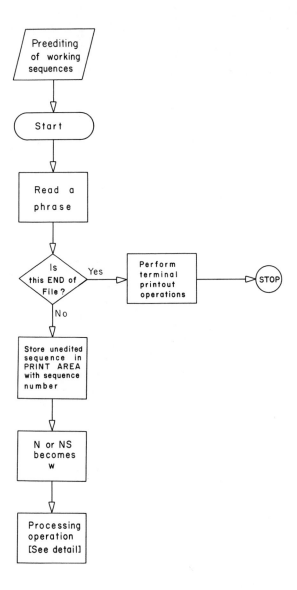

Figure 8.2   Summary   Flowchart

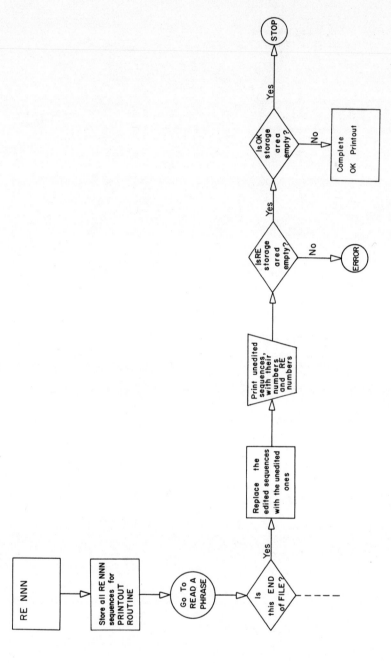

Figure 8.3   Suggested Detail of a RE Terminal Routine

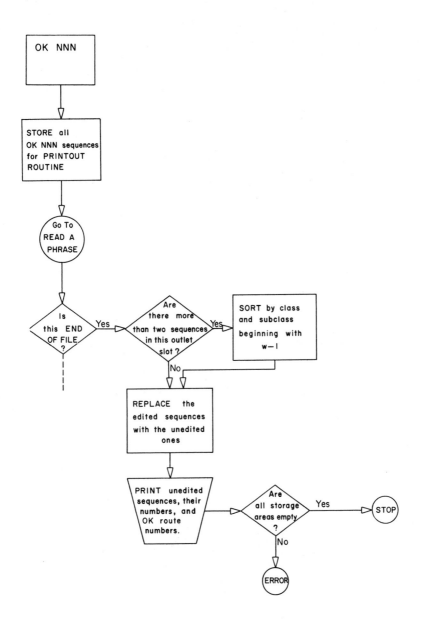

Figure 8.4 Suggested Detail of an OK Terminal Routine

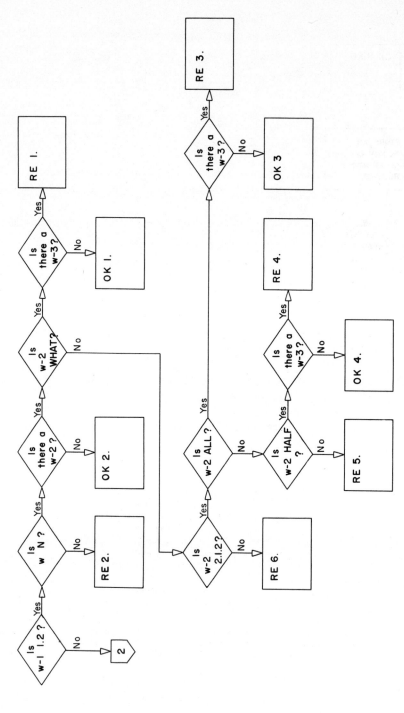

Figure 8.5   DETAIL OF PROCESSING OPERATION

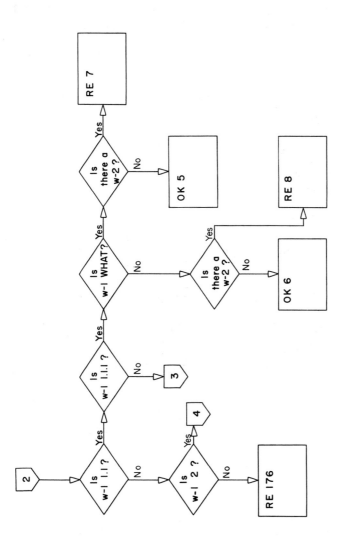

Figure 8.6

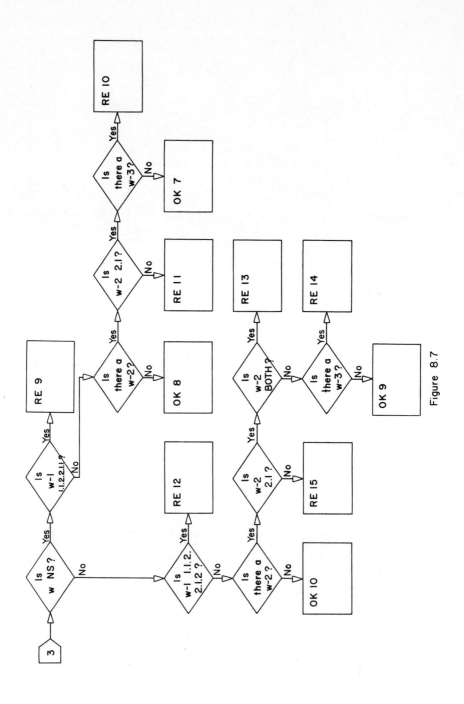

Figure 8.7

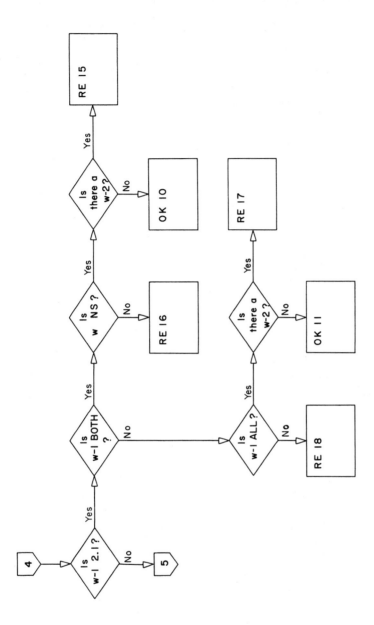

Figure 8.8

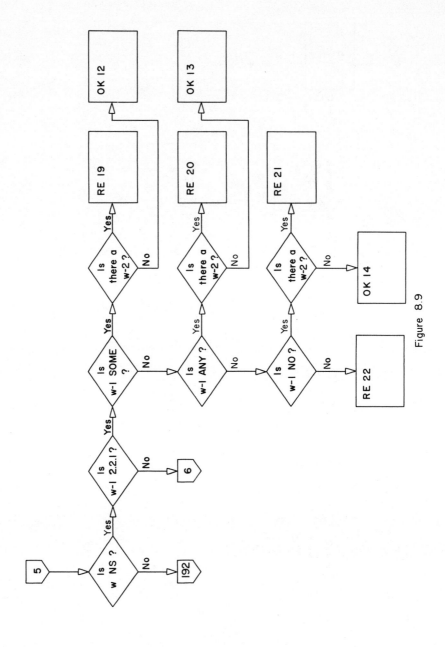

Figure 8.9

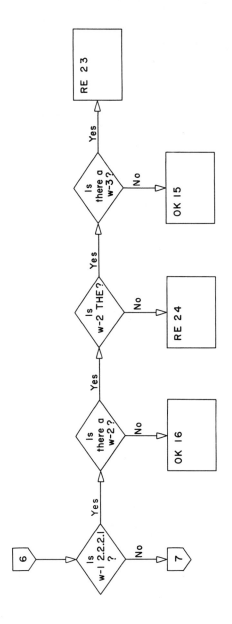

Figure 8.10

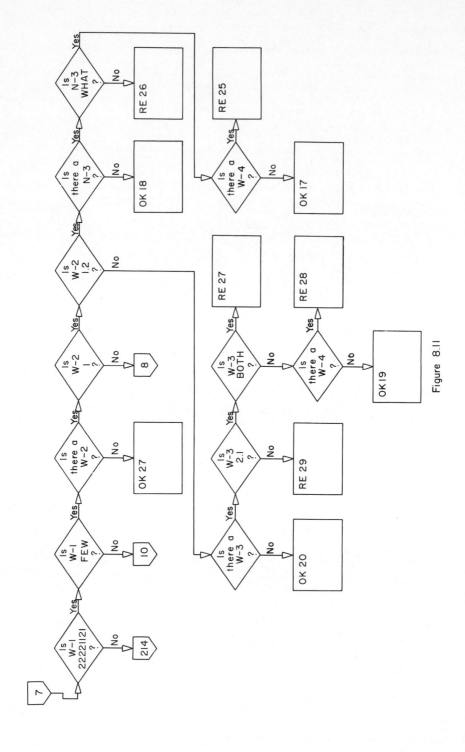

Figure 8.11

Chapter 9

A Structural Recognition Routine for the Noun
Phrases of Standard Chinese

Fred C. C. Peng

1 INTRODUCTION

1.0 This study presents an attempt at the automatic parsing of standard Chinese (hereafter SC), the official language of Formosa and mainland China. The processing involves a recognition routine which, given an SC sentence, will identify, on the basis of the grammar we are to describe, the structures of those phrases which will be called basic substantive phrases (hereafter BSP).

1.10 The data which this routine will process are written texts in SC. Thus, in addition to a necessary description of SC grammatical structure, which will be restricted to a syntactic analysis of BSP, we shall take into consideration the functions and meanings of SC characters and punctuation marks.

1.20 The processing of text by the routine, which is intended for an MT program the completion of which falls beyond the scope of this paper, is to be manually simulated. Our processing will be the result of (1) establishing a system of grammar-coding, (2) describing the structure of SC-BSP, and finally (3) flowcharting the routine itself. Our approach will in general follow that of the fulcrum technique;[1] but, our attention will be focused on only the first of several proposed passes.

1.21 The first part of this paper will discuss the grammar code for use in the processing. This grammar code will be based on the taxonomy of SC word classes worked out by the author.[2]

1.22 The second part of this paper will be devoted to the description of the characteristics and relationships of the items which enter into the structures of BSP. The description will primarily be based on an item-and-arrangement model, showing the occurrences, distributions, and classes of the items involved.

1.23 The third part will then utilize the preceding parts in the form of flowcharts for the mechanization of the recognition of linguistic items pertinent to SC-BSP.

1.30 In the course of the processing as proposed in this study, the recognition routine will be applied to one sentence at a time. Each sentence will be scanned from right to left, assuming that the beginning of a sentence is to the left and the end of it is to the right. The right-to-left technique is favored at this stage, because (1) SC endocentric constructions are usually of the attribute-head type, and (2) punctuation marks used in SC often help differentiate meanings of homographs and/or homophones, as shown in Figure 9.1.

Traditionally, the two occurrences of 幾 chi in these contexts are regarded as two separate homophonous-and-homographic forms, because one means 'how many (or much)' and the other 'several'. However, in this research it has been found that the two are actually instances of one morpheme; the differences in meaning are added to the morpheme by the intonations, for which two grammar codes, // and # respectively, will be designed to account, the former being interrogative, the latter declarative. These intonations are inferred on the basis of punctuation marks (cf. 2.12).

In both cases, it should be noted that the right-to-left scan will permit the detection of the greatest source of syntactic information — head of the attribute-head construction and punctuation marks — first.

1.4 We shall select texts written by educated native writers for processing in order to be able to assume that they contain no grammatical errors. This assumption is based on the following observation.

There are in SC, as in any language, many ways to make a grammatical sentence ungrammatical. For example, 兩 條 狗 liang t'iao kou 'two dogs' is a grammatical phrase consisting of numeral + measure + noun. By use of permutation one can produce five more sequences, each being distinctively different, not to mention various kinds of transitions from word to word. Of these new sequences only one can be considered grammatical, namely, noun + numeral + measure, the literal translation of which is 'dog two'. Ungrammatically ordered sequences are, however, not the only source of error; without appropriate restrictions, wrong cooccurrences by the hundreds could be generated, should t'iao in the above sequences be replaced by other measures. Fortunately, the educated native writers know exactly which sequenced order and cooccurrence

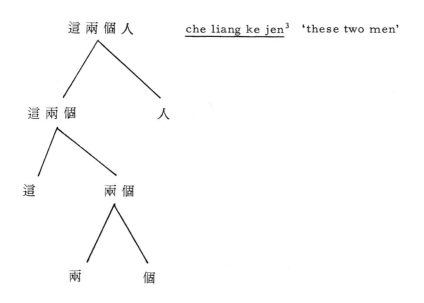

che liang ke jen[3] 'these two men'

幾 個 人 **?**   chi ke jen 'how many people?'

幾 個 人 .   chi ke jen 'several people.'

Figure 9.1

is grammatically acceptable, and hence will use just the right one.
That is to say, they know of six possible sequences of three lexical
units, liang, t'iao, and kou, when, where, and how to use the correct two sequences; and they also know which of several hundred
measures (in this case, only 隻 chih), can replace t'iao in the
correct sequences.

If we do not assume that no grammatical error exists in our
data, we would have (1) to expect that our data might contain any
conceivable grammatical error which had to be detected, and (2) to
construct a routine capable of identifying not only the grammatical
but also the ungrammatical phrases, to be corrected by the routine.
Such a routine would go far beyond the domain of our immediate
concern (cf. 1.0).

2.   PROCESSING I — CODING SYSTEM

2.0 A complete automatic parsing program for SC will have to
be preceded by a dictionary look-up and begin with a word-class
ambiguity resolution routine. These two steps, however, are not
included in the present study. Rather, the recognition routine for
BSP has been developed as if the dictionary look-up and ambiguity
resolution had already been accomplished by the time this routine
goes into effect. It is believed that this research strategy makes
it possible both to develop the BSP routine independently and to
thoroughly study the requirements for the ambiguity resolution that
will be needed for the complete parsing program.

2.1 Grammar code. Two types of grammar codes will ultimately be required for the automatic parsing of SC, namely, (1) a
word-class code and (2) a government code. However, only the
first type is needed for the BSP routine. It consists of (1) a functional code and (2) an expressive code. The functional code stands
for the parts of speech of SC (to be discussed in a subsequent section), and is made up of a list of one-digit capital letters. The
expressive code stands for special types of words and word substitutes, such as interjections, onomatopoeia, and punctuation marks,
and is made up of a list of two one-digit capital letters plus three
special signs.

2.11 Functional code. The functional code is the following:

J	Adjunctivals
A	Adverbials
B	Adverbializing particle
X	Approximals

T	Attributive particles
L	Auxiliaries
C	Conjunctions
D	Demonstratives
R	Derivative particles
H	Ergatives
F	Final particles
I	Instrumentals
M	Measures
G	Negatives
N	Nouns
U	Numerals
P	Pronouns
Z	Stative verbs
V	Verbs

The taxonomy of these codes in terms of SC word-classes may be summarized as shown in Figure 9. 3

2. 12 <u>Expressive code.</u>   The expressive code is the following:

K	Interjection
O	Onomatopoetics
#	Declarative marker
=	Exclamatory marker
//	Interrogative marker

The taxonomy of these codes is shown in Figure 9. 2.

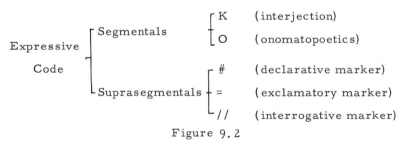

Figure 9. 2

It should be noted that we are for the time being ignoring three punctuation marks: (1) some instances of comma, (2) quotation marks, and (3) parentheses. This means that, in line with (1) above, instances of comma which are not ignored are conveniently interpreted as equivalent to a period, and hence coded as #. Moreover, colon as well as semicolon are treated as periods, since they indicate the declarative intonation;[4] hence, they are also coded as #.

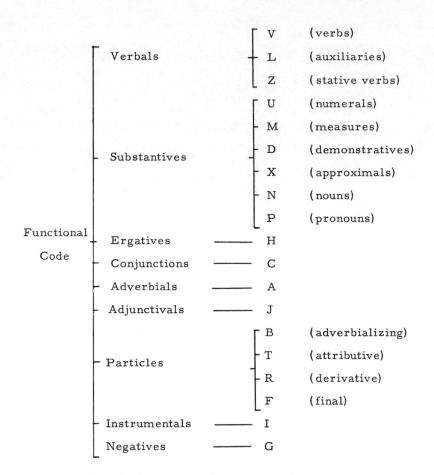

Figure 9. 3

2.2 PROCESSING II — STRUCTURAL DESCRIPTION

2.20 <u>Grammatical characteristics.</u> In the following sections
we analyze the grammatical characteristics of the items of which
SC-BSP are made up. In order to discuss this, we need to know
exactly what items are pertinent to the structure of BSP.

There are five relevant items, each one of which is a class of
forms: (1) numerals, (2) measures, (3) demonstratives, (4) approximals, and (5) nouns. Each form in these classes consists of
most often one, but sometimes more than one, character with a
single set of lexical meanings and grammatical functions. We will
now discuss the grammatical characteristics of these five classes
of forms.

2.21 <u>Numerals.</u> A numeral is defined as a form which consists
of one or several numeric character(s). There are in SC 19 such
numeric characters which can be divided into two sets, each being
subdivided into two types, as shown in Table 9.1.

Types 1 and 3 consist of free forms, whereas types 2 and 4
of bound forms. In terms of meaning, each character of types 1
and 3 expresses an independent number, while those of types 2 and
4 do not, except under special conditions. These conditions are
the following: (1) Each character of type 2 can express its meaning
as a number, if and only if it is bound to a nonnumeric character,
e.g. 零 度   <u>ling tu</u> 'zero degree'. (2) The first three characters
of type 4 as numeric units (cf. note 8) can express the approximate
meanings of their values, if and only if they are bound to nonnumeric
characters, e.g. 百 人 大 合 唱   <u>pai jen ta he ch'ang</u> 'the chorus
of (about) a hundred voices'.

All four types of numeric characters, however, may combine
in various ways to express independent numbers higher than 10,
e.g. 三 百 五 十   <u>san pai wu shih</u> 'three hundred and fifty'. It
should be noted that one of the numeric characters of type 4, namely,
万   <u>wan</u> 'ten thousand', may be reduplicated when combined with
others, especially with those of types 1 and 3, to express independent
numbers, e.g. 五 万 万   <u>wu wan wan</u> 'five hundred million'. The
reduplicated form <u>wan wan</u>, therefore, is freely interchangeable with
a different numeric character, namely 億   <u>i</u>. In this case, <u>wu wan</u>
<u>wan</u> is equivalent to <u>wu i</u> 'five hundred million'.

Two more instances of interchangeability are worthy of mention:

(1) The numeric character 兆 <u>chao</u>, which constitutes a form
wherever it combines with other numeric character(s) to express
a possible independent number, may be freely replaced by the

Table 9. 1.   Numeric Characters

Set I

Type 1

一 i 'one'

二 erh 'two'

三 san 'three'

四 ssu 'four'

五 wu 'five'

六 liu 'six'

七 ch'i 'seven'

八 pa 'eight'

九 chiu 'nine'

Type 2

零 ling 'zero'

幾 chi 'several'[5]

兩 liang 'two'[6]

數 shu 'several'

Set II

Type 3

十 shih 'ten'

Type 4[7]

百 pai 'hundred'

千 ch'ien 'thousand'

万 wan 'ten thousand'

億 i 'hundred million'

兆 chao 'thousand billion'

numeric characters 万 <u>wan</u> and 億 <u>i</u>, combined together into the form <u>wan i</u>. However, any number containing either one of these two forms seldom appears in practice.

(2)　二 <u>erh</u> and 兩 <u>liang</u> are to some extent interchangeable. However, their interchangeability is by no means as free as in the cases mentioned earlier; there are certain environmental restrictions involved. The conditions under which <u>erh</u> and <u>liang</u> may be interchanged are as follows:

(a)　<u>Liang</u> may replace <u>erh</u> if

   (i)　The latter precedes, in a given number, any numeric character of type 4, e.g. 二 千 <u>erh ch'ien</u> 'two thousand' can freely become 兩 千 <u>liang ch'ien</u> 'two thousand'.

  (ii)　The latter does not precede 十 <u>shih</u> in a number the value of which is larger than 10, e.g. in 二 百 二 十 <u>erh pai erh shih</u> 'two hundred and twenty' only the first occurrence of <u>erh</u> can be replaced by <u>liang</u>, as in 兩 百 二 十 <u>liang pai erh shih</u> 'two hundred and twenty'.

 (iii)　The latter does not follow 十 <u>shih</u> in a number the value of which is larger than 10, e.g. in 二 百 十 二 <u>erh pai shih erh</u> 'two hundred and twelve' only the first occurrence of <u>erh</u> can be replaced by <u>liang</u>, as in 兩 百 十 二 <u>liang pai shih erh</u> 'two hundred and twelve'.

  (iv)　The latter does not follow 零 <u>ling</u> in a number the value of which is larger than one hundred, e.g. in 二 百 零 二 <u>erh pai ling erh</u> 'two hundred and two' only the first occurrence of <u>erh</u> can be replaced by <u>liang</u>, as in 兩 百 零 二 <u>liang pai ling erh</u> 'two hundred and two'.

However, it is interesting to note that <u>liang</u> may not replace <u>erh</u> at all, if the latter is used along with such special nouns as 夫 人 <u>fu jen</u> 'madam' and such special kinship terms as 哥 <u>ko</u> 'older brother'. In such instances, the use of <u>erh</u> is culturally fixed and cannot be altered in any way, although the meaning of <u>erh</u> is slightly changed. Thus, <u>erh fu jen</u>[8] no longer means 'two madams' but 'number two madam', and <u>erh ko</u> does not mean 'two older brothers' but 'number two elder brother'.

(b)　On the other hand, <u>erh</u> may replace <u>liang</u> in any context, so long as the latter is used with other numeric characters

in expressing a number. Only two minor restrictions
apply to this: erh may not replace liang if
(i) The latter is used with nouns which are paired, e.g.
夫婦倆   fu fu liang[9] 'a couple, the two of them'.
(ii) The latter immediately precedes such characters as
個 ko,   條 t'iao, and 双 shuang.[10]
While the discussion of the detailed combinations of these
numeric characters is not within the purview of this presentation, it will hereafter be considered that (1) each
independent number constitutes a numeral, inasmuch as it
is expressed (a) by a numeric character, when possible,
or (b) by a grammatical combination of the numeric characters, and that (2) each numeric character constitutes a
numeral when it is appropriately bound.

    2.22 Measures.[11] A measure is best defined as a form which
can at least follow a numeral, as in 十個   shih ko 'ten ke things',
to form a construction of the attribute-head type. Syntactically,
measures function more often than not as parts of attribute-head
constructions. Thus, when a numeral and a measure are accompanied by a noun, they each form part of the attribute to the noun
which is head. But when an attribute-head construction consists
only of a numeral and a measure, the measure functions as head,
the numeral as attribute. And when an attribute-head construction
consists of a numeral, a measure, and a noun such that the construction is immediately preceded by a verb, the numeral may be
optionally omitted if and only if it is the numeral 'one'. If the
numeral is so omitted, the measure alone functions as the attribute
to the noun which is head. (A more detailed distributional description of individual measures will be given later.)
    A measure always consists of a single character. But the
form 奌兒 tien erh[12] is an exception in that the presence of the
second characters is quite optional; it is more readily omitted in
writing than it is in speaking. For example, 一奌錢   i tien ch'ien
'a small amount of money' is as grammatical as   一奌兒錢
i tien erh ch'ien 'a small amount of money'.
    The exact number of measures in SC is unknown. Our guess
is that it is close to several hundred. (According to Professor Y.
R. Chao, there are about 350 measures plus an unlimited number
of container measures, e.g. t'ung 'pail', and temporary measures,
e.g. wu tsu 'room'. However, wu tzu and the like are treated as
nouns in 2.324 of this study.)

2.23 <u>Demonstratives</u>. A demonstrative may be defined as a
form which can precede a construction consisting of a numeral and
a measure, or precede just a numeral. For example, 這 兩 個
<u>che liang ko</u> 'these two <u>ke</u> things', or 星 期 二 <u>hsing ch'i erh</u>
'Tuesday'. An alternative definition can be given as follows: A
demonstrative is a form which may precede a measure in a given
construction.

Whether or not a demonstrative is identified in terms of the
primary or the alternative definition, we need to point out that in
a given construction it is always the attribute.

A demonstrative normally consists of a single character, with
two exceptions, 礼 拜 <u>li pai</u> and 星 期 <u>hsing ch'i</u>; the two characters
in each form are obligatorily bound together.

There are, like numerals, a few interchangeable forms. First,
the two exceptional forms given in the preceding paragraph are
completely interchangeable; one substitutes for the other under all
conditions. Second, 唯 <u>wei</u> may interchange with 惟 <u>wei</u> in a few
contexts. Notice that they are homophonous but not homographic.

There are 39 demonstratives in SC. They are listed in Table
9.2.

2.24 <u>Approximals</u>. An approximal is best defined as a form
which must be preceded by a numeral and at the same time followed
by a measure. For example, 十 來 個 <u>shih lai ko</u> 'ten or so <u>ko</u>
things'. The numerals with which approximals occur must be those
which designate numbers higher than 10. There are only three
approximals, each consisting of a single character, viz. 來 <u>lai</u>,
餘 <u>yü</u>, and 多 <u>tuo</u>.

2.25 <u>Nouns</u>. In SC, as in other languages, while a noun, or
rather nominal material, is relatively easy to identify referentially,
it is difficult to give a theoretically adequate definition. A first
approximation toward such a definition is here attempted as follows:
A noun is a form which can follow a measure in a given construction,
where the noun always functions as the head of the construction; for
example, 兩 頭 牛 <u>liang t'ou niu</u> 'two head of cattle'.

The following additional distributional characteristics of nouns
may serve as secondary defining criteria.

2.251 A noun may follow a stative verb. The stative verb and
the noun constitute a construction in which the former is always
the attribute and the latter the head; for example, 好 人 <u>hao jen</u>
'a good man'.

Table 9.2 <u>Demonstratives</u>

這 chei[13] 'this'   牛 <u>pan</u> 'half'

那 <u>nei</u>[13] 'that   礼 拜 <u>li pai</u> 'weekly'

哪 <u>nei</u>[13] 'which'   星 期 <u>hsing ch'i</u> 'weekly'

每 <u>mei</u> 'every'   中 <u>chung</u> 'middle'

第 <u>ti</u> ' — th'[14]   初 <u>ch'u</u> 'beginning'

頭 <u>t'ou</u> 'beginning'   老 <u>lao</u> 'respectable'

末 <u>muo</u> 'last'   今 <u>chin</u> 'present'

另 <u>ling</u> 'other'   明 <u>ming</u> 'bright'

各 <u>ke</u> 'each'   昨 <u>tsuo</u> 'past'

諸 <u>chu</u> 'all'   次 <u>tz'u</u> 'next'

整 <u>cheng</u> 'whole'   前 <u>ch'ien</u> 'before'

該 <u>kai</u> 'that'   後 <u>hou</u> 'after'

其 <u>ch'i</u> 'that specific'   去 <u>ch'ü</u> 'past'

別 <u>pie</u> 'the other'   上 <u>shang</u> 'above'

單 <u>tan</u> 'single'   下 <u>hsia</u> 'below'

此 <u>tz'u</u> 'this'   甚 <u>shen</u> 'what'

双 <u>shuang</u> 'double'   怎 <u>tsen</u> 'how'

翌 <u>i</u> 'next'   本 <u>pen</u> 'self'

唯 <u>wei</u> 'only'   少 <u>shao</u> 'juvenile'

惟 <u>wei</u> 'just'

2.252 A noun may follow 有 yu 'to have' (a verb). In this
sequence, the verb and the noun give rise to a construction which
is often called a verb-object construction. Such a construction
may or may not function as a predication. When it does, yu is the
main verb of the sentence in which the construction occurs, and the
noun which yu precedes becomes the direct object of yu. If not, the
construction, which can be an attribute modifying another noun to
form a larger attribute-head construction, is in itself an attribute-
head construction in which yu is the attribute while the noun preceded by yu is the head. Examples are the following: 他 有 錢
t'a yu ch'ien[15] 'he has money'; 有 錢 人 yu ch'ien jen 'rich people'.

It should be noted that yu ch'ien jen may be regarded as equivalent to 有 錢 的 人 yu ch'ien te jen which has the inserted particle te.
(Yu ch'ien te jen is ambiguous in meaning; it means (1) rich people
and (2) the people who have money (with them).) If ch'ien is replaced by another noun, say, 趣 ch'ü 'interest',[16] the noun requires
the presence of the particle te in order to modify 人 jen, because
* 有 趣 人   *yu ch'ü jen is ungrammatical. (In this case, 有 趣 的 人
yu ch'ü te jen is also ambiguous in meaning; it means (1) interesting
people and (2) the people who are interested.)

However, a noun such as 機 chi 'organ', if preceded by yu, is
a special form, because the verb-object construction, 有 機
yu chi 'organic', when it becomes an attribute, always directly
modifies the head-noun: e.g. 有 機 物 yu chi wu 'organic matter';
有 機 化 合 物   yu chi hua he wu 'organic compounds'. Should
te be used after chi in a larger construction, e.g. 有 機 的 東 西
yu chi te tung hsi[17] 'something which is organic', chi allows no
ambiguity in meaning.

2.253 A noun may follow 無 wu 'no' (a negative). They also
form an attribute-head construction, wu being the attribute and the
noun the head; for example, 無 恥 wu ch'ih 'shameless'. If, however, wu is followed by a noun such as 機 chi 'organ', the function
of wu chi 'inorganic' is quite similar to that of yu chi 'organic', as
an attribute, or as a part of an attribute; for example, 無 機 物
wu chi wu 'inorganic matter', 無 機 的 東 西 wu chi te tung hsi
'something which is inorganic'.

2.254 A noun may follow 之 chih (a particle)[18] while another
noun precedes it. Such a sequence (noun + particle + noun) always
constitutes a construction in that the first noun and the particle
together as attribute modify the second noun which is head. The

attribute is in turn a construction in that the particle is subordinate to the noun; for example, 房子之前 <u>fang tzu chih ch'ien</u> 'the front of the house'.

In the light of the preceding sequence, it is worth noting that one of the nouns, more often than not the first noun, may substitute for material which is a construction. Such a construction may be (1) a nominal construction, (2) a verb-object construction, (3) a verbal construction, or (4) a complete sentence. Examples are the following: 新房子之前 <u>hsin fang tzu chih ch'ien</u> 'the front of a new house'; 開車之前 <u>k'ai ch'eh chih ch'ien</u> 'before driving'; 走出去之前 <u>tsou ch'u ch'ü chih ch'ien</u> 'before going out'; 我去買菜之前 <u>wo ch'ü mai ts'ai chih ch'ien</u> 'before I go marketing'.

Should the second noun in the sequence mentioned substitute for material which is a construction, such a construction must be nominal, e.g. 房子之大門 <u>fang tzu chih ta men</u> 'the front door of the house'.

It is also possible that both nouns in the said sequence substitute for other material. Such material always follows the restrictions mentioned previously. For example, 新房子之大門 <u>hsin fang tzu chih ta men</u> 'the front door of the new house' has the following sequential order: nominal construction + particle + nominal construction.

2.255 A noun may follow 的 <u>te</u> (a particle)[19] which in turn follows other material. Such material may or may not be a construction. When a noun follows <u>te</u> which in turn follows other material, the material (whatever it is) together with <u>te</u> becomes the attribute to the noun which is head. The attribute is also a construction in that <u>te</u> is subordinate to whatever precedes it.

The noun which is the head of the preceding endocentric construction may be omitted from it; for example, 我的書 <u>wo te shu</u> 'my book' versus 我的 <u>wo te</u> 'mine'.

The omission serves the following purpose: The absence of the head in what would otherwise be an attribute-head construction automatically nominalizes the attribute. The function of this absent noun as the head of the construction is understood from the context. The identity of this absent noun can be inferred from the environments in which the nominalized attribute is used.

The noun following <u>te</u> in the previously discussed attribute-head construction may be replaced by a construction. Such a construction must be nominal. For example 我的書 <u>wo te shu</u> 'my book' may become 我的新房子 <u>wo te hsin fang tzu</u> 'my new house'.

On the other hand, the material preceding <u>te</u>, if it is a construction, may be (1) a nominal construction, (2) a verb-object
construction, (3) a verbal construction, or (4) a complete sentence;
if it is not a construction, it may be (1) a noun, (2) a stative verb,
or (3) a verb. Examples of constructions are the following: 老 先
生 的 書   <u>lao hsien sheng te shu</u> 'the old teacher's book'; 有 價 值
的 書 <u>yu chia chih te shu</u> 'books of great value';   買 回 來 的 書
<u>mai huei lai te shu</u> 'the book which has been brought back';   我 送
給 她 的 書   <u>wo sung kei t'a te shu</u> 'the book I sent her'.   Examples
that are not constructions are the following: 爸 爸 的 書 <u>pa pa te shu</u>
'father's book'; 新 的 書 <u>hsin te shu</u> 'new books'; 買 的 書 <u>mai te shu</u>
'the book which is bought'.

2.256 A noun may follow a certain demonstrative. The demonstrative and the noun form a construction in which the former always
modifies the latter, thus constituting an attribute-head construction;
for example, 唯 物 <u>wei wu</u> 'materialistic'. There are altogether 17
such demonstratives (see 2. 315).

Nouns may vary greatly in terms of the number of characters
comprised, ranging from one to three or four, or possibly five,
characters. The large number of characters for a given noun is
historically due to (1) borrowings, e. g. 斯 蒂 克 <u>ssu t'i k'e</u> 'stick'[20]
and 玻 璃 <u>puo li</u> 'glass',[21] and (2) loan translation, e. g. 機 關 鎗
<u>chi kuan ch'iang</u> 'machine guns'. Native nouns normally consist of
one, most often two, and relatively rarely three, characters.

2. 30 <u>Distributional relationships</u>. In the preceding, we have
stated the principal characteristics of the items pertinent to the
structures of SC-BSP, by giving distributional definitions (or ap-
proximations of these) in terms of the other items that are permitted to precede or follow the defined items. We now propose to
discuss the distribution of these items further, by presenting their
cooccurrence possibilities in terms of pairs, triples, quadruples,
and quintuples.

2. 310 <u>Cooccurrence in pairs</u>. By pairs are meant two items
considered jointly. The manner and extent in which the members
of the items concerned may cooccur is examined. There are five
items (cf. 2. 2), but only seven pairs can be discussed: (1) numerals
and measures; (2) demonstratives and measures; (3) demonstratives
and numerals; (4) numerals and nouns; (5) demonstratives and
nouns; (6) measures and nouns; and (7) measures and measures.

Each pair, except the last, is a set of endocentric constructions;
the last pair is a set of exocentric constructions.

2.311 <u>Numerals and measures</u>. In considering the pairing of numerals and measures, beside noting that the latter usually follow the former, it must be kept in mind that not every measure can follow every numeral. Two special cases may be noted in this connection.

First, there are four measures, viz. 些 <u>hsieh</u>, 臭兒 <u>tia(r)</u>, 會兒 <u>hue(r)</u>, 切 <u>ch'ieh</u>, which have unusual distribution: they can, in meaningful contexts, be preceded by only one particular numeral, namely, 一 <u>i</u> 'one'. The first three measures may drop <u>i</u> from their respective endocentric construction, provided the pairs are preceded by certain demonstratives (see 2.321), without change in denotative meanings, though some connotative differences are introduced. The other measure must keep <u>i</u> in every occurrence, otherwise the sequences in which the measure is used become ungrammatical.

Second, there are three measures, viz. 兒 <u>erh</u>, 裡 <u>li</u>, and 麽 <u>ma</u>, which under no circumstances follow any numeral; they may, however, follow a few demonstratives (see 2.312).

2.312 Demonstratives and measures. There are three measures, viz. 切 <u>ch'ieh</u>, 會兒 <u>hue(r)</u>, and 絲 <u>ssu</u>, which do not follow any demonstratives. Moreover, 兒 <u>erh</u>, 裡 <u>li</u>, and 麽 <u>ma</u>, which were stated previously to follow no numeral, may follow only a few demonstratives; the first two can follow 這 <u>chei</u>, 那 <u>nei</u>, and 哪 <u>nei</u>, while the third one can follow 甚 <u>shen</u>, 怎 <u>tsen</u>, 這 <u>chei</u>, and 那 <u>nei</u>. Note that 兒 <u>erh</u> and 裡 <u>li</u> are quite freely interchangeable, when occurring in these environments.

In addition to these restricted cooccurrences, it is worth noting that the combinations of the 39 demonstratives with the several hundred measures are not evenly distributed. While there are demonstratives, e.g. 少 <u>shao</u> and 別 <u>pieh</u>, which occur with only a few measures, there are also demonstratives, such as 這 <u>chei</u> and 那 <u>nei</u>, which are extremely versatile.

Finally, there are a few demonstratives which precede no measures, no matter under what conditions they occur. They are 第 <u>ti</u>, 另 <u>ling</u>, 唯 <u>wei</u>, and 惟 <u>wei</u>.

2.313 <u>Demonstratives and numerals</u>. First, we should note that, of the 39 demonstratives, 18 never precede numerals under any conditions, and that of those which do, 10 are allowed to combine with only a restricted number of numerals (with one exception), when measures are not used. These two distributionally restricted subclasses of demonstratives are listed in Table 9.3 under I and II, respectively.

Table 9.3 <u>Distributionally Restricted Demonstratives</u>

I		II	
甚	<u>shen</u>	初	<u>ch'u</u>
怎	<u>tsen</u>	老	<u>lao</u>
各	<u>ke</u>	双	<u>shuang</u>
該	<u>kai</u>	半	<u>pan</u>
別	<u>pieh</u>	礼拜	<u>li pai</u>
單	<u>tan</u>	星期	<u>hsing ch'i</u>
次	<u>tz'u</u>	其	<u>ch'i</u>
本	<u>pen</u>	唯	<u>wei</u> (= 惟 <u>wei</u>)
少	<u>shao</u>	第	<u>ti</u>
中	<u>chung</u>		
整	<u>cheng</u>		
諸	<u>chu</u>		
今	<u>chin</u>		
明	<u>ming</u>		
昨	<u>tsuo</u>		
此	<u>ch'ih</u>		
去	<u>ch'ü</u>		
翌	<u>i</u>		

Second, the limitations on the cooccurrences of the 10 demonstratives and numerals must be stated. In this connection, we note that except for 第 ti, which can cooccur with virtually every numeral expressing an independent number, the other nine demonstratives rarely cooccur with numerals higher than 10. Nevertheless, there is one demonstrative, namely 半 pan 'half', which can cooccur with a numeral higher than 10. But the cooccurrence, 半百 pan pai '(about) half of a hundred', is the only instance.

The particular combination of pan and pai constitutes a unique idiom. Thus, no other numerals may combine with pan. Although it is logically conceivable to combine pan with such numeric characters as 千 ch'ien 'thousand' and 万 wan 'ten thousand', the resulting sequences, * 半千 *pan ch'ien and * 半万 *pan wan, are culturally inappropriate and hence ungrammatical.

Further, it should be noted that 双 shuang can only cooccur with 十 shih 'ten';[22] 唯 wei and 惟 wei seldom cooccur with numerals higher than two; 其 ch'i, 初 ch'u, and 老 lao hardly ever cooccur with numerals higher than 10; and 礼拜 li pai and 星期 hsing ch'i never cooccur with numerals higher than 6.

2.314 <u>Numerals and nouns</u>. Numerals form pairs with nouns, without intervening measure, to constitute idioms of varying frequency of occurrence. Most such idioms contain numerals lower than 10.

The numerals 一 i 'one', 二 erh 'two', and 三 san 'three', are used relatively frequently in sequence with certain nouns with which they form idioms; for example: 一心 i hsin 'one heart — loyal'; 二心 erh hsin 'two hearts[23] — double-minded'; and 三心 san hsin 'three hearts — changeable'.

The numerals, 四 ssu 'four', 五 wu 'five', 六 liu 'six', 七 ch'i 'seven', 八 pa 'eight', and 九 chiu 'nine', are used only occasionally in sequence with certain nouns with which they form idioms; for example: 四寶 ssu pao 'the four treasures — brush-pen, paper, ink, and ink-slab'; 五臟 wu tsang 'the five viscera — the heart, the lungs, the liver, the kidneys, and the stomach'; 六義 liu i 'the six components (of Chinese characters)'; 七竅 ch'i ch'iao 'the seven apertures in the human head — eyes, ears, nose, and mouth'; 八仙 pa hsien 'the eight immortals of Taoism'; and 九泉 chiu ch'üan 'the nine springs — the grave, Hades'.

The numeral 十 shih 'ten' is used even less frequently in sequence with nouns to form idioms. However, there are a few instances; for example: 十誡 shih chieh 'The Decalogue'; and 十成 shih ch'eng 'one hundred per cent — complete'.

The numerals 十 一 <u>shih i</u> 'eleven' and 十 二 <u>shih erh</u> 'twelve' form idioms with even fewer nouns. Examples are 十 一 月 <u>shih i yüeh</u> 'November' and 十 二 月 <u>shih erh yüeh</u> 'December'.

In addition to these numerals, the numerals 百 <u>pai</u> 'hundred', 千 <u>ch'ien</u> 'thousand', and 万 <u>wan</u> 'ten thousand' may occasionally form idioms with a few nouns; for example: 百 姓 <u>pai hsing</u> 'a hundred surnames — the people (population) '; 千 金 <u>ch'ien chin</u> 'a thousand gold — (your) precious daughter'; and 万 物 <u>wan wu</u> 'all things — all creation'.

The previously described list of idioms consisting of numerals followed by nouns is by no means closed. It is quite reasonable to assume that new idioms may be created on this same pattern.

It is important to note that all instances of the pair numeral + noun (without intervening measure) have been found to be idioms. The meanings of these idioms are more often than not metaphorical, and the actual numeric values of the numerals involved are to some extent lost.

2.315 <u>Demonstratives and noun</u>. There are 17 demonstratives which can form pairs with a few nouns, and most pairs constitute idioms, as shown in Table 9.4.

Some of these pairs are less frequently encountered, in spoken as well as written SC, than the others. For example, while <u>the feudal princes</u>, <u>old master</u>, and <u>young master</u> are rarely used nowadays, the others are commonplace in SC.

In addition, it should be pointed out that these cooccurrences in pairs do not behave alike. Of the 17 cooccurrences five, viz. <u>the feudal princes</u>, <u>old master</u>, <u>young master</u>, <u>high school</u>, and <u>God</u>, share some characteristics of nouns; that is they function like nouns and can be preceded by certain measures, though their distributional patterns vary: for example, 兩 位 諸 侯 <u>liang wei chu hou</u> 'two feudal princes', and 這 位 老 爺 <u>chei wei lao yeh</u> 'this old master'. But note that in the former instance, if hou is replaced by 君 <u>chün</u> 'gentleman', the construction 諸 君 <u>chu chün</u>, as a pair, can no longer function as a noun; consequently, * 兩 位 諸 君 *<u>liang wei chu chün</u>, or any similar utterance, is ungrammatical, and that in the latter instance, if yeh is replaced by 家 <u>chia</u> 'home', the construction 老 家 <u>lao chia</u> 'home town', as a pair, even though it still functions as a noun, can no longer be preceded by a measure but by 的 <u>te</u>, as in 你 的 老 家 <u>ni te lao chia</u> 'your home town'.

Table 9.4 Demonstrative-noun idioms

Demonstratives	Nouns	Pairs
諸 chu 'individual'	侯 hou 'duke'	諸侯 chu hou[24] 'the feudal princes'
其 ch'i 'specific'	時 shih 'time'	其時 ch'i shih 'at that time'
唯 wei 'only'	物 wu 'thing'	唯物 wei wu 'materialistic'
本 pen 'self'	書 shu 'book'	本書 pen shu 'this book'
該 kai 'that'	書 shu 'book'	該書 kai shu 'that book'
老 lao 'respectable'	爺 yeh 'master'	老爺 lao yeh[24] 'old master'
少 shao 'juvenile'	爺 yeh 'master'	少爺 shao yeh[24] 'young master'
單 tan 'single'	刀 tao 'knife'	單刀 tan tao 'single-handed'
中 chung 'middle'	學 hsüeh 'learning'	中學 chung hsüeh 'high school'
前 ch'ien 'before'	夫 fu 'husband'	前夫 ch'ien fu 'the former husband'
後 hou 'after'	妻 ch'i 'wife'	後妻 hou ch'i 'a second wife'
上 shang 'above'	帝 ti 'emperor'	上帝 shang ti 'God'
下 hsia 'below'	文 wen 'text'	下文 hsia wen 'the text below'
次 ts'u 'next'	子 tzu 'son'	次子 ts'u tzu 'the second son'
這 chei 'this'	人 jen 'man'	這人 chei jen 'this man'[25]
每 mei 'every'	人 jen 'man'	每人 mei jen 'every man'[25]
那 nei 'that'	人 jen 'man'	那人 nei jen 'that man'[25]

2.316 <u>Measures and nouns</u>. Some extremely versatile measures may combine with nouns alone without the presence of numerals. Although there are only a few such measures, they can
combine with many nouns, again resulting in idioms. Examples
are given in Table 9.5.

Some of these pairs may function as nouns, e.g. <u>treaties</u>, as
in 三 個 條 約   san ke t'iao yüeh 'three treaties', but   the
others, though only a few, never function as nouns, e.g. <u>individual</u>.

2.317 <u>Measures and measures</u>. The versatile measures mentioned previously may be reduplicated; that is, two exactly identical
measures cooccur, forming an idiom: for example, 個 個   ko ko
'everyone', 件 件   chien chien 'everything'. However, it should
be noted that such reduplicated pairs occur only in casual speech
(and writing).

These reduplicated pairs seem to be the casual equivalents of
more formal pairs, consisting of <u>mei</u> 'every', or <u>ke</u> 'each', plus
the measure found in reduplication. Thus, 個 個   ke ke is the
casual equivalent of 每 個   mei ke, or 各 個   ko ko   the latter
has wider application and fewer syntactic restrictions.

2.320 <u>Cooccurrence in triples</u>. Since cooccurrence possibilities
of the five word-classes in triples differ significantly from those in
pairs, we will now examine the manner and extent in which the members of the items concerned may cooccur in sequences of three.
There are seven triples: (1) numerals, measures, and nouns;
(2) demonstratives, measures, and nouns; (3) numerals, approximals, and measures; (4) numerals, nouns, and nouns; (5) demonstratives, nouns, and nouns; (6) demonstratives, numerals, and
nouns; and (7) demonstratives, numerals, and measures.

These triples are sets of endocentric constructions, but their
structures are not identical. If we let I represent the first item,
II the second item, and III the third item, the structures of these
triples can be analyzed as follows: (1), (2), (3), (4), (5), and
(6) may be analyzed as ((I II) III), while (7) may be analyzed as
(I (II III)).

Triple (3) can be analyzed in an alternative way: (I...III) and
II are the immediate constituents where the constituent II modifies
the discontinuous constituent (I ... III). The discontinuous constituent in turn forms a construction which also occurs as a continuous one, with I modifying III (cf. the constituent (I II) of triple
(1)).

The constituent (I II) of triples (1), (2), (4), (5), and (6) constitutes an endocentric construction of the attribute-head type. The

Table 9.5 Measure-noun idioms

Measures	Nouns	Pairs
個 ko	人 jen 'man'	個人 ko jen 'individual'
	性 hsing 'nature'	個性 ko hsing 'personality'
團 t'uan	体 t'i 'body'	團体 t'uan t'i 'group'
課 k'o	文 wen 'literature'	課文 k'e wen 'lessons'
	程 ch'eng 'journey'	課程 k'o ch'eng 'curriculum'
條 t'iao	裡 li 'reason'	條理 t'iao li 'method'
	約 yüeh 'promise'	條約 t'iao yüeh 'treaties'

constituent (I II) of triple (3), following the first and not the alternative analysis, on the other hand, constitutes an endocentric construction of the head-attribute type.

In triple (7), the ICs are I and (II III), where the former modifies the latter. The ICs of the second constituent are in turn II and
III, II modifying III.

2.321 <u>Numerals, measures, and nouns</u>. Since the first two
items of each of these triples are the same as the previously described pairs of numerals and measures (cf. 2.311), the cooccurrence possibilities of these triples are extremely high. Two
important points may be raised in this connection.

First, if <u>i</u> 'one' is used in a triple, and if such a triple is
preceded by a verb, the numeral can be optionally omitted. As
a result, the second and the third items of the triple form a
quasipair in which, though such a pair normally does not occur by
itself as an endocentric construction, the first item, namely the
measure, behaves like an attribute directly modifying the second
item, namely the noun, which is head (cf. 2.22).

Second, if we require detailed distributional patterns of these
triples, a detailed description regarding the cooccurrence possibilities of measures and nouns is most important. Such a description
is at present beyond our capability; one means for achieving this
goal would be to ascertain the semantic characteristics of both
measures and nouns. (An approach such as testing the semantic
features of nouns, e.g. concrete versus abstract, or the shapes
of referents, would probably result in a fruitful classification.)

Our knowledge of the relationship between measures and nouns
in these triples may be summarized as follows: a given noun is
always modified only by one measure; a given measure, on the
other hand, may often be used to modify more than one noun. It
thus follows that there are measures which are rather versatile,
in terms of the number and varieties of nouns which each can
modify, e.g. 個 <u>ko</u>, and there are other measures each one of
which is limited to modifying only a few nouns, e.g. 絲 <u>ssu</u>.

2.322 <u>Demonstratives, measures, and nouns</u>. In these triples,
the distributional relationships between demonstratives and measures often determine those between measures and nouns. That is
to say, certain pairs of measures and nouns are preceded only by
certain demonstratives to form triples. There are three restrictions involved for these triples.

First, from the 39 demonstratives must be excluded four
which cannot precede any measure (cf. 2. 312), and thirteen, viz.
其 ch'i, 別 pie, 此 tz'u, 翌 i, 礼拜 li pai, 星期 hsing ch'i,
今 chin, 昨 tsuo, 去 ch'u, 前 ch'ien, 後 hou, 明 ming, and
末 mo, the presence of which prohibits the measures which they
precede from cooccurring with nouns.

Second, there are three measures (cf. 2. 312) which do not
follow any demonstratives, even though their cooccurrence with
a few nouns is otherwise acceptable.

Third and most important of all, there are a few measures
which may cooccur with certain nouns in triples if and only if such
measures are preceded by certain demonstratives. For example,
the measure 麼 ma may cooccur with such nouns as 事 shih
'business' and 樣 yang 'manner' if and only if ma is preceded by
the demonstrative 甚 shen, for the first noun, and by the demonstrative 怎 tsen, for the second noun, as in 甚麼事 shen ma
shih 'what's the matter?' and the idiom 怎麼樣 tsen ma yang
'how is the situation?'

A similar example is that of the measure 個 ko, which normally
does not cooccur with the noun 河 ho 'river', if the measure is
preceded by a numeral, for example, 一 i 'one', but can and does
cooccur with 河 ho, if and only if the measure is preceded by the
demonstrative 這 chei 'this' or 那 nei 'that', as in 這個河
chei ko ho 'this river' and 那個河 nei ko ho 'that river'.[26]

2. 323 Numerals, approximals, and measures. Since approximals always cooccur with both numerals and measures simultaneously, their relationships are discussed together. From these
relationships are first excluded those measures which cannot follow
numerals and those which can only follow 一 i 'one' (cf. 2. 311),
for approximals by definition (cf. 2. 24) follow numerals, the values
of which are larger than, or at least equal to, 10. Moreover, these
combinations may include only those numerals which end in a
numeric character of type 3 and 4 as stated earlier (cf. 2. 21).

Within these limits, the three approximals are further differ-
entiated into two subclasses: (1) 多 tuo, and (2) 來 and 餘 lai
and yü; the former occurs with every numeral that qualifies, the
latter two only with those which end in 十 shih.

2. 324 Numerals, nouns, and nouns. These triples are, generally speaking, formed by adding a third item, an additional noun,
to a pair of numeral and noun (cf. 2. 314), and in some cases, constitute idioms. The cooccurrence possibilities of the pairs of

numerals and nouns, forming the first and second items, are quite
restricted within these triples; fewer triples than pairs are found,
including numerals not higher than 10. For example, 七竅
ch'i ch'iao 'the seven apertures' is a pair, but the same pair does
not occur as part of a triple. On the other hand, 十字 shih tzu
'a cross-shaped character' not only constitutes a pair but also
occurs very commonly as part of such triples as 十字架 shih
tzu chia 'The Cross'.

Normally, the second item in these triples is a noun consisting
of a single character. However, three nouns, namely, 屋子
wu tzu 'house', 桌子 cho tzu 'table', and 車子 ch'e tzu
'vehicle', each consisting of two characters, may also constitute
the second item, as in 一屋子人 [27] i wu tzu jen 'a houseful
of people', 一桌子菜 [27] cho tzu ts'ai 'a tableful of dishes',
and 一車子人 [27] i ch'e tzu jen 'a carful of people', respectively. Notice that the first item in each instance is always
the numeral 'one'.

It should also be mentioned that the third item in these triples
is restricted to only a few nouns, e.g. 論 lun 'theory', 架 chia
'frame', and 說 shuo 'viewpoint'. Furthermore, we must note
that not every noun in the third item can cooccur with every noun
in the second item. For example, the idiom 一神論 i shen
lun 'monotheism' is grammatical but * 一神架 *i shen chia
is not; likewise, the idiom 十字架 shih tzu chia 'The Cross'
is grammatical but * 十字論 * shih tzu lun is not.

In addition to these, we find that the numerals 百 pai 'hundred',
千 ch'ien 'thousand', and 万 wan 'ten thousand', though permis-
sible in a few triples (as in the idioms 百家姓 pai chia hsing
'the Book of Family Names', 千字文 ch'ien tzu wen 'The One-
Thousand-Character Book', and 万靈丹 wan ling tan 'all-
powerful pills') are less frequently used in triples than in pairs
(cf. 2.314), and their cooccurrences with nouns in triples sound
rather old fashioned.

2.325 Demonstratives, nouns, and nouns. These triples, like
those discussed previously, are formed by adding a third item,
nouns, to the pairs of demonstratives and nouns (cf. 2.315). However, the cooccurrence possibilities of demonstratives and nouns,
in the pairs formed by the first and second items, are thereby
drastically reduced. Of the 17 demonstratives which have been
stated to cooccur with nouns in pairs (cf. 2.315), only four, viz.
唯 wei, 單 tan, 老 lao, and 中 chung, can cooccur with nouns

in triples. Examples are the idioms 唯 物 論   <u>wei wu lun</u>
'materialism', 單 身 漢   <u>tan shen han</u> 'unmarried man',
老 爺 車 <u>lao ye ch'e</u> 'old cars', and   中 學 生   <u>chung hsüeh sheng</u>
'high school students'.

The second and third items of these triples are also restricted
to a few nouns; the restriction is due to the cooccurrence possibilities
between the nouns constituting the second item and those constituting
the third item. It thus follows that if the noun forming the second
item is replaced, that forming the third item may also have to be
replaced in order to form a new triple. For example, <u>wei wu lun</u>
may become 唯 神 論   <u>wei hsin lun</u> 'idealism' by replacing the
noun which forms the second item, but <u>tan shen han</u> must become
單 行 道   <u>tan hsing tao</u> 'one-way road', by replacing the nouns
forming both the second and the third items.

In general, it is correct to state that the cooccurrence possibilities between nouns and nouns in triples of demonstratives, noun,
and nouns — or in triples of numerals, nouns, and nouns (cf. 2. 324)
— are much more restricted than those between measures and
nouns in triples of demonstratives, measures, and nouns (cf. 2. 322)
or in those of numerals, measures, and nouns (cf. 2. 321).

2. 326 <u>Demonstratives, numerals, and nouns.</u> When numerals
and nouns cooccur in pairs, it has been stated that numerals higher
than 10 are seldom used, except 十 一   <u>shih i,</u> 十 二   <u>shih erh,</u>
百   <u>pai,</u> 千 <u>ch'ien,</u> and 万 <u>wan</u> (cf. 2. 314). If demonstratives
are added to such pairs in order to form acceptable triples, it is
found that numerals higher than two are seldom used, except 十
<u>shih</u> 'ten'. In addition, we find that of the 39 demonstratives only
two, and possibly three, are acceptable in the triples, namely,
<u>wei</u> which may interchange with 惟 <u>wei,</u> as in 唯 一 論   <u>wei i</u>
<u>lun</u> 'Monism', and 双 <u>shuang</u> 'double', as in 双 十 節   <u>shuang shih</u>
<u>chieh</u> 'the Double Ten Festival'.

Regarding the third item in these cooccurrences, it is worthy
of mention that only one other noun, namely, 說 <u>shuo</u> 'viewpoint',
is acceptable in cooccurrence with <u>wei,</u> as in   唯 一 說   <u>wei i</u>
<u>shuo</u> 'monistic viewpoint', and that <u>chieh</u> is the only noun which
can cooccur with <u>shuang</u> as shown in the preceding triple. Note
that these triples constitute idioms.

2. 327 <u>Demonstratives, numerals, and measures.</u> Two distributional patterns deserve mention here. First, only one of the 10
demonstratives (listed under II in 2. 313), namely, 第 <u>ti</u> ' 一 th',

occurs in triples. This demonstrative combines freely with
numerals and measures; virtually every numeral and every measure can cooccur with the demonstrative, except seven measures
(cf. 2.311).

Second, 11 demonstratives, which do not combine with numerals
when no measures are present (cf. 2.313), may combine with
numerals when measures are present. These demonstratives are:
另 ling, 這 che, 那 na, 每 mei, 頭 t'ou, 末 mo, 哪 na, 前
ch'ien, 後 hou, 上 shang, and 下 hsia. The first seven of these
are extremely versatile. The last four are more restricted in
terms of the varieties and number of numerals and measures with
which they can combine.

2.33 Cooccurrence in quadruples. We now consider the extent
to which items cooccur in sequences of four. There are only three
quadruples: (1) numerals, approximals, measures, and nouns;
(2) demonstratives, numerals, measures, and nouns; and (3) demonstratives, numerals, approximals, and measures. These
quadruples likewise form sets of endocentric constructions.

If we let I represent the first item, II the second item, III the
third item, and IV the fourth item, these quadruples may be analyzed as follows: (1) becomes (((I II) III) IV); (2) becomes ((I (II III))
IV); and (3) becomes (I ((II III) IV)).

Note that (1) and (3) may also be analyzed differently. The
alternative solution follows exactly the way in which numerals,
approximals, and measures are analyzed as triples (cf. 2.32).
That is to say, the constituent (I II III) of (1) and the constituent
(II III IV) of (3) may be analyzed as having discontinuous ICs (see
2.32 for details).

The first solution, however, entails assigning the endocentricity
of the head-attribute type to the constituent (I II) of (1) as well as
to the constituent (II III) of (3), while keeping that of the attribute-
head type for the constituent (II III) of (2), for the other constituents
when possible, and finally for each set of quadruple constructions.

2.331 Numerals, approximals, measures, and nouns. These
quadruples are formed by adding a fourth item, nouns, to the triples
of numerals, approximals, and measures (cf. 2.323). As a result,
beside noting that all the distributional relationships in those triples
also hold for these quadruples, it should be noted that the relationships between measures and nouns in quadruples also hold for those
between measures and nouns in triples (cf. 2.321). One point in

this connection deserves some attention, namely the fact that, because of the presence of approximals in the quadruples, the cooccurrence possibilities of measures and nouns are considerably
reduced. First, those measures which only follow 一 i 'one' (cf.
2. 311) must be excluded (cf. 2. 323). Second, those measures
which hardly ever follow 十 shih 'ten', or any numeral higher than
that must also be excluded. Two such measures are 絲 ssu and
縷 lü. (When excluding these measures, we automatically preclude
a few nouns from following them in any quadruple.)

2. 332 Demonstratives, numerals, measures, and nouns. These
quadruples are formed by placing a fourth item, nouns, after the
triples of demonstratives, numerals, and measures (cf. 2. 327).
The cooccurrences in these quadruples are highly productive —
perhaps more productive than most cooccurrences in SC. In addition to the relatively high cooccurrence possibilities of demonstratives, numerals, and measures in triples, a measure, if it can
be used in such triples, may normally cooccur with more than one
noun (cf. 2. 321) to form many acceptable quadruples.

However, there are certain limitations. First, note that 双
shuang, which has been used in a triple (cf. 2. 327), no longer occurs
in quadruples. Second, note that 前 ch'ien, and 後 hou (cf. 2. 327)
with which it has been said that only a restricted number of numerals
and measures can combine, have also a very limited number of
nouns with which to combine in quadruples. Examples are the following: 前 五 位 數   ch'ien wu wei shu 'the five digital numbers
in the front', and 後 五 位 數   hou wu wei shu 'the five digital
numbers in the back'. But note that 上 shang and 下 hsia, which
have some cooccurrence possibilities with numerals and measures
in triples (cf. 2. 327), should be excluded from any cooccurrence in
quadruples.

2. 333 Demonstratives, numerals, approximals, and measures.
Unlike the other quadruples, these are formed by adding a first item,
demonstratives, to the triples of numerals, approximals, and measures (cf. 2. 323). However, note that all the distributional relationships in those triples also hold in these quadruples, as they do in
the quadruples of numerals, approximals, measures, and nouns
(cf. 2. 331).

When demonstratives cooccur with numerals, approximals,
and measures in quadruples, however, only three of the 39 demonstratives can be used. They are 這 chei, 每 mei, and 那

nei; for example: 這 十 來 張   <u>chei shih lai chang</u> 'these ten
or so sheets (of paper) ';   每 一 百 多 個   <u>mei i pai tuo ko</u>
'every one hundred or so (people) '; and   那 一 千 零 十 餘 位
<u>nei i ch'ien ling shih yü wei</u> 'those one thousand and ten or so (stu-
dents) '.

Although it is possible to use 那 <u>nei</u> in a quadruple (cf. 2. 332),
there are two limitations which prevent <u>nei</u> from being used in
these quadruples.

First, <u>nei</u> is normally used with a numeral which refers to a
specific number, higher or lower than 10. Since approximals are
present in these quadruples (this means that the numerals used
with them do not and cannot specify the values of the numbers referred to), it must follow that <u>nei</u> cannot cooccur with numerals in
these quadruples. (However, if one wishes to be very specific and
particular, instead of using <u>chi</u>, he could use <u>nei</u> with a numeral
followed by an approximal in questions such as <u>nei shih lai chang a</u>?
'which ten or so sheets? ', when <u>chei shih lai chang</u> 'these ten or
so sheets' as a statement is not heard clearly.)

Second, if <u>nei</u> is to cooccur with a numeral which need not
specify the precise value of a number higher or lower than 10, it
usually cooccurs with 幾 <u>chi</u>. In this case, the numeral is custom-
arily immediately followed by a measure which in turn may or may
not be followed by a noun. Thus, it must also follow that <u>nei</u> cannot occur in quadruples containing approximals.

2. 340 <u>Cooccurrence in quintuples</u>. Finally we consider the
extent to which items cooccur in sequences of five. Since there
are altogether five items under study, it follows that we have only
one set of quintuples. The items making up the quintuples occur
in the following order: demonstratives, numerals, approximals,
measures, and nouns. The quintuples are endocentric constructions.

If we let I represent the first item, II the second item, III the
third item, IV the fourth item, and V the fifth item, two structures
may be given to each quintuple as follows: (1) ((I((II III) IV)) V);
(2) (I (((II III) IV) V)).

Since these quintuples also contain the triples of numerals,
approximals, and measures (cf. 2. 32), it then follows that each
structure has an alternative analysis: the constituent (II III IV) in
each structure may be analyzed as having discontinuous ICs (see
2. 32 for the detail).

The first solution for each structure entails endocentricity of
the head-attribute type for the constituent (II III).

2.341 <u>Demonstratives, numerals, approximals, measures, and nouns</u>. These quintuples are formed by adding either (1) a fifth item, nouns, to the quadruples of demonstratives, numerals, approximals, and measures (cf. 2.333), or (2) a first item demonstratives, to the quadruples of numerals, approximals, measures, and nouns (cf. 2.331).

In the first case, all of the distributional relationships in the quintuples follow (1) those in the quadruples mentioned, and (2) those between measures and nouns (cf. 2.321). In the second case, the cooccurrence possibilities of the five items concerned are in line with (1) those of the four items mentioned, and with (2) those between demonstratives and numerals mentioned in 2.333. Examples are the following: 這十來張紙 <u>chei shih lai chang chih</u> 'these ten or so sheets of paper'; 每一百多個人 <u>mei i pai tuo ko jen</u> 'every one hundred or so people'; and 那一千零十餘位同學 <u>nei i ch'ien ling shih yü wei t'ung hsüeh</u> 'those one thousand and ten or so (students)'.

2.4 PROCESSING III — FLOWCHARTING

This section of the paper discusses the essentials of the flowcharts that have been prepared to effect the recognition routine for the BSP of SC.

2.40 <u>Types of BSP</u>. In the light of the preceding analysis, we may now establish 21 types of BSP. These are listed under four headings, as shown in Table 9.6.

Each type, characterized by a string of grammar codes established earlier, represents a set of phrases. The number of phrases contained in each type varies, ranging from a few to denumerable infinity.[28]

2.50 <u>Abbreviation</u>. The following abbreviations are employed in this analysis.

E	Current element in code
E + 1	Element in code next to the right of E
E - 1	Element in code next to the left of E
GC	Grammar code(s)
period	Sentence boundary marker
S	Current sentence
S + 1	Sentence next to the right of S
S - 1	Sentence next to the left of S

Table 9.6 <u>Types of BSP</u>

N-Group	M-Group	U-Group	D-Group
N	MM	U	D
MN	UM	DU	
UN	DM		
DN	DUM		
UNN	UXM		
DNN	DUXM		
UMN			
DMN			
DUN			
DUMN			
UXMN			
DUXMN			

2.60 <u>Problem description</u>. To recognize BSP, we have flow-charted six routines: (1) initializing routine (Fig. 9.4), (2) finalizing routine (Fig. 9.5), (3) N-routine (Figs. 9.6, 9.7), (4) M-routine (Figs. 9.8, 9.9), (5) U-routine (Fig. 9.10), and (6) D-routine (Fig. 9.11).

2.61 <u>Initializing routine</u>. This routine accomplishes four tasks:

(1)   It inputs sequences of GC for recognition.
(2)   It recognizes the first E in a sequence of GC:
        (a) If it is #, =, or //, it takes E - 1 for further recognition.
        (b) If it is not, it gets the next sequence of GC for recognition.
(3)   It recognizes E - 1 as N, M, U, or D.
(4)   It stops the entire program.

2.62 <u>Finalizing routine</u>. This routine follows the initializing routine and accomplishes two tasks:

(1)   It recognizes E - 1 if it is not N, M, U, or D.
(2)   It returns to the initializing routine.

2.63 <u>N-routine</u>. The N-routine accomplishes three tasks which give varying results.

(1)   If there is no E to the left of N, it prints N and takes the <u>nx</u> exit.
(2)   If there is an E to the left of N, but it is not M, U, or D, it prints N and takes the <u>ny</u> exit.
(3)   If there is an E to the left of N and it is either M, U, or D, several legal combinations of elements may be permitted. These are listed under N-group. If any of these combinations are found, they are printed and then the <u>nx</u> exit is taken.

2.64 <u>M-routine</u>. The M-routine accomplishes only one task which gives varying results. When there is an E to the left of M and it is either M, U, D, or X, several legal combinations of elements may be permitted. These are listed under M-group. If any of these combinations are found, they are printed and then the <u>mx</u> exit is taken.

2.65 <u>U-routine</u>. The U-routine accomplishes three tasks which give varying results. First, if there is no E to the left of U, it prints U and takes the <u>ux</u> exit. Second, if there is an E to the left of U but it is not D, it prints U and takes the <u>uy</u> exit.

Third, if there is an E to the left of U and it is D, only one legal combination of elements may be permitted. It is listed under U-group. This combination is printed and then the ux exit is taken.

2.66 D-routine. The D-routine accomplishes one task which gives just one result. When there is no E to the left of D, it prints D and takes the dx exit.

2.67 Flowcharts. Note that, other than the initializing and the finalizing routines, there are only four routines to accomplish the task of recognizing all and only SC-BSP on the basis of their syntactic structures. Note also that the finalizing routine comprises 10 routines which have not been flowcharted in full. These routines, however, will be flowcharted in greater detail when more information about the total structure of SC becomes available.

In addition, it must be noted that the semantic structure of SC will also have to be explored. The present study shows that a description of the formal structure alone of SC is apparently insufficient. To overcome this insufficiency, more should be known about the semantic features of measures and nouns. This will most likely require a study of multiple meanings, which will concern not only lexical units but also phrases.

In summary, Garvin's view of the role of linguistics in machine translation can be quoted:

The emphasis on centers of grammatical information (fulcra) and on properly sequenced search patterns (the pass method) is a reasonable point of departure for developing a more advanced operational grammar for MT purposes. [29]

NOTES

1. Cf. Paul L. Garvin, 'Syntax in Machine Translation', Natural Language and the Computer 223-32 ed. Garvin (New York, 1963).

2. Fred C. C. Peng, A Grammatical Analysis of Standard Chinese (Buffalo, 1964).

3. The romanization hereafter follows the Wade-Giles system.

4. It must be borne in mind that intonations in SC are not as clearly audibly distinguishable as in English, because intonations in SC are more often than not obscured by tones. Moreover, the convention of punctuation marks has been established only rather recently.

5. This form, when used with 這 chei (or 那 nei) and measures, may interchange with 些 hsieh to mean only 'several', as
in chei hsieh wei 'these several (people)'. However, the latter is
less preferable in such an instance; its use often marks the user's
special written style and reflects his dialectal idiosyncracy.

6. This is a bound form, hence should not be regarded as expressing an independent number, even though it is glossed 'two'.

7. These are also bound forms and express numeric units;
thus they do not constitute independent numbers by themselves.

8. This refers as a title to a man's concubine, in the old days,
when addressed by her servants or anybody inferior to her. Such a
title, with which the people in modern Chinese society are still
familiar, is nowadays out of fashion; although it can frequently be
found in writing, especially in novels, it will perhaps eventually
cease to be used, as monogamy prevails over polygamy in Chinese
culture.

9. The morpheme represented by character 倆 is considered
the same as the one represented by character 兩 ; though the two
characters are written slightly differently, they are pronounced
homophonously, as indicated in their romanizations. (See Harvard
Journal of Asiatic Studies, 1. 33-38 (1936) for a note on lia, sa,
etc., by Y. R. Chao)

10. These characters are called measures, in terms of their
grammatical functions (cf. 2. 22). But this restriction is less
strict in writing than in speaking, and should necessitate an eventual
investigation concerning stylistic as well as semantic factors involved, for other measures such as 位 wei and 本 pen freely permit either liang or erh to precede them in their occurrences in
both writing and speaking.

11. It is extremely difficult to gloss an SC measure in English.
However an English example can be cited to illustrate the function
of an SC measure: a head of cattle. The word head used in this
context is comparable to an SC measure. Because of the difficulty
just shown, measures given in the examples cited in our study will
not be glossed.

12. See Peng, 'On the Concept of Affixes in Standard Chinese',
Archiv Orientální, 34. 1 (1966).

13.   These three forms often morphophonemically become <u>che</u>, <u>na</u>, and <u>na</u>, respectively, when used in contexts.

14.   As in eleven<u>th</u>.

15.   This sentence is ambiguous. It has two meanings: 'he has money (with him)' and 'he is rich'. The ambiguity can be clarified by adding another word, namely, 很 <u>hen</u>, between t'a and <u>yu</u>, becoming 他 很 有 錢   t'a hen yu ch'ien which only means 'he is (very) rich'. Orally, however, one can make the distinction, without inserting <u>hen</u>, by putting a slight pause before <u>yu</u> for the second meaning.

16.   If ch'ü is used with <u>yu</u> as a predication in a sentence, e.g. 他 有 趣   t'a yu ch'ü, such a sentence can only mean 'he is interesting'. In this case, native speakers often add 很 <u>hen</u> to the sentence, yielding 他 很 有 趣   t'a hen yu ch'ü 'he is (very) interesting'. The same is true of a disyllabic noun, e.g. 勇 氣 yung ch'i 'courage'.

17.   In this case, the noun after 的 <u>te</u> always consists of two or more characters. Note that while   有 機 的 化 合 物 <u>yu chi te hua he wu</u> 'organic compounds' is grammatical in conjunction with 有 機 化 合 物   <u>yu chi hua he wu</u>, the former being less formally and technically used than the latter, * 有 機 東 西   * <u>yu chi tung hsi</u> is ungrammatical.

18.   This is an attributive particle.

19.   This is also an attributive particle.

20.   From English.

21.   From Sanskrit.

22.   This cooccurrence 双 十   <u>shuang</u> <u>shih</u> 'double ten' is an expression culturally fixed; that is, no other numeral can replace <u>shih</u> in the same environment unless an innovation calls for such a replacement.

23.   兩   <u>liang</u> as an alternative is rarely used with nouns, but the author has encountered one instance frequently, namely 兩 意 <u>liang i</u> 'two minds' as in 三 心 兩 意   <u>san hsin liang i</u>, the figurative meaning of which is 'indecisive; uncertain'.

24.   However, 諸 君   <u>chu chün</u> '(you) Gentlemen', 老 家 <u>lao chia</u> 'home town', and 少 女   <u>shao nü</u> 'maidens' are modern expressions, and are frequently used.

25. These are collapsed forms of 這個人   chei ko jen 'this man', 那個人   mei ko jen 'every man', and 每個人   nei ko jen 'that man', respectively.

26. The author is indebted to Professor Y. R. Chao for this example (private communication).

27. These expressions may be regarded by some speakers as equivalent to 一屋子的人   i wu tzu te jen, 一桌子的菜 i cho te ts'ai, and 一車子的人   i ch'e tzu te jen, respectively. However, the author feels that whether or not the particle te is present makes a great difference in meaning, not to mention the syntactic differences. To him, i wu tzu jen means 'a houseful of people' while i wu tzu te jen should mean '*a house of people' which, unfortunately, is ungrammatical in English. Nevertheless, a comparable example in English is available: a cupful of tea versus a cup of tea. This English example illustrates the distinction made here between i wu tzu jen and i wu tzu te jen, between i cho tzu ts'ai and i cho tzu te ts'ai, or between i ch'e tzu jen and i ch'e tzu te jen. This distinction can further be evidenced syntactically: If we substitute another numeral for 一 i 'one' in the preceding series of expressions, we find that only those which contain the particle te remain grammatical; the others become ungrammatical. That is, 三屋子的人   san wu tzu te jen 'three houses full of people' is grammatical but * 三屋子人 * san wu tzu jen is ungrammatical, and so on. Note that in English one can say 'three cupfuls of tea' as well as 'three cups of tea'.

28. Cf. the use of this term in E. Bach, An Introduction to Transformational Grammars 151 (New York, Chicago, San Francisco, 1964). See also Peng's review of this book, Lingua 13 (1965).

29. Garvin, 'An Informal Survey of Modern Linguistics', to appear in American Documentation.

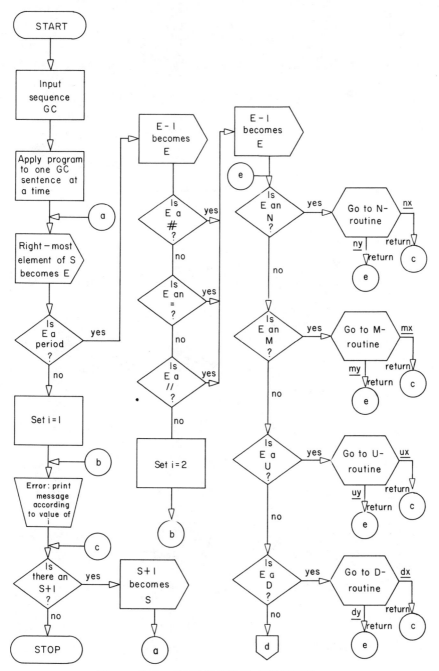

Figure 9.4 INITIALIZING ROUTINE

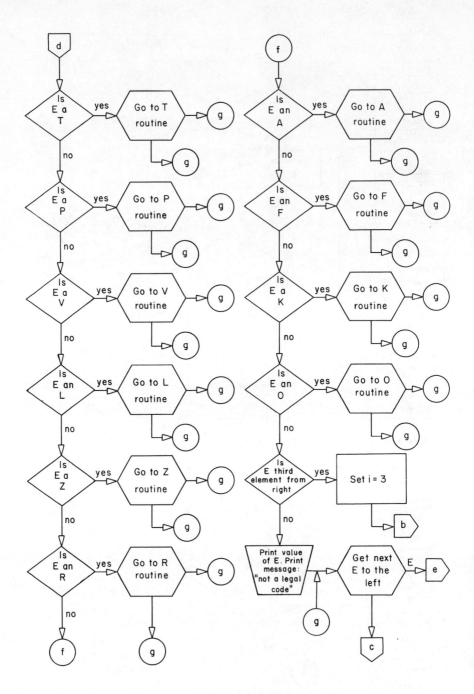

Figure 9.5 FINALIZING ROUTINE

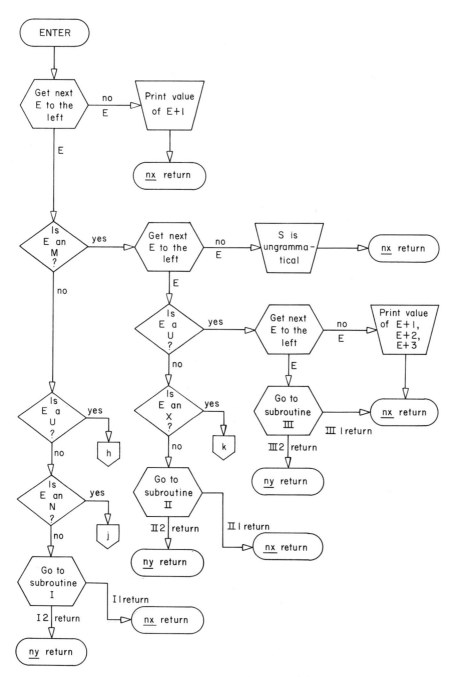

Figure 9.6   N-ROUTINE (I)

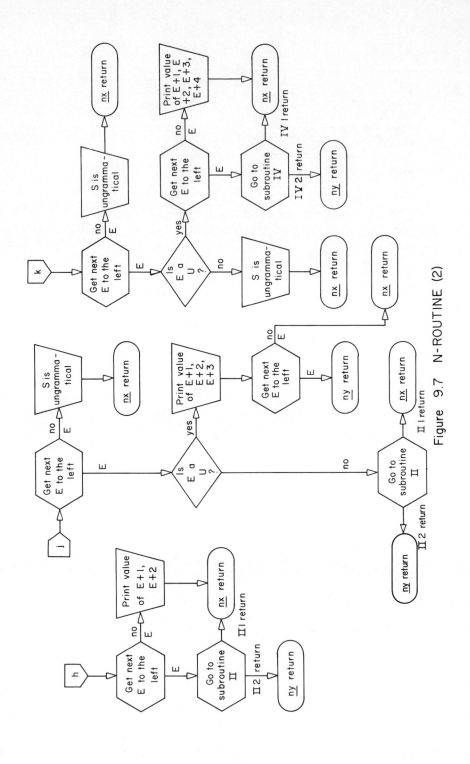

Figure 9.7 N-ROUTINE (2)

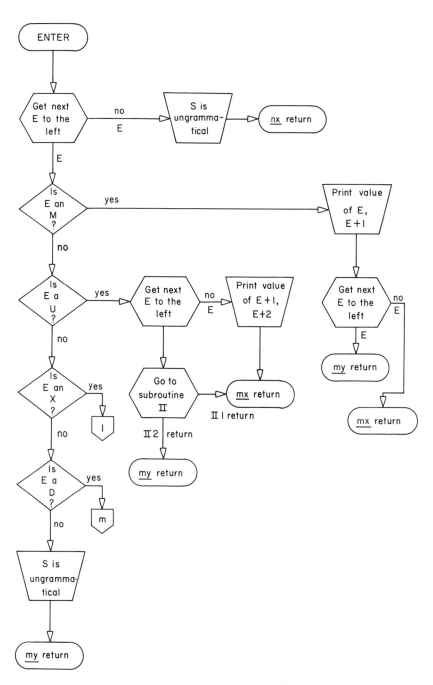

Figure 9.8 M-ROUTINE (1)

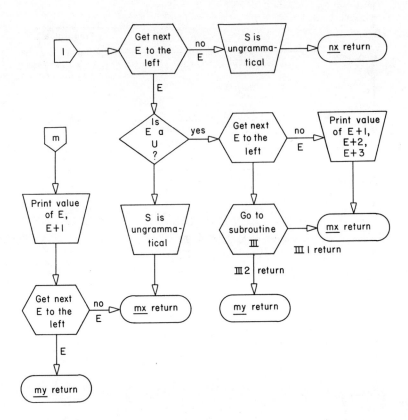

Figure 9.9 M-ROUTINE (2)

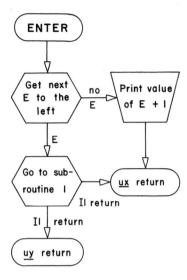

Figure 9.10   U-ROUTINE

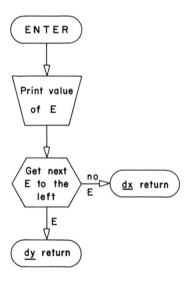

Figure 9.11   D-ROUTINE

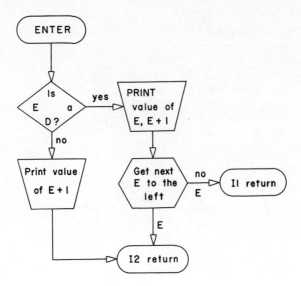

Figure 9.12 SUBROUTINE I

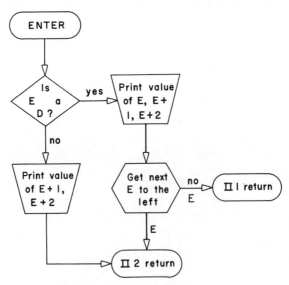

Figure 9.13 SUBROUTINE II

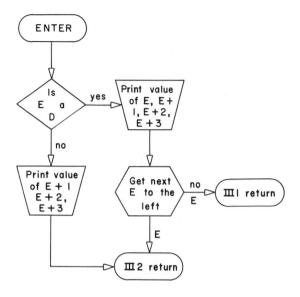

Figure 9.14 SUBROUTINE III

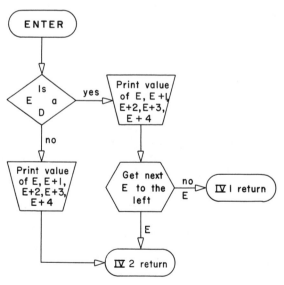

Figure 9.15 SUBROUTINE IV

Chapter 10

The Participle in Modern Hebrew — A Study in Automatic Ambiguity Resolution

Paul O. Samuelsdorff

1.0 THE GENERAL PROJECT

This research project is part of a larger project to analyze
the modern Hebrew language with the aim of translating by computer
from Hebrew into another language. With this aim in view we hope
on the one hand to get a satisfactory description of the structure of
the Hebrew language and on the other hand to contribute to the development of an efficient method of applying the computer to linguistic
work.

1.1 The problem of homograph resolution. One of the most
difficult problems of machine translation is the resolution of homographs, i.e. words with the same spelling but different grammatical
functions or meanings. This problem is of particular significance
in the Semitic languages, where only part of the spoken vowels are
written. That means that not only words of different grammatical
function or meaning but also words of different pronunciation (having
the same consonants but different vowels) may be spelled identically.
While in English most of the words that have the same spelling are
also pronounced the same way and even many words with the same
pronunciation (homophones) have a different spelling, in Hebrew
many words whose pronunciation differs have the same spelling.
Thus many words that are unambiguous to the hearer will be ambiguous to the reader. If a method could be found to solve the
problem of homographs, it would be an important step forward in
the development of a system for machine translation.

1.2 The fulcrum approach. The method adopted for the syntactic analysis of Modern Hebrew is in principle the same as that
described by Paul L. Garvin.[1] According to this method a sentence is analyzed in several passes. At each pass certain

grammatical information is retrieved from a sentence to be analyzed. This information enables the program to group lower syntactic units into higher syntactic units. This method Garvin calls
'the fulcrum approach to syntax' as it looks for pivot words or fulcra that determine the syntactic function of the word group (word
package) to which they belong. According to this method a sentence is analyzed in four series of passes.

1) Preliminary passes during which all words and strings are
   provided with unambiguous grammar codes.
2) Minor syntax passes during which word packages are identified and labeled according to whether they are to be included
   in, or excluded from, the major sentence portions upon which
   the third series of passes operates.
3) Major syntax passes during which the major components of the
   sentence (subject, predicate, and object) are identified and
   labeled.
4) Terminal passes during which previously unidentified word
   packages (like adverbial phrases and genitive nominal blocks)
   are identified and included in the major components of the
   sentence.

   The multiple-pass method has the advantage over the one-pass
methods that it does more justice to linguistic theory, since passes
follow a linguistic conception of the various structural aspects of
language (levels). Several passes allow treatment of one set of
problems (one level) at a time. Separate programs will therefore
have to be written for different languages, each program matching
the structure of the language dealt with.

   1.3 Transliteration. In order to keep the preediting of the
Hebrew input to a minimum, a simple method of transliteration
has been adopted, replacing — for purpose of keypunching — each
letter of the Hebrew alphabet by one letter of the Latin alphabet:

א = a, ב = b, ג = g, ד = d ה = h, ו = u, ז = z, ח = h, ט = j, י = i,
כ = k, ל = l, מ = m, נ = n, ס = s, ע = y, פ = p, צ = c, ק = q, ר = r,
ש = w, ת = t

This means that any Hebrew text can be punched without difficulty
on a keypunch machine with Latin characters. In order to facilitate reading, the keypunching convention will be abandoned in the
examples below for the letters ט and ש , and they will be

represented by ŧ and š respectively, which are closer to phonetic
equivalents.

1.4 <u>Modified approach</u>. Since the fulcrum approach was developed for analyzing Russian, it could not be adopted for the analysis of Hebrew without alterations. Hebrew in distinction from
Russian is not an inflectional language of the same type, since there
are no case endings in Hebrew. A word in isolation is therefore
not as clearly recognizable as belonging to a certain word-class,
i. e. having a certain syntactic function, as in Russian. If by definition the same sequence of letters between blanks is one word, irrespective of whether it has one or several functions or meanings,
many more words than in Russian may have two or more functions
depending on the environment. Thus the sentence <u>hua ktb</u> [hu katáv]
may mean 'he wrote' or 'he is a journalist', since there is no equivalent to the copula <u>is</u> in Hebrew, and the word <u>ktb</u> may have verbal
or nominal function. Only by means of its environment can we decide what function the word has. Thus, if <u>ktb</u> is preceded by the
third person pronoun and followed by the accusative particle <u>at</u> [et],
we know that it has verbal function. The sentence <u>hua ktb at hmiktb</u>
[hu katáv et hamixtáv] may therefore be translated unambiguously
as 'he wrote the letter'.

1.5 <u>Ambiguity</u>. Before finding the fulcrum word of a certain
word-group we have to determine what function each word has in a
certain sentence. This can easily be done when a certain word
belongs to only one word-class and this word-class can only have
one function in the sentence. We can define an adjective for instance
as the class of words that have the function of modifying a noun. A
noun on the other hand may be defined as a class of words that may
have several functions in a sentence, such as being the subject, the
object, or part of an adverbial phrase introduced by a preposition.
Since all nouns may have all of these functions, we do not have three
or more word-classes on the lexical level for all of these nouns but
assign all of them to one class of nouns. Some words however may
have the function of both adjective and noun. (In Hebrew this is the
case with all adjectives.) This is what we call syntactic ambiguity
in contrast to semantic ambiguity, where two words of the same
word-class have a totally different meaning. An example of the
latter is the English word <u>bat</u> which can mean 'mouse-like flying
mammal' or 'implement for striking a ball'. An example of syntactic ambiguity is <u>love</u>, which may have nominal or verbal function.

2.0 SCOPE OF THIS PAPER

The present paper deals with a specific problem of syntactic
ambiguity resolution, namely the participle. The practical investigations done in connection with this paper concern mainly the active
participle, but the flowchart that has been developed should also
work for the passive participle or for any other word of the same
triple (verbal, nominal, or adjectival) ambiguity. The active
participle in Hebrew can have the same three functions as the present participle in English. While the meaning of the participle in
its verbal or adjectival function is similar to its English equivalents,
its meaning differs when it has nominal function. The Hebrew
active participle has the meaning of the actor and not of the verbal
noun when it has nominal function in a certain environment. Thus
the Hebrew word šupṭ [šofet] will have the same meaning as 'judging'
when it has verbal or adjectival function, but will have the meaning
of 'judge' when it has nominal function. When it has verbal function,
the Hebrew active participle is equivalent to the English present
continuous or the simple present since Modern Hebrew has only one
present tense and the present of to be has no equivalent. How the
various functions of the participles can be recognized will be
exemplified below.

2.1 Overall method. A detailed elaboration of all passes that
will lead to a complete analysis of the language will have to await
future investigations. The general method is to solve all ambiguities
in the preliminary passes and then to start with the identification of
word packages. Some groupings will have to be done at an earlier
stage. In order to solve the ambiguity of the participle it is advisable to combine nouns with their preceding prepositions to form
adverbs, since this combination always has adverbial function. We
shall then avoid testing the grammar code of the word preceding
the noun each time a participle follows a noun, because the ambiguity
of the participle following a noun will, in all cases where the noun
is not preceded by a preposition, be resolved by testing only the code
or codes of the word or words following the participle. By combining
the noun with the preceding preposition before the participle ambiguity
resolution, we avoid testing the codes of a preposition.

2.2 Motivation for this paper. The problem of the grammatical
ambiguity of the Hebrew participle was chosen as a first step toward
syntactic analysis for mainly two reasons: 1) A participle occurs in
almost every Hebrew sentence, and many sentences contain more

than one. It is therefore of vital importance for the mechanical
analysis of almost any Hebrew sentence that the program have
some way of finding out the syntactic function of the participle.
2) The participle in Hebrew may have verbal, nominal, or adjectival function. Verb, noun, and adjective are the three main
parts of speech. If a method is found that will solve the ambiguity
of a word that can have these three functions, one may hope that
it will be a significantly easier task to solve the ambiguity of many
other words that can have only two out of these three functions.

3.0 THE PROPOSED FULL PROGRAM

Before going into the details of the present project we wish to
give an outline of the analysis as it is planned for the future, so
that the reader may have a clear picture of how the ambiguity resolution of the participle fits into the whole syntactic analysis. The
general method of analysis is shown in Figure 10.1.

3.1 Dictionary look-up. The analysis starts with a written
Hebrew sentence. First each word is looked up in the dictionary
and replaced by the grammar code found there. That means that
this method of analysis presupposes a dictionary where next to each
word we find the code of the word-class or classes to which it belongs.
A period is in this process considered the last word of the sentence.
When a period is read into the machine, the program recognizes
the end of the sentence and can start again from the beginning and
go through the first pass. If the word is not a period, it is replaced
by the grammar code found in the dictionary. The new sentence,
ready for the first pass, consists of grammar codes only. As an
example we take the English sentence I hear a voice. After the dictionary look-up it might read 'PRONOUN VERB ARTICLE VERNOM
PERIOD'.[2]

3.2 Ambiguities in the Look-up. When a word belongs to more
than one word-class, the codes of all these classes are not put into the dictionary, but a special code is given depending upon the
classes to which the word belongs, as we saw above in the case of
voice. If all the classes to which the word belongs were marked,
then the question about the membership in any of these classes
would be answered affirmatively, even if the word in the sentence
under discussion does not have the function of a certain class in
that context. We want to make this clear on a very simple example.
The word love in English belongs to the classes 'verb' and 'noun'.

If during the analysis of the sentence <u>They love plays.</u> the question
'Is the word preceding <u>plays</u> a noun? ' is answered in the affirmative,
the program might decide that <u>plays</u> in that sentence is a verb. If
a special code indicating the functional ambiguity is given to words
belonging to more than one class, this wrong decision is avoided;
e. g. if we give <u>love</u> the ambiguous code 'vernom', the question 'Is
the word preceding <u>plays</u> a noun? ' will be answered in the negative.
The ambiguous code is changed to its respective unambiguous code
in a specific sentence during the ambiguity resolution. There are
of course other ways of dealing with this problem. One might for
instance ask whether a certain word-class code is the only one. If
it is, its function is unambiguous; if it is not, the ambiguity has to
be resolved. In our view this complicates the program, since it
demands an additional question each time a word is tested.

  3. 3 <u>Unambiguous classes.</u> The words are classified according
to the environment in which they may appear in a sentence. These
word-classes do not always coincide with the traditional parts of
speech. We have therefore adopted the names 'nominal', 'verbal',
and 'adjectival' for the unambiguous functions of a word in a specific sentence, instead of the traditional terms 'noun', 'verb', and
'adjective'. We use the traditional terms for the coding of a word
in the dictionary according to the various functions that this word
may have in different sentences. That means that the traditional
terms that are used as codes for some ambiguous word-classes
in the dictionary will be changed to unambiguous codes during the
analysis process in the same manner as all other ambiguous
codes are. The grammar codes in the dictionary are the starting
point, not the outcome, of the syntactic analysis. Starting with
the traditional parts of speech as grammar codes in the dictionary
seems to us to be the most efficient method. If, as an outcome of
our analysis, a more efficient codification will be found, then the
dictionary codes may be changed later. As an example we may
take the traditional term 'adjective' that would in Hebrew be the
name of the ambiguous class of words that may have nominal or
adjectival function, i. e. may in different environments have the
function of one of the unambiguous word-classes 'nominal' or
'adjectival'. The code 'participle' is used for a word that may belong to any of the three classes 'nominal', 'verbal', or 'adjectival'.

  3. 4 <u>The first set of passes.</u> It is a working assumption of the
present project that all ambiguities apart from that of the participle
are solved before resolution of participial ambiguity. This is done

in the first pass. [3]   Taking again as an example the English sentence
They love plays. , the input for the first set of passes would be
'PRONOUN VERNOM VERNOM PERIOD'.   In the output of the first
set of passes the above sentence would read 'PRONOUN VERB
NOUN PERIOD' (or whatever unambiguous codes we choose for the
syntactic analysis of English).

3.5 The problem of particles. For purposes of automatic
analysis we define a word as a concatenation of letters between
blanks. The present Hebrew orthography complicates the dictionary look-up, since not all forms of all words will be in the dictionary. One-letter particles like the conjunction u 'and', the definite
article h 'the', the prepositions b 'in, at, with', k 'like', l 'to, for',
m 'from', and the relative particle š 'that' combine in the spelling
with the following word to form a new word. Thus miktb 'letter',
hmiktb 'the letter', and uhmiktb 'and the letter' are each considered
one word in the orthography, but only miktb will be found in the
dictionary. This delimitation of word boundaries is linguistically
unsatisfactory, since the function of a one-letter preposition joined
to the following word does not differ from the function of a preposition that consists of several letters and is written as a separate
word. During the analysis process this discrepancy is remedied. In the
dictionary look-up or in the first set of passes, words preceded by a preposition, a relative particle, or a conjunction will get two codes, namely
the code of the major word, as found in the dictionary, preceded by the code
of the particle. They will therefore subsequently be treated the same way
as the functionally equivalent sequence of two separate orthographic words

The conjunction u 'and' will be treated slightly differently from
the one-letter preposition or the relative particle. Its code will be
replaced during the first set of passes by one of two separate codes,
according to whether it joins two words or phrases or whether it
joins two clauses. This is important for the ambiguity resolution
of the participle. No method has as yet been developed for the program to decide by testing the environment which of the two functions
u has. For the present project it is presupposed that this question
is solved with the other ambiguities that are handled during the
first set of passes.

The words combined with the preceding h (definite article or
relative particle) will get one code during the dictionary look-up.
This code represents a definite nominal, a definite adjectival, or
a definite participle. This is done in order to facilitate the ambiguity resolution of the participle. Since the participle is
frequently preceded by h it is more efficient to create a new

ambiguous unit with its own ambiguity resolution than to test each
participle for a preceding h; in case there is a preceding h we would
have to go through the same ambiguity resolution as we would if we
had never separated the h from the participle. Another reason for
regarding the definite participle as a separate unit is that the h is
itself ambiguous as long as the ambiguity of the participle has not
been resolved.[4] In case the h has another function apart from that
of article or relative particle (e. g. that of being the first letter of
a word that is spelled the same way as a participle with preceding
article), its ambiguity is to be resolved together with the others
that are handled in the first set of passes. This does not apply to
the h in its function of a relative particle preceding a participle
with verbal function, because this ambiguity can only be resolved
in the second pass. In this case the input to the second pass will
be one code for the definite participle, and the output two codes,
one for the relative particle and one for the verbal. In the succeeding passes the relative h will be treated in exactly the same
way as another relative particle, namely š.

     3. 6 Other ambiguities. We have already mentioned two cases
of ambiguity that are solved in the first set of passes, namely the
ambiguity of the conjunction u and the ambiguity of the morph represented by the letter h. A similar ambiguity to be solved in the
first set of passes is that of the morphs represented by the letters
b, l, m, and k, each of which can be a preposition or the first
letter of a word that is spelled the same way as another word joined
to its preceding preposition. Another ambiguity to be solved in the
first set of passes is that of the adjectives, all of which can have
adjectival or nominal function. The rare cases where adjectives
may have verbal function do not justify giving them the code 'participle', since the environments where this occurs are limited. It
is therefore advisable to solve this ambiguity before we solve that
of the participle, which is much more complicated. For the same
reason we may decide to code some of the passive participles as
adjectives in the dictionary, when their function is more like those
of the adjectives than like those of the majority of the participles.

     3. 7 The second pass. After having resolved all ambiguities
apart from that of the participle in the first set of passes, we still
have to resolve the ambiguity of two kinds of words in the second
pass: the participle and the definite participle. The second pass
is described below in detail, since it is the subject of the present
paper.

3.8 <u>The third pass</u>. In the third pass or set of passes, words of various classes are grouped together. The aim of this grouping is to recognize phrases and give them an appropriate code so that during the fourth pass the program may find out whether it has correctly analyzed the sentence. Thus for instance adjectivals and nominals are grouped together to form nominal phrases, and prepositions followed by nominals or nominal phrases are changed to adverbial phrases. For example a masculine singular predicate may be formed from a masculine singular verbal and an adverbial phrase, which itself was formed from a nominal preceded by a preposition. As in the first set of passes more than one pass may be needed for the grouping.

3.9 <u>The fourth pass</u>. In the fourth pass the program compares the output of the third pass with a list of sentence rules. If it finds the rule, it has made a possible analysis and can start translating; if it does not find the rule, it prints out an error message. A sentence rule may for instance require that the sentence contain a masculine singular nominal phrase and a masculine singular predicate.

4.0 THE PRESENT PROGRAM

The problem of resolving the ambiguity of the participle was tackled in two stages:

1) A flowchart was drawn that indicates resolution of the ambiguity of constructed sentences consisting entirely of participles. The assumption was that, if the program can solve the ambiguity of these sentences, it will be an easy matter to solve the ambiguity of the participle in sentences which consist only partially of participles and contain no more than one, two, or three of the latter. As a result of a program based on the above flowchart, we expected to get an output of a sequence of unambiguous grammar codes in each case where the constructed sentence has an unambiguous meaning to the native speaker. In those cases where the meaning of a sentence is ambiguous to a native speaker the output codes are unambiguous only up to and excluding the first ambiguous participle.

2) After completing the flowchart for sentences containing only participles or participles preceded by particles, we developed rules for solving the ambiguity of the participle in sentences taken from actual texts. It is our belief that if an efficient

algorithm for analysis and translation is to be developed, it must be based on actual texts rather than on constructed sentences. The program developed on the basis of constructed sentences composed of participles only may still be used as a subroutine in a general analysis program. The input for the program based on the rules developed from the analysis of actual text is a sequence of codes replacing the words of the actual text, such that all the words apart from the participle and the definite participle are replaced by their respective unambiguous codes, which they are presupposed to have received as a result of the dictionary look-up and the subsequent first set of passes. The output of the program will be the same sequence of codes, with the difference that the codes of the participles and definite participles will have been replaced by unambiguous codes. As an illustration we shall discuss below that part of the flowchart that indicates the resolution of the ambiguity of the definite participle.

4.10 <u>Sentences containing only participles.</u> Figures 10.2, 10.3, and 10.4 show the flowchart of the questions to be asked in order to resolve the ambiguity of constructed meaningful sentences that consist entirely of participles. The original flowchart was drawn to provide also for sentences containing definite participles and participles preceded by the conjunction <u>u</u>. For illustrative purposes the flowchart has been reduced to sentences containing only participles without preceding particles.

4.11 <u>Grammar code.</u> The grammar code for the first experiment has been devised as follows. The code for each word in the sentence is stored in one machine word of 36 bit positions.[5] A certain meaning is assigned to each of the 36 bit positions. We give below the meanings of those bit positions that are relevant to the identification of the participles in sentences consisting entirely of participles:

0.	Period	9.	Masculine Singular
1.	Participle	10.	Feminine Singular
2.	Nominal	11.	Masculine Plural
3.	Adjectival	12.	Feminine Plural
4.	Verbal	17.	Verbal Priority

Bit position No. 17 needs some explanation. In order to resolve the ambiguity that is not resolved by the word order, we

mark some participles by indicating verbal priority in the 17th bit
position. That means that in certain cases where the participle
ambiguity cannot be resolved by testing the environment it may be
resolved by testing the 17th bit position. A '1' is stored in this
position with all four forms (masculine singular, feminine singular,
masculine plural, and feminine plural) of those participles that in
ambiguous cases usually do not have nominal function. Examples
are the participles ruah 'seeing' and luqx 'taking'. Words like
šupť 'judging, judge' and suxr 'trading, merchant', that frequently
have nominal function, will not be assigned verbal priority. An
example of a participle ambiguity that is not solved by testing the
environment, but may be solved by testing whether the participle
has been assigned verbal priority or not, is a sentence starting
with a masculine plural participle. Since the usual word order
in Modern Hebrew is subject-verb-object, we assume that, unless
the sentence starts with a masculine plural, the participle at the
beginning of the sentence has nominal function for the following
reason: When the participle in Modern Hebrew is masculine singular, feminine singular, or feminine plural and has verbal function,
the subject is always expressed separately and usually precedes the
participle. When the participle is masculine plural and has verbal
function, the subject need not be separately expressed when it is
impersonal, e.g. ruaim [ro'im] 'one sees, they see'. If therefore
the first word in the sentence is masculine plural and has verbal
priority, it is recognized as a verbal. If however (in a sentence
consisting of participles only) the first word is masculine plural
and the second word is not masculine plural, the first word has
verbal function irrespective of whether it has verbal priority or
not; for if the first word is a nominal, the following verbal or
adjectival must also be masculine plural.

　　4. 12 Bit pattern code. The bit pattern code works as follows.
Each function of a word is represented by a '1' in the respective bit
position of the machine word that contains its code. All other bit
positions of the machine word are zero. E.g., the code of a masculine singular participle will be '1' in bit positions No. 1 and No. 9
and 'O' in all other 34 bit positions, unless it has verbal priority,
in which case it will have an additional '1' in bit position No. 17.
After the ambiguity resolution of the second pass, bit position No. 1 will be 'O' and any one of bit positions No. 2, 3,
or 4 will be '1', i.e. the code will show that the word has
one of the three unambiguous functions of nominal, verbal, or

adjectival. It is irrelevant for the subsequent recognition of the sentence that the word was previously a participle.

4.13 Input of second pass. The sentence to be analyzed is supposed to be stored in the work area of the machine. As we are starting the second pass, the input consists of unambiguous grammar codes or the ambiguous participle codes only, since all ambiguities apart from those of the participles were resolved in the first set of passes. There is no dictionary look-up in the second pass. The dictionary look-up occurs only once during the whole syntactic analysis program, at the beginning, when each Hebrew word is replaced by its respective grammar code.

4.20 Analysis of artificial sentences. We are now ready to describe the second pass. Note that we presuppose that the dictionary look-up and the first set of passes have already taken place. While the original Hebrew word is read into the machine together with its grammar code so that we may see in the output which code belongs to which Hebrew word, the test questions of the routine concern the grammar code only. At this stage, where we are dealing with constructed sentences, the main job of the routine is to confirm that the assumptions of the flowchart are correct. The task of the extended routine that will be developed on the basis of our experience with this routine will of course be to resolve the ambiguity of the participles in sentences from actual texts.

4.21 Some examples in detail. In order to see how the ambiguities are resolved or, in those cases where they are not solved, to show the reasons, we shall follow one sentence consisting of four participles through the flowchart. We shall then introduce slight variations to this sentence and trace these through the flowchart. The first question on the flowchart, 'Is W period?', [6] is asked for the first word of the sentence. The first question will of course be answered in the negative for the first word of any sentence. It is a bookkeeping device to insure that the program recognizes the end of the sentence by noting the period. When the period is reached the participle codes will have been replaced by the codes for 'NOMINAL', 'VERBAL', or 'ADJECTIVAL', and the new sentence of grammar codes will be printed out together with the original Hebrew words. As can be seen, the flowchart displays the questions that the program asks, and shows that when the program arrives at an unambiguous answer, it will replace the ambiguous grammar code by

an unambiguous one. If it cannot resolve the ambiguity, then it will
print out: 'AMBIGUITY UNRESOLVED'.

Let us take as an example the sentence ruaim suxrim mnhlim
puylim 'They see merchants manage workers' or rather 'Merchants
are seen managing workers'. It could also mean 'Managing merchants are seen acting'. If we leave out the last word, we will get
the unambiguous sentence ruaim suxrim mnhlim 'They see managing
merchants' or 'Managing merchants are seen'. The ambiguity resolution does not depend entirely on the word order. In the above
sentence the first participle has verbal function. If we exchange
the first two words, we get a second sentence suxrim ruaim mnhlim
puylim. Here the first word has nominal function. The meaning
of this sentence is also ambiguous and can be translated as either
'Merchants see managers acting' or 'Seeing merchants manage
workers'. The second interpretation will be excluded by the routine
as being unlikely. The first interpretation may still be translated
into English in two ways, namely as 'Merchants see acting managers'
and 'Merchants see managers acting'. In spite of this stylistic
difference in English, we do not regard the Hebrew puylim 'acting'
as being functionally ambiguous, because in order to be classed as
a verbal it would have to be the nucleus of a verbal phrase. Since
it is not followed by an object, a complement, or an adverbial
phrase, and since it is preceded by a verbal in the sentence, it is
unambiguously classed as an adjectival.

The above examples are intended to show that there are two
ways of treating words whose ambiguity cannot be resolved immediately by testing the environment. One way is to regard this
ambiguity as unresolvable as long as we deal with separate sentences and to postpone their resolution until we find a way of including surrounding sentences in our resolution program. Another
way is to reject a certain solution as being an unlikely interpretation of an ambiguous sentence. We sometimes find that a certain
type of ambiguity will rarely be recognized as ambiguous by the
native speaker. In this case we shall use the second solution and
have the routine discard the rarer ambiguity in order to obtain
some solution. We have to be careful not to reject meaningful
sentences this way. This can only be done by trying out our rules
on actual texts.

4.22 Tracing the examples through the flowcharts. We shall
now trace the two sentences ruaim suxrim mnhlim puylim (sentence
1) and suxrim ruaim mnhlim puylim (sentence 2) through the

flowchart. Both are represented by a sequence of four participle
codes followed by a period. The difference between them is that
in the first sentence the first word and in the second sentence the
second word are assigned verbal priority. In order to be able to
follow the subsequent argument the reader is requested to compare
each step with the flowchart in Figures 10.2, 10.3, and 10.4.

Going through the flowchart we move to the right when the
answer to a question is 'no' and down when the answer is 'yes'. As
the first word in both sentences is a participle, we go to the right
until we reach the question 'Is W-1 period?'. For the first word
in the first sentence, ruaim, we go down the column until we reach
the question 'Has W+1 verbal priority?'. Since suxrim has not,
the first word is a verbal. The reason for this was given when we
discussed 'verbal priority' (see above). All other questions on the
way down were answered 'yes'.

Let us discuss the questions that lie on the way down to 'Has
W+1 verbal priority?':

'Is W masculine plural?' If the first word of a sentence
containing only participles is not masculine plural, we assume
that it is a nominal (subject of the sentence). This also was
explained when we discussed 'verbal priority'.

'Is W+1 participle?' If not, it must be a period, since we
are discussing sentences that consist of participles only.[7] If
the word following the first word in the sentence is a period, we
have a one-word sentence. This word could be a nominal, e.g.
in answer to a question, or a verbal, in case of a masculine
plural participle that expresses both subject and predicate. A
one-word sentence consisting of a masculine plural participle
is therefore ambiguous. When the participle has no verbal
priority it remains ambiguous; when it has verbal priority, we
have decided to resolve the syntactical ambiguity in favor of
the verbal, as was explained above.

'Is W+1 masculine plural?' If it is not, it can be neither
an adjectival nor a verbal dependent upon W, because the question 'Is W masculine plural?' was answered in the affirmative
and in Hebrew the verbal or adjectival following the nominal
it modifies has to agree with it in gender and number; so W+1
must be a nominal, i.e. W is a verbal (containing subject and
predicate) irrespective of whether it has verbal priority or
not. An example would be šuptim puyl 'They judge a worker',

'They are judging a worker', or 'A worker is judged'. If W+1
is masculine plural, the function of W depends on whether
either W or W+1 has verbal priority. If only W+1 has verbal
priority, then W is a nominal (W+1 may in this case be a verbal or an adjectival). This result is based on our argument that
in unambiguous cases participles with verbal priority usually
do not have nominal function. Examples would be the two sentences šupt̃im luqxim nusyim 'Judges take travelers' and luqxim
šupt̃im nusyim 'They take traveling judges' or 'Traveling judges
are taken'. (We could also take as an example the first three
words of our original pattern sentences ruaim suxrim mnhlim
'They see managing merchants' and suxrim ruaim mnhlim
'Merchants see managers'.) The interpretations 'They judge
traveling takers' and 'Traveling judges are taken' are unlikely
and excluded by the routine. The interpretation 'Taking judges
travel' (for the first sentence) is also excluded, since it is
indeed unlikely. This same pattern may however be less unambiguous in other cases. For instance supt̃im ruaim nusyim
could be interpreted as 'Seeing judges travel'. Work with
actual texts will show whether the routine will have to be altered
to treat sentences of this structure as ambiguous, or whether
there are other ways of dealing with this ambiguity. If both W
and W+1 have verbal priority (which is unlikely), the ambiguity
will not be resolved. If neither W nor W+1 has verbal priority,
the ambiguity will only be resolved if W+2 has verbal priority.
In that case W will be a nominal and W+1 an adjectival.

In the second sentence the first word suxrim has no verbal
priority, so we have to go to the right from the question 'Has W
verbal priority?'. Since W+1 has verbal priority, we go down to
'N', which is the label of the rectangle 'W = nominal'. Since the
first word of the sentence cannot be an adjectival and two verbals
cannot follow each other and an adjectival can only follow a nominal,
one of the first two participles must be a nominal. Since the second
participle has verbal priority, we decide that the first participle is
a nominal.

Sentence 1, word 2 suxrim: We go down from the question 'Is
W−1 verbal?' to the rectangle labeled 'N', i. e. the second word is
a nominal. In Hebrew a verbal can be followed neither by an adjectival nor by another verbal.

Sentence 2, word 2 ruaim: We go to the right till we reach the
question 'Is W−1 nominal?'; since it is, we go down to the question

'Is W+1 period?', then to the right to the question 'Is W+1 participle?', then down past the question 'Is there syntactic agreement between W and W+1?' to the question 'Has W+1 verbal priority?'; since it has not, we have to go to the right to the question 'Has W verbal priority?'. Since it has, W is a verbal. (This is only correct if W+1 is a possible object of the transitive verbal W. We shall take up this point later.) If there had been no syntactic agreement between W and W+1 (i.e. gender or number in one of them had differed from the other), W+1 would have been the object of a verbal and W a verbal, regardless of its verbal priority or lack of it. If instead of mnhlim 'managers, managing' the word following ruaim had been luqxim 'taking, takers', a participle with verbal priority, ruaim would have been recognized as having adjectival function, since it is more likely for a participle with verbal priority to have adjectival function than to have nominal function, so that if two participles following a nominal and in syntactic agreement with the nominal both have verbal priority, then the first will be recognized as an adjectival and the second as a verbal. If the first had been recognized as a verbal, the second would have to be a nominal. Therefore the sentence suxrim ruaim luqxim puylim would be translated as 'Seeing merchants take workers', which is indeed a more likely translation than 'Merchants see acting takers'.

Sentence 1, word 3 mnhlim: We go to the right till we reach the question 'Is W−1 nominal?' and follow the same path as we did for ruaim (word 2) in sentence 2, except that in this case W has no verbal priority, so that the function of the participle remains ambiguous. Indeed mnhlim can have verbal function, as in the interpretation 'Merchants are seen managing workers', or adjectival function as in the interpretation, 'Managing merchants are seen acting'. If mnhlim had been followed by a period, we would have gone down the column from 'Is W+1 period?' and mnhlim would have been recognized as an adjectival. In the two-word sentence suxrim mnhlim, mnhlim would have been recognized as a verbal, since the question 'Is any previous word verbal?' would have been answered in the negative.

Sentence 2, word 3 mnhlim: We go to the question 'Is W−1 verbal?'. Since it is, mnhlim has nominal function. The reason is that two participles with verbal function cannot follow each other and a verbal or an adjectival can only follow a nominal, as we mentioned above.

Sentence 1, word 4 puylim: If the ambiguity of one participle in a sentence consisting only of participles cannot be resolved, then the ambiguity of succeeding words cannot be solved either, since the ambiguity of the participle is resolved by testing the unambiguous code of the preceding word at least in all cases where the following word is still ambiguous.

Sentence 2, word 4 <u>puylim</u>: We go to the right till we reach the question 'Is W-1 nominal?' then down to 'W = adjectival', since W+1 is a period and there is a verbal in the sentence.

We therefore got an unambiguous resolution of Sentence 2. The same routine was tried on the sentence <u>suxrim kutbim mnhlim puylim</u>. This sentence means unambiguously 'Writing merchants manage workers'. Since <u>kutb</u> usually has verbal function, we assigned verbal priority to it. As a result the machine analyzed the sentence as meaning 'Merchants write acting managers'. If we do not assign verbal priority to <u>kutb</u>, then the result will be ambiguous, since neither W nor W+1 have verbal priority (W being <u>kutb</u>, following the nominal <u>suxrim</u>). This is an unsatisfactory solution for an unambiguous sentence. The solution will be to add another test question to the routine, namely 'Is W+1 a possible object of W?'. In order to be able to answer this question correctly, all transitive verbs will have to be marked with the classes of nominals that can follow them as objects and vice versa. We call this semantic agreement, as distinct from syntactic agreement (gender and number). The revised part of the flowchart in Figure 10.4 is shown in Figure 10.5.

The program based on the extended flowchart for resolving the ambiguity of sentences included analysis of the definite participle and participles preceded by the conjunction <u>u</u> which works in the same manner.

4.30 <u>Analysis of sentences from actual texts</u>. The following part of the paper demonstrates how to develop a program for syntactic analysis that is based on actual texts. The method does not differ from the one used for analyzing constructed sentences. It is more complicated, however, because of the variety of codes that have to be used for indicating the function of the words that are not participles. These codes are the output of the first set of passes that is presupposed to have resolved all ambiguities apart from that of the participles.

4.31 <u>Procedure</u>. The method for choosing the rules from actual texts is by discovery of criteria by which a native speaker recognizes the function of a certain participle and by formulation of

these criteria as a rule for the machine. After the rule is written,
it is tried out on other sentences. If it does not work, it is altered
or a new rule is added to cover both sentences. The rule is constructed by stating the conditions under which we can determine the
word-class membership of W. This can often be done by giving the
word-class membership of W-1 and/or W+1 as a condition. If the
function of the participle W can be determined by one condition, then
the rule is complete. Thus, 'If the word preceding the participle
is a definite nominal, then the participle has verbal function' is a
complete rule. It is usually not sufficient to state merely the word-
class membership of the word preceding or following the participle.
For instance, a participle following a noun can have verbal or adjectival (or in case of the construct state[8] even nominal) function.
We have therefore frequently to state more than one condition in
order to formulate a rule.

If we use actual texts for developing the recognition rules, the
rules that are formulated are specific for the cases that have been
examined. A rule will however by rejected as soon as, in the light
of more material, a new rule will have been developed that accounts
for the same case as a previous rule, or if a rule is correct for
some cases but will give the wrong answer in other cases. The
rules will thus be improved by this process of trial and evaluation.

4.4 <u>The definite participle</u>. As a first text, a hundred sentences from the newspaper extracts published in the textbook by
A. Rozen, <u>Elef Millim</u> (Jerusalem, 1962) were chosen. As the
flowchart for all occurrences of the participle would be too complicated, we shall here take as an example the flowchart for the
definite participle. This will be sufficient for the illustration of
the principle of ambiguity resolution. In order to explain this principle it will not be necessary to take entire sentences and trace
them through the flowchart, since there are usually no more than
one or two definite participles in a sentence. We shall therefore
discuss the flowchart in Figures 10.6, 10.7, 10.8, and 10.9 and
illustrate certain points with appropriate examples. The reader
is again requested to follow the subsequent argument through the
flowchart.

We first ask four questions concerning the word-class membership of W+1, since these cases (except for the definite nominal
following a definite participle) are fairly frequent and we avoid
repeating these questions each time the word-class membership
of W-1 does not solve the ambiguity of the participle. In the first

two cases and the fourth case the definite participle has the function
of a relative particle plus a verbal. Examples are: ...hbunh bit...
'who builds a house...': W+1 is a nominal; ...hmuca (at) drku...
'who finds his way...': W+1 is either the accusative particle or a
definite nominal. The latter case is rare, since the definite nominal
following the relative particle h plus a verbal is usually preceded by
the accusative particle at. If the word following a definite participle is
a definite adjectival, the definite participle must have nominal function,
since a definite adjectival is always preceded by a definite nominal.

If W-1 is a period, W (which is then the first word of the sentence) will in most cases be a definite nominal. Some sentences
however start with a relative particle followed by a verbal. Those
verbals followed by the accusative particle or a nominal have already been identified by testing the word-class membership of W+1.
If the definite participle in question is followed by a verbal or a
participle (without article), it has nominal function (remembering
that the first four test questions about W+1 were answered negatively).

If the definite participle is followed by an adverbial, it can be
either a nominal or a verbal. The provisional solution is that those
definite participles to which verbal priority has been assigned will
be identified as verbals, while the others will be recognized as
nominals. The latter will probably not always be correct, and more
rules will have to be developed to achieve correct solutions. Some
classes will have to remain ambiguous or an arbitrary decision will
have to be made. Thus, hpuylim bisral itplu bynin zh may be translated as 'the workers in Israel will deal with this matter' or as
'those who act in Israel will deal with this matter'. In newspaper
style, the former will probably in most cases be the correct translation and the above rule may prove satisfactory also for similar
cases.

If W-1 is an adjectival (without article), i.e. if the participle
under discussion follows an indefinite nominal phrase, W must be
a relative particle plus a verbal. The same is the case when the
previous word is a definite adjectival, for if two definite adjectivals
modify the same nominal, they are usually separated by a conjunction
or a comma.

In most cases the relative particle followed by a verbal is preceded by a comma. For the definite participle preceded by a comma
we have developed the following rules: If W+1 is a verbal, W is a
definite nominal. W cannot be a relative particle plus a verbal,
since two verbals cannot immediately follow each other. Theoretically it might be an adjectival, namely when the comma is preceded

by another adjectival; but since the last adjectival modifying a
nominal is usually separated from the preceding adjectival by the
conjunction u and not by a comma, it is in practice almost always
a definite nominal. W must be a definite nominal (or a definite
adjectival) when it is followed by the relative particle š, since the
latter is never preceded by a verbal. The possibility of W being
a definite adjectival is rejected for similar reasons as those given
above. If W+1 is a definite participle, W is a definite nominal, because W+1 has either adjectival or verbal function. We exclude the
possibility that if two definite participles follow each other, the
second one is a definite nominal (which makes the first a relative
particle followed by a verbal), since we assume that in this case
the definite nominal would be preceded by the accusative particle.
The case of W+1 being a definite adjectival has already been covered
at the beginning of the flowchart. If W+1 is the coordinate conjunction u, the identification of W depends on W+2. If the word
following the conjunction is a definite adjectival, the word under
discussion must also be a definite adjectival; if W+2 is a definite
nominal, W must also be a definite nominal. In all other cases we
assume that the definite participle following the comma is a relative
particle plus a verbal.

If W-1 is a preposition, the word šl 'of', or the accusative
particle at, W is a definite nominal.[9]

The definite participle following a verbal will also be a definite
nominal. This will usually be the case when the verbal follows an
adverbial or an adverbial phrase; in that case the definite participle
will be the subject, since in Hebrew the order of subject and predicate
is frequently reversed when the sentence starts with an adverbial or
an adverbial phrase. In some cases, namely when the accusative
particle at is omitted, the definite participle may be the object
following a transitive verbal.

If the preceding word is kl 'each, every, all', the function of
the definite participle depends mainly on whether it is masculine
singular or not. In the first case it will usually have verbal function,
otherwise nominal function. Thus kl hšupt barc ... will be translated as 'All those who judge in the land ...' or 'Everyone who judges
in the land ...' which kl hšuptim barc ... will be translated as
'All the judges in the land ...'. A routine has still to be developed for the deviant cases. (For instance, when kl is preceded
by a preposition, the following definite participle has always
nominal function.)

If the preceding word is a nominal (without article), W is a
relative particle followed by a verbal unless the two are in construct
state. For the latter case it is proposed that words in construct
state will consistently be joined by a hyphen, as is already done
occasionally, so that this ambiguity does not have to be dealt with.
Then bn šupṭ would unambiguously be translated as 'a judging son'
and 'a judge's son' would be bn-šupṭ.

If the preceding word is a definite nominal, the word under
discussion is a definite adjectival in the following cases: if the
following word is a period, a comma, šl, or a definite participle.
If the following word is an adverbial, W is a relative particle
followed by a verbal if it has verbal priority, otherwise it remains
ambiguous. If the following word is a participle not in syntactic
agreement with W, W is a relative particle followed by a verbal
and W+1 a nominal. If there is syntactic agreement between W and
W+1, W is a definite adjectival if W+1 has verbal priority, but W
is a verbal preceded by a relative particle if it has verbal priority
itself; otherwise it remains ambiguous. The case of both W and
W+1 having verbal priority is rare but would be solved in favor of
W having adjectival function. Thus haiš hluqx muca ... would be
translated as 'The taking man finds ...' and not as 'The man who
takes a finder ...'.

If the preceding word is an adverbial, we distinguish two cases:
1) W-1 is a simple adverb like ykšu 'now', atmul 'yesterday' etc.
2) The adverbial is composed of a prepositional particle and a
nominal. In the latter case it will be marked by gender and number.
A definite participle following a simple adverb or an adverb composed of a prepositional particle and a nominal of different gender
and number will be recognized as a definite nominal, because a
relative particle followed by a verbal is usually preceded by a
comma, unless it follows directly the nominal to which it is related.
If there is syntactic agreement between W and W-1, W is a definite
adjectival modifying the nominal part of the preceding adverbial in
the following cases: if W+1 is a comma, a period, a verbal, or the
conjunction u, unless this conjunction is followed by a definite
nominal.[10] If W+1 is an adverbial, W is a relative plus a verbal
modifying the nominal part of the preceding adverbial. In all other
cases, the ambiguity has not yet been solved.

4.5 Future plans. The flowchart has been checked manually
on fifty sentences containing definite participles, taken at random
from Hebrew daily papers. As a next stage it is planned to develop

the other preliminary passes which are needed to obtain a complete
syntactic analysis by machine.

NOTES

1. Paul L. Garvin 'Syntax in Machine Translation', ed. Garvin,
Natural Language and the Computer (New York, 1963).

2. 'Vernom' is the class of words whose members can function
as both verbs and nouns. In the proper coding person and number
would also have to be taken into account. How the classes are defined depends on the particular analysis of English followed.

3. In practice more than one pass may be needed. We may
therefore talk of the first set of passes. The first set of passes is
intended to accomplish the resolution of all ambiguities whose solution is a necessary assumption for the success of the present project.
The order of some steps may be changed later on.

4. The h has the function of a definite article when the participle
has nominal or adjectival function and the function of a relative particle when the participle has verbal function.

5. A bit position represents a unit of the computer that may be
in either of two states, depending on the direction of the flow of
current. The two states are represented by 'O' and '1' respectively.

6. The word under discussion is always symbolized by 'W',
the following word in the sentence by 'W+1', the word following the
following word by 'W+2', etc. The word preceding 'W' in the sentence is symbolized by 'W-1', the word preceding 'W-1' by 'W-2',
etc.

7. We have excluded the possibility of W being a definite participle or a participle preceded by u 'and', or š 'that', in order to
limit the size of the flowchart.

8. The construct state is the Hebrew equivalent of a noun with
its genitive modifier. The modifying noun follows the modified
noun and the latter loses its stress. Because of this loss of stress
the modified noun may undergo some change in its vowels or its
ending, while the modifying noun remains in its basic form.

9.   Whether šl and at may also be considered prepositions is
irrelevant in this context. The definition of a preposition will
probably be that it can only stand in front of nominals or definite
nominals, so that šl and at may be included in this class; on the
other hand šl and at differ from other prepositions in the classes
of words which they can follow, so that it is advisable to keep them
separate in order to facilitate some ambiguity resolutions.

10.   In this case the conjunction u may join two definite nominals,
e. g. btnaim dumim ybdu šm hnšim uhildim 'the women and the
children worked under similar conditions there'; here it is important
to distinguish between the conjunction u joining two words and the
same conjunction joining two clauses, for in the latter case W will
be a definite adjectival even if u is followed by a definite nominal,
e. g. asy bšna hbah uhmšpxh tbua axri 'I shall go next year and my
family will come after me'.

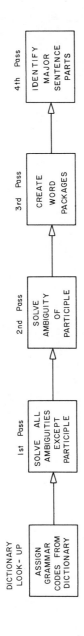

DICTIONARY
LOOK-UP

ASSIGN
GRAMMAR
CODES FROM
DICTIONARY

1st Pass

SOLVE ALL
AMBIGUITIES
EXCEPT
PARTICIPLE

2nd Pass

SOLVE
AMBIGUITY
OF
PARTICIPLE

3rd Pass

CREATE
WORD
PACKAGES

4th Pass

IDENTIFY
MAJOR
SENTENCE
PARTS

Figure 10.1

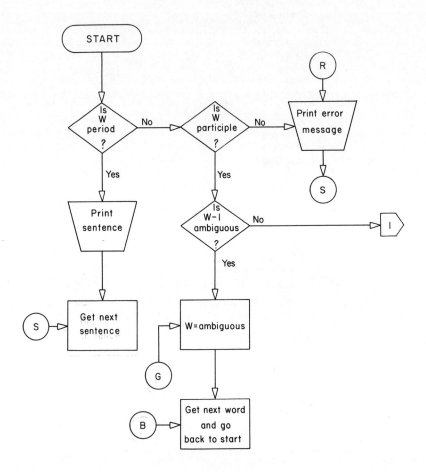

Figure 10.2

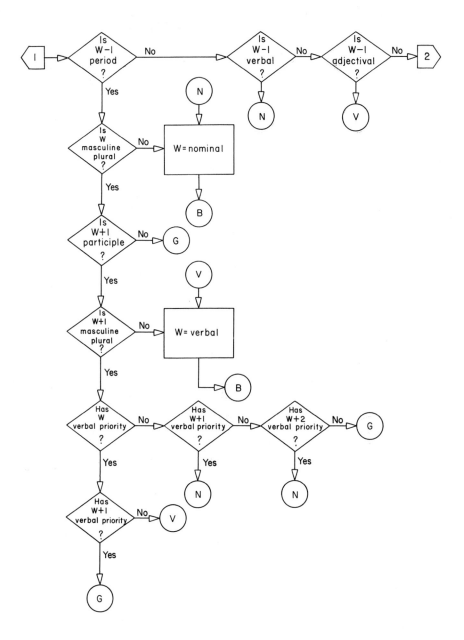

Figure 10.3

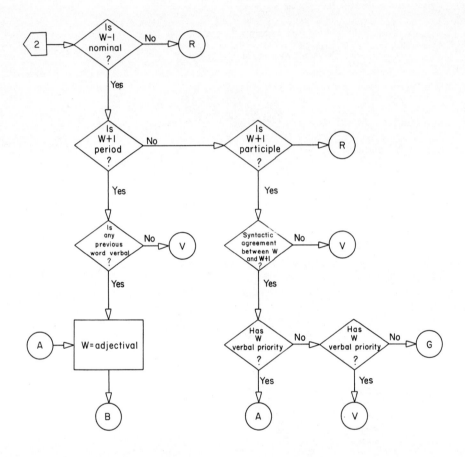

Figure 10.4

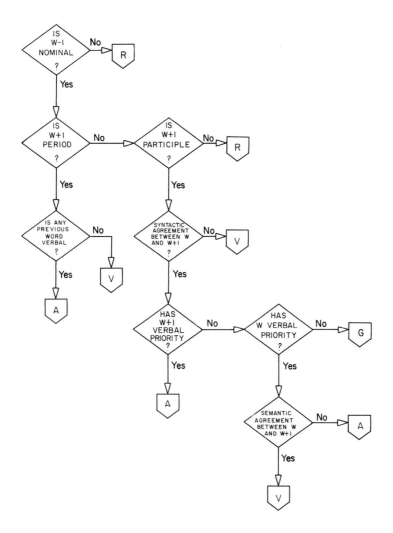

Figure 10.5

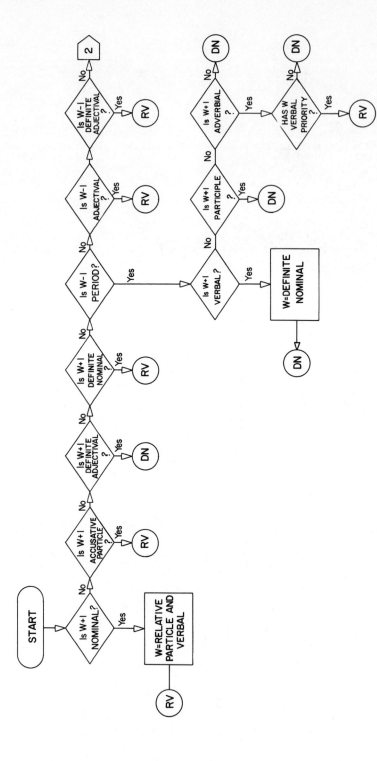

Figure 10.6

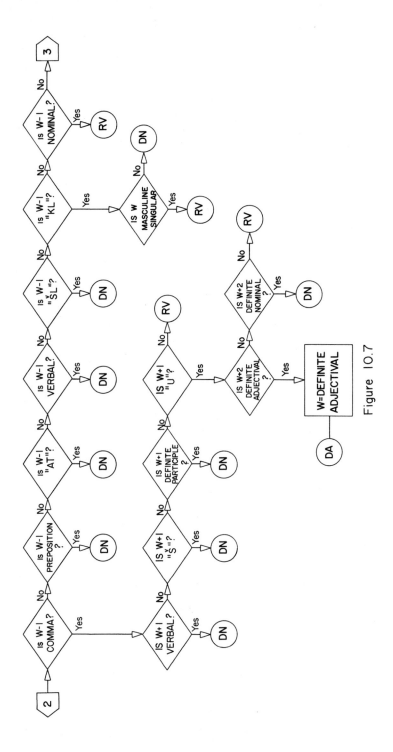

Figure 10.7

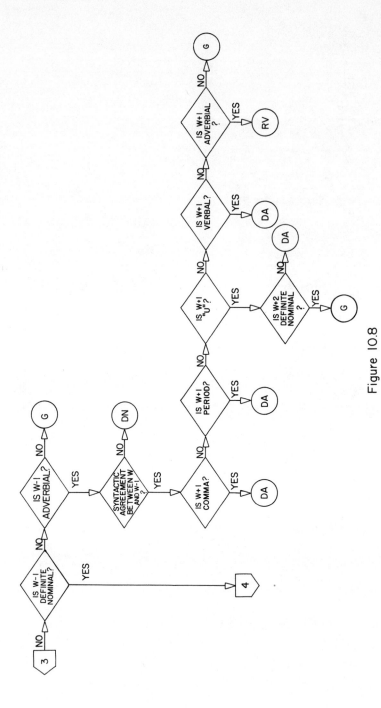

Figure 10.8

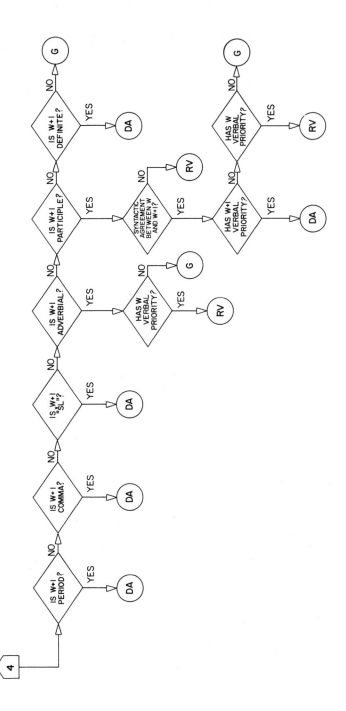

Figure 10.9

Chapter 11

A Modifiable Routine for Connecting Related Sentences of English Text

S. N. Jacobson

1.0 INTRODUCTION

This is a report on a computational approach to the relations between the sentences of a text. These relations organize the text into paragraph-like groups of sentences, each group dealing with a separate topic. To make the discussion concrete, a computer application which produces text abstracts is described. This application makes use of the relations between sentences to extract sentences from the sentence groups in order to form an abstract. The emphasis will be on the way in which these relations organize the sentences of the text rather than on the programming details required to set up the application on an actual computer.

The easiest way to follow a computational approach is to perform the computations. First we will discuss how and why the computations work on the text. Then, an example will be given of the application of the computational rules to a short text. The computation makes use of a dictionary and rules for when and how to use the dictionary. The text determines when to use the dictionary.

The computational task is in some ways similar to reading a text in a foreign language with the help of a dictionary. In both cases, the text determines when the dictionary is to be used. When several alternatives are given by the dictionary, the text determines which one is the appropriate choice. The result of using our dictionary however is not an understanding of the sentences of the text, but an explicit diagram of the significant relations between sentences of the text. This diagram is used to produce abstracts.

2.0 PRACTICAL AND THEORETICAL MOTIVATION

For purposes of this discussion, an abstract is a selection of sentences from a text which is sufficient to allow a reader to decide if he should read the entire text. When this selection is done by a computer whose processing is directed and organized entirely by the words and sentences of the text and a computer program, the result will be called an auto-abstract.

The most obvious way to prepare an abstract would be to ask a person capable of understanding the text to select a set of sentences which would represent it. The author of the text is such a person. The practical goal of auto-abstracting[1] is to make it unnecessary to use a person who understands the text. Instead, auto-abstracting procedures make use of the organization imposed on the text by its author. This organization is based on the clues given by the author to help the reader follow the text. The various auto-abstracting procedures which have been developed make use of different aspects of this organization. But all assume that there is sufficient organization of the text, either by vocabulary statistics or sentence arrangements, to recognize the important sentences which represent the text.

The manual equivalent of auto-abstracting would be to go through a text on an unfamiliar topic and underline those sentences which seem important. Even when the subject matter is unfamiliar, it is still possible to recognize the sentences that hold the text together.

The procedure to be described here focuses on those clues which indicate that groups of sentences should be considered together and independently of other sentences. The result is very much as if the text had been reparagraphed, but the paragraphing is much more detailed than usual. Each group of sentences includes either a topic or summary sentence which is identified by the way the sentences are grouped together. By extracting these special sentences, an auto-abstract is produced.

The relations between sentences which make possible this sort of organization of text are discussed in the body of the paper. The point of practical interest is that they can be recognized without understanding the text as a whole or any individual sentence. This means that an abstractor need not understand the text or be familiar with the subject matter in order to select out the important sentences for representing the text. If clues to these relations can be precisely stated, a computer program can be written to select them.

However, this claim must be qualified. No auto-abstracting procedure can guarantee that the sentences it selects out will be interesting to a specialist in the subject matter. Important is defined entirely by the particular text and its organization. Selection of interesting sentences requires knowledge of the subject matter, in other words, information relating the sentences from more than

a single text. Insofar as the author treated interesting sentences
as important they will be in the auto-abstract. If the requirement
were that the auto-abstract include interesting sentences instead of
important sentences, there might be no sentences extracted since
it is quite possible that there are no interesting sentences in the
text.

The theoretically pertinent point for linguists is that the sentences of the text need not be understood in order to recognize the
important sentences. Just as the task of syntactic analysis does
not require knowledge of the meaning of the individual words in a
sentence, the analysis of a text does not require knowledge of the
meaning of the individual sentences which are related to each other.
Since the most obvious way to recognize the important sentences
is to understand them, this suggests that at least part of the meaning of a sentence depends on the overall organization of the text
rather than the other way around.

This dependence is made computationally explicit by the decision
to select certain sentences for the auto-abstract. The computation
can be varied to determine the consequences of adding, deleting, or
otherwise reordering and reinterpreting the clues to the organization
of the text. This makes auto-abstracting procedures useful experimental devices for testing specific ideas of how text is organized.

3.0 HOW TEXT IS ORGANIZED

The auto-abstracting procedure to be discussed links the sentences of the text on the basis of clues which occur in the sentences.
Figure 11.1 is an example of the diagram which results. Because
of the way the links are set up, it is possible to construct a variety
of paths through the sentences of the text by traversing the links in
different ways. Just as a reader may decide to skip individual
sentences or whole sections of a text, these alternative paths go
through less than the complete set of sentences of the text.

Links are assigned so that there is always a principal path
through the text. Every sentence of the text is either on the principal path or is linked to a sentence on the principal path, directly
or indirectly. These links to the principal path connect side paths
which link to the skipped sentences. The principal path can be
enlarged to include these sentences by restoring the side paths.

This way of organizing sentences is familiar to anyone who
has written from a sentence outline. The procedure is to write
out a list of sentences covering the main topics to be discussed.
The list is then interrupted to insert additional sentences. These

additional sentences expand on particular sentences in the outline and may themselves be expanded on. By repeating the process of expansion, the entire text is eventually produced. However, the original basic list is never added to.[2]

Consider, for example, the following section from a sentence outline for description of a diplomatic crisis:

I. ....
II. The acute phase of the crisis is quickly reached.
   1. Nation Xau denounces Nation Yau.
      a. ....
   2. Nation Yau responds by severing diplomatic relations.
      a. Ambassador Mau is recalled to the capital.
      b. A meeting of the signers of treaty Oau is called.
      c. ....
   3. ....
III. ....

In this outline, sentences of equal importance are placed directly under each other. Less important sentences are indented and placed under the sentence to which they are related. The same relations between sentences as are represented in the sentence outline can be recognized in text using the procedures described in sections 4 through 8. Although the diagram resulting from these procedures takes a form different from that of a sentence outline, the same structures occur.

The principal path is the set of sentences to which all the other sentences are related. Accordingly, sentences I, II, III are on the principal path, sentences 1, 2, 3 are a related sidepath, and 2a, 2b, 2c is a sidepath related to the first sidepath. The addition or deletion of sidepaths in going through the text represents decisions as to how deep to go in the outline for sentences.

It is not possible to freely insert sentences in a sentence outline when preparing text. If sentences were freely expanded, the organization of the outline as an outline would be destoryed. The same restrictions on using a sentence outline as a basis for preparing text also apply to the diagram of Figure 11.1. They are stated in detail in section 7.

Basically, there are two different ways to use a sentence outline for the preparation of text. The first treats the outline as an incomplete sketch of the text. It takes an incomplete sentence outline and expands it to increase the number of sentences included in the actual text. This is the equivalent of the procedure for

restoring sentences to an auto-abstract as described in section 9.

In terms of this procedure, a sentence can be 'expanded' by
placing an additional sentence directly under it so as to align the
pair of sentences. This was done when sentence 2b was placed
under sentence 2a in the outline. Alternatively, a sentence can be
expanded by indenting another sentence under it as was done with
sentence 2a under 2. Any sentence on the outline can be expanded
by indenting any number of times to add additional sentences to
the outline. In addition, any sentence, except those on the basic
list, can be expanded by aligning any number of times to add additional sentences to the outline. Both of these methods of expansion
are represented by 'vertical paths' in the diagram.

The second way to use a sentence outline takes it as the source
of the sentences available for inclusion in the actual text. Applying
this second technique, the sentence outline may include more sentences than occur in the actual text. It is the equivalent of the procedure for forming an abstract as described in section 8. As each
sentence in the outline is encountered, a decision is made whether
or not to include it in the text and where to look in the outline for
the next sentence. The sentence chosen can prevent the inclusion
of other sentences from the outline.

The freedom to expand on sentences in the outline does not
apply to the use of expansions in the text: (1) Whenever a sentence
is not included in the text from the outline, no expansion on it may
be included in the text. Thus if sentence 1 is not included in the
text, sentence 1a cannot be included either. (2) As soon as a sentence is included which is an expansion by alignment of a preceding
sentence and is not immediately adjacent to that sentence, no additional expansions can be made on the preceding sentences which
have not already been included in the text. Thus the list of sentences which expand sentence 2 by indenting to include sentences
2a-2b-2c cannot be further expanded as soon as sentence 3 is included in the text. The sentence sequence 2-2a-3-2b cannot occur,
but the sequence 2-2a-2b-3 may. As a result of the list 2-2a-2b-2c
in the text being closed to the addition of more sentences, no
sentence following 3 can be a member of the same list of sentences
which includes 2c unless the list also includes II. This restriction
is the basis for constructing 'bow paths' in the diagram. The
concept of bow path is explained in section 7.

The sentence outline requires that every sentence be either
on the principal path or related to it. In text, however, this is

not a necessary requirement. The outline corresponding to the text may include another outline which is not connected to it and which produces an independent text. The following sentence could serve as such an additional sentence outline for our example:

The private life of the leader of Nation Xau is notorious.

There is no obvious sentence to which it could be related in our outline. If it were used in the actual text, it would probably function as an excursus which adds nothing about the diplomatic crisis and may entertain the reader.

The bow paths in the sentence diagram function as such an extra outline. Thus sentences B-4-8-11-12 in the diagram may be treated as a principal path for an independent text which has been inserted in the text. In order to treat this independent outline as part of the overall outline, the 'dummy sentence' was inserted. The dummy sentence is a sentence number that acts as a structural element in the diagram but does not correspond to any actual sentence in the text. It functions exactly like the footnote convention in scholarly prose. Although it does not occur as a sentence in the actual text, it preserves the requirement of the outline organization that every sentence is either on the principal path or related to a sentence on the principal path. Sentences on a bow path have only an indirect relation to the other sentences in the text. This is through a 'dummy sentence' which has been inserted to allow that connection.

4.0 THE COMPONENTS OF THE COMPUTATION

The various components of the sentence-linking computation are:

1) A dictionary of clues (cf. sections 5, 6 and dictionary appendix)
   The clues in a sentence instruct the computational device to
   a) make a prediction, and
   b) set up a test for the prediction.
   If a prediction is satisfied, a link is constructed between the two sentences.

2) A routing procedure (cf. sections 6 and 7, Figures 11.2, 11.3, 11.4)
   This instructs the computational device
   a) to continue or terminate testing the current prediction;
   b) to assign links to pairs of sentences and modify previously constructed links where necessary; and

   c) where to look for the next clue which the procedure
       designates.

3) <u>Text to be processed</u> (cf. Figure 11.5)
As the sentences of the text are processed, various kinds of
information are required. Syntactical information is required
so that clues can be properly used in making predictions. The
information associated with the clues in the dictionary is also
utilized in making predictions. Finally, as links are constructed
between the sentences, they are recorded as intermediate results
which are utilized by the processing along with subsequent clues
to determine what action to take next.
The text functions as a kind of scratchpad in which are recorded:
   a) the results of a syntax analysis which brackets noun
       phrases and indicates the main verbs of sentences for
       use in making predictions;
   b) the values of the clues as supplied by the dictionary;
       and
   c) the links constructed as the result of successful predic-
       tion.
The sample text given in Figure 11.5 has had the results of a
syntax analysis and the values of the clues in the dictionary
inserted for the convenience of the reader.

4) <u>A procedure for producing a principal path using the text diagram clues</u> (cf. sections 7 and 8, Figure 11.1.)

5.0 CLUES

Consider the following set of sentences:

1) Nitrogen is an element.
2) Nitrogen is an element of the inert gases.
3) Nitrogen is not an element of the inert gases.

As additional words are inserted into the first sentence of the
set, it becomes increasingly unable to stand alone without additional
sentences to provide it with context. The first sentence is an
assertion but the last sentence, because of the qualifications placed
on the assertion, requires more discussion to make its occurrence
meaningful. Though still a grammatical sentence of the same kind
(in some significant way), it has changed from an independent
sentence to a text-dependent sentence. Because it is now a text-
dependent sentence, [3] the reader expects additional sentences as
explication.

The following set of sentences starts with a text-dependent sentence:

1) However, this is merely a psychological theory.
2) This is merely a psychological theory.
3) This is a psychological theory.
4) Gestalt theory is a psychological theory.

As words are deleted or replaced, the sentence becomes increasingly independent. The first sentence in the set is a dependent sentence which definitely requires additional text. The last sentence is a relatively independent assertion of fact.

The words which were deleted, replaced, or added are clues. These clues signal the independent or dependent status of sentences. In addition, they make it possible to recognize other sentences in the text to which a dependent sentence is especially closely related. These two functions make it possible to organize the text into larger units than individual sentences.

In general, a potential clue is either

1)   A word or construction which can be replaced by any one of a small list of items of which it is a member, such that this replacement does not modify the sentence structure in a significant way. An example would be the word this which can be replaced by the word that in the first sentence of the preceding example.

2)   A word or construction which can be deleted without destroying the grammatical function of at least one of the constructions in which it occurs. Examples would be the words however and merely in the second set of sentences. Their deletion still leaves a grammatical sentence.

The clues seem to serve to relate the clauses of the text to other clauses in the text. Clues are not significantly involved in the grammatical structure of the clauses and phrases in which they occur since they can always be either deleted or replaced without disrupting the structures. Clues relate a dependent sentence to the other sentences in the text in two ways: (1) they arouse the expectation that there is another sentence in the text to which a dependent sentence is especially related, and (2) they permit the reader to make a prediction about this other sentence so he can recognize it if he encounters it in the text.

Predictions are either predictions about the recurrence of nouns which occur in noun phrases marked by clues or about the

recurrence of a clause type as specified by a clue marking a clause.
The predictions based on noun phrases are quite specific. For
example, the phrase this task suggests that there has been an
earlier use of the word task. Predictions based on clauses are
much less specific though they are also testable. An example is
a clause introduced by the clue however. This suggests only that
there was an earlier clause to which the clause is related. While
this is a relatively unspecific prediction, it can fail since there
may be no clause preceding in the text.

6.0 MAKING PREDICTIONS

Predictions are used to set up paths through the text. If a
prediction is satisfied, a link is set up connecting the two sentences
concerned. The following information is supplied in the dictionary
for each class of clues, as the basis for making a prediction: The
clues tell where to look for related sentences, how to decide whether
or not the related sentence has been encountered, and when to give
up trying to find the related sentence.

Each prediction is based on the occurrence of a clue and the
phrase or clause structure in which it occurs. If the structure
marked by the clue is a noun phrase, the clue determines what
part of the noun phrase must reoccur and under what conditions
it must reoccur in another sentence in order to be treated as a
match. When a match is made, a link is constructed joining the
two sentences as related. If the marked structure is a clause, the
clue determines what clause type must reoccur and under what conditions it should be matched in another sentence to set up the link.
In addition, for both noun phrases and clauses, the clue determines
how far and in what direction the text must be searched for a match.

As stated above, the information used to make these predictions
is contained in a dictionary. An abridged version of the dictionary
is given in the appendix. Its entries include only those clues used
in processing the sample text. This dictionary was abridged from
a larger dictionary which has been used to process other texts.

The dictionary contains an entry for each clue; each field of
the dictionary entry is devoted to a single piece of information used
in setting up and testing the prediction. The following is the organization of the dictionary entry or format into separate fields of information. Field 1 specifies the conditions under which the occurrence of a clue should be ignored. Fields 2 and 3 specify what must
be matched to satisfy the prediction. Fields 4 and 5 specify the

direction and distance in which the text must be searched to test
the prediction. The general format for the information in the
dictionary entries is:

Field 1:	Field 2, 3:	Field 4, 5:
Conditions when clue is ignored	Specify item to be matched to satisfy prediction	Determine direction and distance of text search for item

The information placed in these different fields can be interpreted as instructions to the computational device. Each field of
the format acts as a subinstruction.   Thus, the dictionary entry
for the clue <u>would</u> is:

$$\text{NOT-1/SELF/TYPE-}\phi\text{/LEFT/NEXT}$$

which tells the computational device to do as follows:

Field-1 NOT-1 ....do <u>not</u> specify a prediction for this clue which
      makes use of TYPE unless the clue precedes
      the main verb of the sentence.
Field-2 SELF......make a match on the clause type.   Clause type
      is determined by the clue <u>itself</u> and specified
      by Field-3
Field-3 TYPE......the clause-<u>type</u> specified by the clue as TYPE-ϕ
Field-4 LEFT......search <u>left</u> in the text to make the match
Field-5 NEXT......do not search beyond the <u>next</u> sentence in the
      appropriate direction

'Making a match' on clause type means finding a clause having the
specified type. Similarly, making a match on a noun means finding
a noun phrase containing the specified noun.
  An abridged version of the dictionary and a list of the subinstructions is given in the dictionary appendix.

7.0 TESTING PREDICTIONS AND CONSTRUCTING PATHS

  Properly interpreted, the dictionary information serves as an
instruction to the computational device to search the text in order
to test whether a given prediction is satisfied. The test is based
on both the dictionary entry and a record of the previous predictions which had been satisfied. If a prediction made in one sentence

is satisfied in another sentence, the pair of sentences is connected
by a link. In this way, a record of the success or failure of these
predictions is used to construct a diagram from these links.

The failure of a prediction is also used in constructing the
diagram. A prediction can fail under two circumstances. Either
the text is searched without satisfying the predictions so that no
link is constructed, or the text search specified by the dictionary
may be aborted before the text has been completely searched. In
the latter case, predictions which might have been satisfied if more
of the full text had been searched do not result in a link.

The searches to test predictions are aborted in order to prevent links from being constructed which could not be used by our
auto-abstracting procedure. The procedure requires that a special
kind of path be formed from the links produced by the searches.
This path is called the principal path. The principal path is formed
of links between nonadjacent sentences. Only those links are used which
do not connect sentences occurring between linked nonadjacent sentences.
The sentences connected by these links serve to organize the text into maj-
or subunits just as did the sentences on the principal path in the sentence
outline of section 3. Further complications in the assignment of sentences
to the principal path are discussed in section 8.

The principal path has the property that every sentence of the
text is either:

1)   a sentence on the path;
2)   directly linked to a sentence on the path; or
3)   indirectly linked to a sentence on the path (i.e. a link to a
      sentence which is not a sentence on the path).

The restrictions which abort searches arise as follows:

1)   the predictions in each sentence are tested before moving to
      the right in the text to the next sentence;
2)   when two nonadjacent sentences are connected, the sentences
      occurring between them are called 'bracketed sentences'. As
      soon as the sentences have been bracketed, no new link can
      be constructed between them and the other sentences of the
      text. However, the bracketed sentences may have links con-
      structed between them, and these links, or any other links
      constructed before the sentences were bracketed, are pre-
      served.

The results of previous searches must be available each time
a new prediction is tested. This is because as a result of these
restrictions a previously successful search may be used to abort
a later search.

Additional restrictions are imposed on the links after all the searches have been completed. In order to construct a principal path, various links connecting sentences are shifted or deleted. The result is that the diagram of the links between the sentences is modified. The modifications are:

1) If a sentence is connected by searches to immediately neighboring sentences to its left and right, the link to the left is deleted.

2) If two nonadjacent sentences are linked, a dummy sentence is inserted on the link connecting them. As was stated above, a dummy sentence is a sentence number that acts as a structural element in the diagram but does not correspond to any actual sentence in the text. The function of the dummy sentence is to provide a sentence to which the (bracketed) sentences occurring between the nonadjacent sentences can eventually be linked, if they have not previously been linked to a sentence outside the brackets. This is necessary since (1) it would be arbitrary to connect these sentences with either of the nonadjacent sentences rather than the other, (2) every sentence in the text is required to be connected either directly or indirectly to a sentence on the principal path. The sentences 'bracketed' by the nonadjacent sentences and the dummy sentence are linked together in a closed loop or 'bow'. The sentences on the bow are connected to the principal path through the dummy sentence.

3) If a sentence has not been linked to any other sentence or is only linked as the result of searches from adjacent sentences (i. e. by vertical links in the diagram), it is not linked either directly or indirectly to a sentence on the principal path. Therefore an additional link is constructed which directly or indirectly connects it to the principal path. The sentence is placed when possible on the path which includes both its nearest neighbors, so that it occurs between these neighbors. The more complex conditions which may arise are dealt with in the flowchart of figures 11. 2, 11. 3, and 11. 4. The resulting additional link or links are represented in the diagram by dotted line(s). (See examples in Figure 11. 1.)

The detailed way in which these restrictions apply to processing is shown in the flowchart of figures 11.2, 11.3, and 11. 4. The flowchart is intended as a summary of this section. It determines on the basis of the current clue and whatever processing has already been done: (1) whether to continue or terminate testing a prediction,

(2) how to record this decision in the diagram of the text, (3) what the next prediction for testing should be.

Some additional possible restrictions on the processing are given in section 9.

8.0 PROCESSING TEXT PATHS

8.1 <u>Finding the principal path.</u> The diagram produced by processing a short text according to the flowchart of figures 11.2, 11.3, and 11.4 is shown in Figure 11.1. This summarizes the results of making and testing predictions for the text shown in Figure 11.5. The diagram is a record of the paths connecting the sentences of the text.

The diagram is a set of paths constructed out of the three types of links produced by processing the text: horizontal links which connect nonadjacent sentences, bow links which connect sentences bracketed by nonadjacent sentences, vertical links which connect adjacent sentences. A path is a connected set of links, all of the same type. Each of these paths has an interpretation in terms of the relative information content of the sentences on it.

In terms of information content, the most important kind of path is the principal path. This is the set of horizontal links connecting nonadjacent sentences in the diagram of the text. Sentences occurring between a pair of nonadjacent linked sentences are called 'bracketed sentences'. Sentences are assigned to the principal path only if the sentences have not been connected to either of the bracketing sentences prior to the construction of the horizontal link causing the bracketing. The principal path connects only those linked nonadjacent sentences which are not also bracketed sentences. The informational importance of the principal path derives from two facts: (1) its sentences are not dependent on other sentences of the text, (2) all the other sentences of the text are directly or indirectly dependent on the sentences of the principal path. (It should be noted that these properties also characterize those sentences of the text which are not connected by any kind of link to other sentences of the text as a result of the processing described in section 7. For this reason, these unconnected sentences are also assigned to the principal path.)

Any pair of linked nonadjacent sentences has a more significant information content in terms of the text than the sentences they bracket. This is because there is no sentence in the text on which bracketed sentences can be clearly shown dependent. As a result the bow path on which the bracketed sentences occur can be deleted without altering the basic organization of the text. The bow path provides a kind of detour in the text. The sentences on the bow path take up a side issue or comment on the sentences which bracket them. They are not needed by the discussion which includes the sentences which bracket them.

Vertical links connect a sentence to another sentence which is either more directly linked to the principal path or is on the principal path. Sentences on a vertical path elaborate the content of the sentence which is more directly linked to the main path.

If this interpretation of the relative information content of the sentences on the different kinds of paths is correct, dropping all bow paths and vertical paths should produce a reduced version of the text which would provide the basic information content of the text. This was done to the diagram in Figure 11.1b to produce the diagram in Figure 11.1c. Figure 11.1c has reduced the set of paths given in Figure 11.1b to provide only the principal path. The sentences on the principal path can be read as a plausible summary or abstract of the content of the 28 sentence stretch excerpted from D. H. Lawrence in Figure 11.5:

(1) But in Germany, in weird post-war Germany, he seemed snuffed out again. (15) Now, however, some of the coldness of numbed Germany seemed to have got into her breast too. (16) Another world! (21) Phillip shivered and looked yellower. (27) And she felt quite cold about Phillip's shivering. (28) Let him shiver.

This version would be more readable if clues relating the included sentences to sentences in the full text were omitted. The resulting version is:

1. He seemed snuffed out again.
15. Some of the coldness of numbed Germany seemed to have got into her breast too.
18. It was another world!
21. Phillip shivered and looked yellower.
27. She felt quite cold about Phillip's shivering.
28. Let him shiver.

8.2 Restoring paths. An important test of our interpretation of the relative information content of the different kinds of paths is that it can be used to produce successively more informative versions of the text using only the information provided by the diagram of the principal path in Figure 11.1c. In this diagram,

arrowheads were used to indicate a link to a sentence from a
deleted vertical path and dummy sentences were used to indicate
a link to a deleted bow path. According to our interpretation of the
relative information content:

1)   vertical paths are more informative than bow paths; and
2)   sentences which are more directly linked to the principal path
     are more informative than sentences which are less directly
     linked.

     This interpretation suggests the following cycle for gaining
access to and restoring paths. The cycle proceeds through the
principal path from left to right and:

1)   restores all vertical paths whose arrowheads are encountered;
2)   restores all bow paths whose dummy sentence is encountered;
3)   restores all arrowheads for vertical paths not yet restored on
     the restored paths; and
4)   repeats the above cycle on the enlarged path until the original
     set of paths is restored.

     As the cycle is repeated, first the elaborations and side re-
marks or detours on the sentences of the principal path supplied,
and then the elaborations and detours on the referent, are restored.
The result is a very natural way to restore the information content
of the text which suggests that the diagram accurately organizes
the sentences of the text in relation to their information value.

9.0 EXTENSION OF PROCESSING TO MATCHES ON NONIDENTICAL SPELLING

     As we go through the restoring cycle, each new path as it is
brought in has a list of sentences on it. These lists have some
special properties in terms of information content. Each list is
informationally highly coherent and relatively independent of the
other lists of sentences brought back by the restoring cycle. A
list deals with a specific topic and can be read informatively without considering the other lists of the text.

     Consider, for example, the lists which can be brought back
and defined by the restoring cycle for sentences 3-14. First, the
restoring cycle brings back a bow path with sentences 4-8-11-12
on it. These sentences deal with Phillip's feeling of unreality.
They function as a principal path in relation to the lists of sentences
brought back by the next cycle and provide the equivalent of topic

sentences for these lists. Next, the following vertical paths are
restored: sentences 4-5-6-7, dealing with his personal need for
Kathy; sentences 11-10-9, dealing with the consequences of her
presence for his feelings of unreality; sentences 12-13-14, dealing
with the effect of his declarations on Kathy. Finally, another bow
path is restored containing sentence 3 which describes the feelings
of unreality.

The coherence of lists makes possible an extension of processing to construct links between words of different spelling. This
was done informally when matching for clause type, but a specific
extension of processing to extend the conditions under which matches
are plausible is illustrated in what follows.

After lists have been constructed additional searches seem
reasonable within lists using the rules already presented in figures
11.2, 11.3, and 11.4. The plan for extending the processing is
to attempt to validate plausible matches between differently spelled
words for a specific text. If it is possible to construct a link between two vocabulary items which have been treated as equivalent
in other texts, the match is considered to be validated.

The processing to execute this plan is:

1)   make searches on words with unsatisfied predictions. Use the
       same procedure that was used originally, i.e. that described
       in the flowchart of figures 11.2, 11.3, and 11.4;

2)   if a search encounters a word which has been treated as its
       lexical equivalent in other texts, construct a supplementary
       link;

3)   delete this link if it would connect two previously constructed
       lists.

In order to accomplish this processing, a list of lexical equivalents from other texts would be required. How to produce such
lists will not be discussed here. A thesaurus is an example of such
a list. In terms of any specific text, it simply represents a set of
hypotheses to be tested and validated.

The fact of list coherence is the basis for validating these
entries for a particular text. The reasoning is that pairs of equivalents characterize text for particular subject matter areas. Therefore, if two words have previously been treated as equivalent, we
are less surprised if they are equivalent in sentences of the same
text than if the sentences in which they occur are drawn from
more than one document. This is because sentences from a single
text are more likely to be dealing with the same subject area. This

likelihood is greatly increased when they are in the same list,
because this would lead us to expect them to be dealing with the
same topic. Accordingly, if two such words of different spelling
can be used to construct a link within a list, their equivalence has
been validated for the text in which they occur.

One result of contructing this supplementary link is to introduce into the text diagram additional structure which might otherwise have gone unrecognized. A second result is to provide information about the semantic organization of the text. The lexical
equivalents which can be validated for the text lead us to certain
assumptions about the topics it deals with. These help us in
interpreting it. For example, if the pair of words strand and
filament are validated as lexical equivalents for a specific text by
this procedure, it will not be surprising that the text deals with
botany, but it will be surprising if the text deals with geography.

The dictionary does not provide information about lexical
equivalence for the clues used in matching on clause type. These
clues merely mark a clause as dependent and indicate the direction
in which text should be searched in order to test the prediction that
there is another clause on which it is dependent. Unlike the noun
clues, no way is provided for deciding whether or not the clause has
been encountered. The first clause encountered in the appropriate
direction is treated as satisfying the prediction. Since all clauses
are teated as being of the same type for satisfying the prediction,
matches on clause type should strictly be considered as tentative.
Additional information could have been provided in the dictionary to
distinguish the different kinds of clauses marked for clause type.
This would have required the following additional step in the processing in order to validate the tentative links. If the link previously constructed as a tentative link fails because of the dictionary
information, delete the link and replace it with a special link to
indicate a weaker tie. The result of this processing would be to subdivide the lists further. The special link would indicate the breaks
within lists.

When this extension of processing is applied to nouns, it provides semantic information as well as additional list organization to
the text. The fact that certain pairs of lexical items are validated
for a specific text is significant information about the semantic
organization of the text. In the case of nouns, such lexical equivalents are traditionally called synonyms. Although it is not conclusive, by the same reasoning the lack of match between the
words 'creature' (sentence 13) and 'beast' (sentence 16) in the

sample text is also information about the semantic organization
of the text.   The two words are synonyms in some texts but in this
text they do not function as synonyms since they cannot be validated.
Although they refer to the same individual, in fact, 'creature' is
used in affectionate retrospect while 'beast' refers to the harsh
present of the story.

10.0 CONCLUSION

A computational approach has been used here to recognize
the important or significant sentences of a text without knowing
their meaning.   It was first necessary to construct a description
of the organization of the text.   The application of the same computational approach to other texts provides a good test of insights into
text organization.   The prime significance of the computational
approach is that it allows us to convert our insights into processing
which has testable consequences.   The computational method
described in this paper has been experimentally applied to a variety
of texts, both fiction and technical.   Portions of the technique have
been programmed for use in a computer information retrieval
system.

The computational approach can be extended to other texts
only if additional entries are made to the abridged dictionary provided here.   Each dictionary entry represents a minor hypothesis
about how text is organized.   The flowchart represents a major
hypothesis about how these minor hypotheses work together to
organize the text.   Hypotheses can be entered into the processor
either as dictionary entries or modifications of the flowchart.

If a hypothesis can be inserted into the dictionary without
changing the number of fields in the format or the instructions
which occur in particular fields, it is a minor hypothesis.   If its
entry into the dictionary causes wrong processing, the minor
hypothesis is invalidated.   If the hypothesis is not a minor hypothesis,
it is a major hypothesis which may lead to modification in the flowchart as well as the dictionary.

It is by such a process of trial and error within a developing
framework of hypotheses that the technique discussed in this paper
was developed.

DICTIONARY APPENDIX

The functions of the dictionary are described in section 6. The dictionary used in processing the sample text is given at the end of this section. The dictionary is arranged by type of processing and thus avoids repetition because all the clues listed under a particular format have the same information and processing rules associated with them.

The unabridged version of the dictionary includes two items not entered into the abridged version. Neither of these items is used in the processing of the sample text. The information omitted is from Field-3, which additionally specifies the matches proposed by Field-2:

1)   Only the single entry TYPE-ϕ is given for TYPE, although in fact a number of clause types could be distinguished and utilized in different ways in the processing. A possible extension of the processing which utilizes a greater variety of clause types is discussed in section 9.

2)   Not all nouns make equally good matches for linking sentences as the dictionary might suggest. There is a class of nouns whose major function is to provide something to be modified. An example would be the noun issue in the expression clarification of the nuclear issue. Here the modifier is lexically significant while the noun itself is relatively insignificant. The unabridged dictionary distinguishes between these two kinds of nouns in order to organize the processing so that these more significant matches are attempted before the less significant matches. Although this type of processing is necessary for technical prose, it was not needed in the D. H. Lawrence selection and so is not entered into the dictionary.

The formats are named with different letters of the alphabet. Under each format the clues are listed in alphabetical order. The format letters have been inserted into the text to the right of the clue they are associated with. A single clue may have more than one dictionary format associated with it. In that case the convention applies that the earlier alphabet symbol should be tried first. If it succeeds the other is not tried. Format letters have been assigned so that noun matches will be tried before clause-type matches.

Slashes separate the different fields for each entry. An instruction field is ignored in the processing when marked with a dash. As soon as a match is made on a given search, that search is terminated. Instructions in a given field to search in both directions are executed. The order in which searches are made is arbitrary. In the case of a match, only the first successful search in that direction is completed.

The subinstructions are:

Field 1:   NOT-1   do not specify a prediction for this clue which makes use of TYPE-$\emptyset$ unless the clue precedes the main verb of the sentence

            DASH   No instruction given
Field 2:   SELF   match on clause type. Clause type is determined by the clue and specified in Field-3

            NPL   match on a noun of the same spelling as the noun to the left of the clue in the noun phrase containing the clue

            NPR   match on a noun of the same spelling as the noun to the right of the clue in the noun phrase containing the clue
Field 3:   TYPE-$\emptyset$ the clause type specified by the clue is TYPE-$\emptyset$. This is equivalent to a match on the adjacent sentence if there is any. This is true because in this version of the dictionary all clauses have been assigned to this type.

            DASH   No instruction given
Field 4:   LEFT   make a search through the sentences to the left of the current sentence

            RIGHT   make a search through the sentences to the right of the current sentence
Field 5:   END   make a search to the end of the text in order to test the prediction of Fields 2 and 3

            NEXT   make a search no further than the end of the 'next' sentence of the text where 'next' is determined by Field 4

In any field, a dash means that there is no instruction of any kind given by that field.

The formats are:

A: _____/NPR, NPL/_____/LEFT/NEXT
B: _____/NPR, NPL/_____/LEFT, RIGHT/END
C: _____/NPR/_____/LEFT/END
D: _____/NPR/_____/LEFT/NEXT

E: NOT/SELF/TYPE/LEFT/NEXT
F: NOT/SELF/TYPE-ϕ/RIGHT/NEXT
G: NOT/SELF/TYPE-ϕ/LEFT/END

The dictionary is:

A: _____/NPR, NPL/_____/LEFT/NEXT
   even
B: _____/NPR, NPL/_____/LEFT, RIGHT/END
   of
   's
C: _____/NPR/_____/LEFT/END
   all   only
   another   such
   little   this
   most
D: _____/NPR/_____/LEFT/NEXT
   her
   their
E: NOT/SELF/TYPE/LEFT/NEXT

all	hardly	only	preposition + noun
and	how	so	(except of)
another	however	such	
but	little	this	
could	most	truly	
frightfully	now	would	

F: NOT/SELF/TYPE-ϕ/RIGHT/NEXT
   don't
   let
   not
   there
G: NOT/SELF/TYPE-ϕ/LEFT/END
   feel/felt
   seem/seemed
   "

Miscellaneous:

In addition the dictionary may include information of the kind discussed in section 9. An example of such thesaurus information is the entry he = him, which is to be interpreted as he matches him when searches are made on him.

NOTES

1. The more usual term for this process in information retrieval is <u>auto-extracting</u>. <u>Auto-abstracting</u> normally implies that the sentences extracted from the text have been altered to increase their informational value. Nevertheless I have preferred to use this term because of its more familiar associations.

2. Programming languages for dealing with such list structures have been developed. A good introduction to the subject is Newell, A. et al., <u>Information Processing Language—V Manual,</u> The Rand Corporation (Englewood Cliffs, New Jersey, 1964). A programming language for a similar application to the one described in this paper is reported on under the name CORAL in Sutherland, I. E. sketchpad: <u>A Man-machine Communication System</u>, Lincoln Report TR-396 (Cambridge, Massachusetts: MIT, Electronic System Laboratory, January 1963).

3. A review of work on similar dependency phenomena is given in Viola Waterhouse, 'Independent and Dependent Sentences', <u>International Journal of American Linguistics</u> 29: 1. 45-54 (1963). Rules dealing with similar dependencies are discussed in Z. S. Harris, 'Co-occurrence and Transformation in Linguistic Structure', <u>Lg.</u> 33: 3. 283-340 (1957), see especially the section entitled <u>Transformations in Sentence Sequences.</u> An account of dependencies, also embedded in a computational framework, is presented in John C. Olney, 'Some Patterns observed in the Contextual Specialization of Word Senses', <u>Information Storage and Retrieval</u> 2. 79-101.

a. SYMBOLS

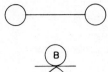

Arrowhead indicates direction of dependence between sentences in diagram.

Horizontal link between nonadjacent sentences which are not included between nonadjacent sentences.

Bow and B-node indicate links between sentences included between nonadjacent sentences. B-node is the dummy sentence thru which these sentences are joined to the principal path.

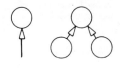

Vertical links between adjacent sentences. Note that a vertical link may be drawn on a slant.

Dotted link(s) join(s) an otherwise unconnected S to the text paths so it is ultimately linked to the principal path.

b. FULL SET OF PATHS THROUGH TEXT

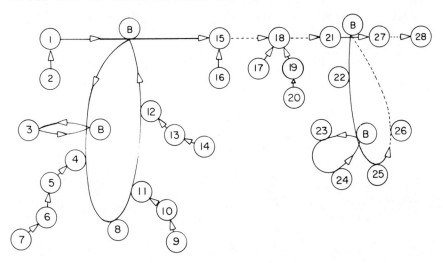

c. REDUCED SET OF PATHS THROUGH TEXT (PRINCIPAL PATH)

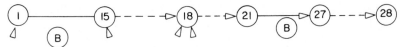

Figure 11.1   Notational Conventions for Paths Through Text

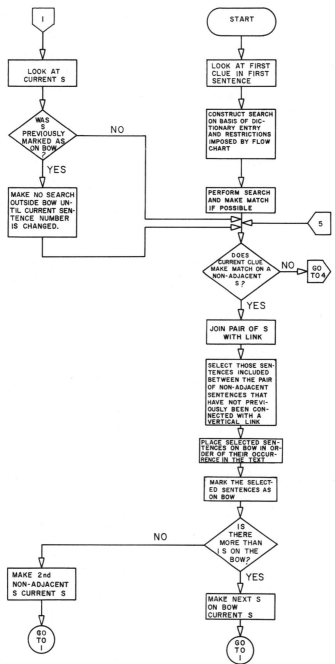

Figure II.2   FLOWCHART FOR CONSTRUCTING A TEXT

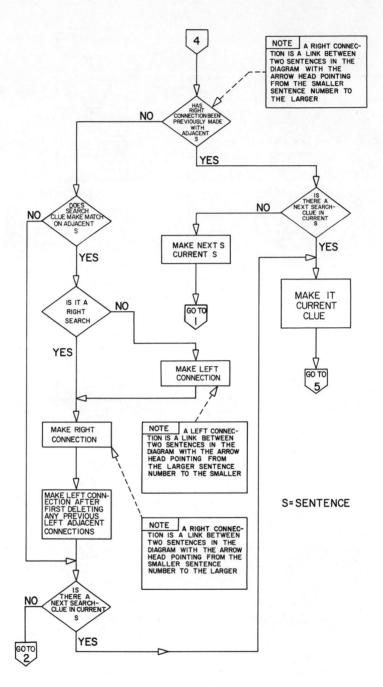

Figure 11.3

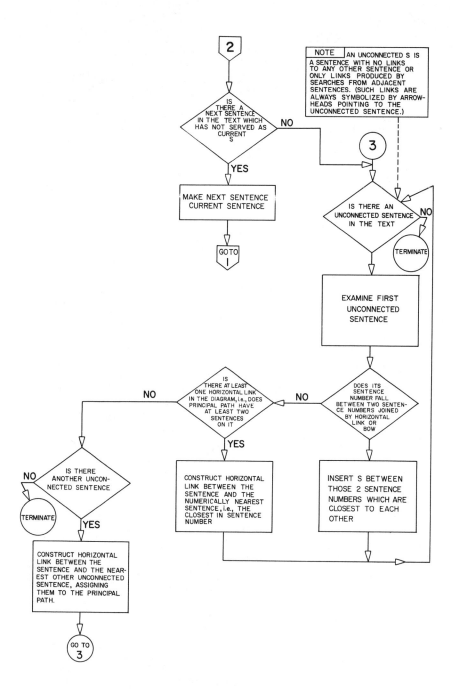

Figure II.4

---

1. But (E) in Germany (E), in weird post-war Germany (E), he
   seemed (G) snuffed out again.

2. The air was so (E) cold and vacant, [That] all (C, E) feeling
   seemed (G) to have gone out of (B) the country.

3. Emotion, even (A) sentiment, was numbed quite (E) dead, as
   in a frost-bitten limb.

4. And (E) if the sentiment were numbed out of (B) him, he was
   truly (E) dead.

5. " (G) I'm most frightfully (E) glad you've come, Kathy," he
   said.

6. " (G) I could (E) hardly (E) have held out another (C, E) day
   here, without you.

7. I feel (G) you're the only (C, E) thing on earth that remains
   real."

8. " (G) You don't (F) seem (G) very real to me," she said.

9. " (G) I'm not (F) real!

10. I'm not (F) ! --not when I'm alone.*

---

* D. H. Lawrence, 'The Border Line', in The Woman Who Rode
Away and Other Stories, Berkley Publishing Corporation, New
York City, January 1962, pp. 84, 85.

Text conventions used in insertion of dictionary information and
marking of constructions:

   ---- main verb: finite verb forms, nonfinite forms govern-
     ed by auxiliaries or modals, predicate adjectives
   ——— clue and the construction it marks
   === clue and the construction it marks where a prediction
     has been satisfied in the text
  ( ) dictionary format symbol

Note: Only those constructions marked by clues are indicated. All
dictionary information which would not have been used because of
information in the first field of the format has been supressed.

Figure 11.5. Sample Text Excerpted from the short story
'The Border Line' by D. H. Lawrence

Figure 11.5, page 2.

11. But (E) when I'm with you I'm the most (C, E) real man alive.

12. I know it!"

13. This (C, E) was the sort of (B) thing that had fetched her in the past, thrilled her through and through in her (D) womanly conceit, even made her fall in love with the little (C) creature who could so generously admit such (C, E) pertinent truths.

14. [It was] so (E) different from the lordly Alan, who expected a woman to bow down to him!

15. Now (E), however (E) some of (B) the coldness of (B) numbed Germany seemed (G) to have got into her (D) breast too.

16. She felt (G) a cruel derision of (B) the whimpering little (C) beast who claimed reality only through a woman.

17. She did not (F) answer him, but looked out at the snow falling between her and the dark trees.

18. Another (C, E) world!

19. When the snow left off, how (E) bristling and ghostly the cold fir-trees looked, tall, conical creatures crowding darkly and half-whitened with snow!

20. So (E) tall, so (E) wolfish!

21. Phillip shivered and looked yellower.

22. There (F) was shortage of (B) fuel, shortage of (C) food, shortage of (B) everything.

23. He wanted (E) Katherine to go to Paris with him.

24. But (E) she would (E) stay at least two weeks near her (D) people.

25. The shortage she would (E) put up with.

26. She saw at evening the string of (B) decent townsfolk waiting in the dark — the town was not half-lighted — to fill their (D) hot-water bottles at the hot spring outside the Kurhaus, silent, spectral, unable to afford fire to heat their (D) own water.

27. And (E) she felt (G) quite cold about Phillip's (B) shivering.

28. Let (F) him shiver.

Chapter 12

Man-Machine Communication in Programmed Instruction

Bernard Spolsky

1.0 BACKGROUND

While the efficacy of programmed instruction as a teaching tool has already been amply demonstrated, there remain many questions as to the most effective form of presentation. Programs may be organized in many different ways (the technical term used for such organization is a paradigm), and may call for various types of responses from the student. This paper presents a programming strategy that will allow students to construct their responses and will provide different branches for different responses.

1.1 Paradigms. The two main classes of paradigms are linear and branching, with the possibility of various degrees of combination of the two extremes. A purely linear program is one in which the frames or items follow in an inflexible order; the student works through them one after the other irrespective of his ability, the accuracy of his responses, or any other individual differences. In a pure branching program, the order in which the frames are presented depends entirely on his responses; a mechanism of some kind decides, on the basis of each response (or of the cumulative history of a number of responses), which frame he should do next.

There are strong arguments in favor of branching. Even if one does not accept the Crowderian model,[1] it is often considered valuable to allow for some degree of branching within a basically linear program (e.g. on the basis of criterial test items, to shunt the student onto a faster or slower program track, or to present more practice items in a matter that has not been mastered). A branching program allows for differences between students; a linear program forces all students to follow the same track. If a linear program is aimed at the slower student, and is successful in ensuring that the student is correct in at least 90 per cent of

his responses,[2] the brighter student is almost certain to be bored
and to find the program insultingly simple-minded; if it is aimed at
the brighter student, it is probable that the slower student will
find many of the steps too large and will consequently make so
many erroneous responses that the effective working of the principle
of reinforcement of desired behavior will be destroyed. There can
be no happy medium, for there will always be students who are
brighter or slower than those for whom the program was constructed.[3]
The only solution to this dilemma is the provision of the maximum
possibility of program branching on the basis of student responses.

1.2 <u>Response modes.</u> The three main types of student response
are covert, overt constructed, and overt multiple-choice. In the
constructed response mode, which is the form favored by those who
follow Skinner most closely, the student makes up his own answer,
writing or speaking it as the program directs.

In the covert mode, the student simply reads the text; he need
make no overt response, for there are no blanks. The program is
however essentially the same as a constructed response one with
the blanks already filled in. For example, a constructed response
frame might appear like this:

The underlined word in 'He <u>ate</u> an apple' is a _____.   verb

In a reading program, this would appear as:

The underlined word in 'He <u>ate</u> an apple' is a verb.

In the multiple-choice mode, the student selects one of a
number of possible responses offered to him. A frame in this
form would appear like this:

What part of speech is the underlined word in the sentence
'He <u>ate</u> an apple. '?
   a. verb
   b. noun
   c. adverb
   d. pronoun

While there is no conclusive evidence as to which type leads
to the most efficient learning, it is a reasonable assumption that
there are areas in which constructed responses are essential.
Foreign language teaching is such an area, for there the aim is
often to teach the student to recall as well as to recognize correct
responses. Even if we accept the hypothesis that training the

student to discriminate correct and incorrect forms will transfer to his being able to produce correct forms, there is a stage at which the student must be able to make up his own responses, and it is these constructed responses which are important in deciding how well he has mastered the material that has been presented so far.

The present state of techniques in programmed instruction permits the use of any response mode with linear programs, but only of multiple-choice responses with branching programs. This paper shows how it is possible to use a computer in order to build a branching program that uses the constructed response mode.

2.0 THE PROBLEM

The crux of the problem that has been described is how to build into a program a device that will analyze the response that the student has made up, and, on the basis of this analysis, decide which branch, or which frame, is to be presented to the student next. The programming logic implied is shown in Figure 12.1. The key problem is in Box 3, where the response is analyzed, and Box 4 where a decision must be made as to which frame should be next presented.

Let us consider some possible solutions. In a program that uses multiple-choice responses, the solution is relatively straight-forward. Consider Example 1.

Example 1.   A branching multiple-choice frame

Make this sentence negative: We went.
a. We went not   (Go to frame 24)
b. We did not go.   (Go to frame 35)
c. We did not gone.   (Go to frame 15)
d. We go not.   (Go to frame 45)

In this example, it will be seen that the solution has been to pro-vide each of the choices offered with the address of the frame that is its appropriate successor; the correct answer will of course carry on with the main line of the program, while the distractors will lead to suitable remedial branches. This system is easily automated,[4] but it is to be noted that it involves two serious limitations:

1)   It calls for the student to recognize the correct answer rather than to produce it.

2)   It identifies only those errors whose possible occurrence has

been predicted by the programmer when he made up the distractors. In Example 1, for instance, there is no allowance
for the student's tendencies to make up such responses as
We not went or We did not went.

Another solution is to have frames in which branching is decided by treating a constructed response as being either right or
wrong. Such a frame is illustrated in Example 2.

Example 2.   A branching either-or constructed response frame

> Make this sentence negative: We went.
> Correct response: We did not go.
> If correct, go to frame 30.
> If wrong, go to frame 15.

In this example, the student makes up his response which is then
compared with the correct response. If he is right (and some degree
of tolerance of, for example, spelling may be built in), he con-
tinues with the main track; if wrong, he may be shunted onto a
remedial loop or returned to go through the previous section again.
Such a frame is used in many linear programs. It is also the type
that has been used in reported computer-based programs because
it lends itself to relatively straight-forward programming. In the
IBM project, for instance,[5] the author of a program specifies not
only the answer or answers which he will accept as correct, but
also any student errors that he anticipates. In this way, provision
is made for dealing with predictable wrong answers. But it is
obvious that this solution too remains severely limited in its
ability to deal with the great variety of erroneous responses that
the student may make.

The solution offered in this paper is a program that will carry
out the following steps:

1)   Analyze any response that the student may construct;
2)   identify as precisely as possible all errors there may be in it;
3)   inform the student of the nature of his error; and
4)   select and present appropriate remedial work.

Such an operation approximates most closely to the behavior of a
good tutor; it can be carried out with the aid of a computer, and its
feasibility is primarily a problem of computational linguistics.

There are a large number of other advantages which accrue
when a computer is used to control programmed instruction; in
this paper, attention will be paid to the possibility of the automatic
generation of frames, and mention will be made of the value of the

computer for gathering statistics and for modifying the operation
of a program in the light of the cumulative history of the experiences
of the student working on it. However, it is clear that one of the
main obstacles to developing a program that will give the maximum
attention to individual differences has been the lack of a method of
dealing satisfactorily with unpredicted erroneous responses. In
this paper, it is shown that this obstacle can be overcome by using
a suitable method of analyzing the material to be taught.

    3. 1 <u>Scope of the program</u>. The preparation of material to be
presented through the medium of programmed instruction calls
first of all for the careful definition, in explicit and operational
terms, of the terminal behavior that the program is designed to
shape. When it is desired to make use of a computer to control
the presentation, this definition must be even more precise than
usual, for it will have to be programmed for computer recognition.
In this paper, therefore, an area to be taught has been selected that
can be more or less exhaustively described.

    The program outlined in this paper is one that will form part
of a course in English as a foreign or second language; it tests
and teaches the formation of English verb phrases. For the purpose of the program, the verb phrase is defined as consisting of
a subject pronoun (which is optional), one or more (optional)
auxiliary verbs, and a verb base. It thus covers phrases ranging
in complexity from <u>Eat!</u> to <u>Might he not have been being eaten?</u>.

    This program is intended to be preparation for one in which
the student will be taught the appropriate uses of the tenses that
he has here learned to form. In other words, at the present stage
he will form the phrase in response to a specific instruction such
as 'Make this sentence past'; in the projected continuation, the
stimulus will be something like 'Add the word <u>yesterday</u> to this
sentence. '

    The terminal behavior that the program aims to shape may
be specified as follows:

When the student is presented with an instruction and an English
verb phrase, he will respond with an appropriate adaptation of
the verb phrase in accordance with the instruction he has been
given.

For example, when he is presented with the instruction 'Make this
sentence negative: <u>We went.</u>', he will respond <u>We did not go</u>. The
full repertory of instructions is detailed in Table 12. 2.

The analysis of the English verb phrase on which the program is based is set out in the state diagram shown in Figure 12.2. [6] Following this, it is possible to consider any verb phrase as consisting of the following elements:

1. Subject pronoun
2. Concord marking
3. Modal auxiliary
4. Perfect auxiliary
5. Continuous (progressive) auxiliary
6. Passive auxiliary
7. Preterit (past) marking
8. Negative marking
9. Question marking
10. Dictionary item (base form).

3.2 <u>Conditions</u>. It has been assumed that the student will type his responses into a console connected with the computer. Frames will be either typed out on the same console or displayed by some other device. The student's ability to use a keyboard is therefore assumed.

4.0 PEDAGOGICAL STRATEGY

One of the greatest values of programmed instruction is that it can be used as an instrument of research into the value of different teaching methods, to the extent that it makes it possible to control many variables in the learning situation and provides a clear and precise record of how certain material has been presented to the learner. This program has been planned to take full advantage of this point; the various strategies that have been built into it may easily be modified if it is desired to test their relative effectiveness.

The decision to build a remedial program rather than one which presents totally new material has been arrived at for two reasons:

1) Most programmed work in foreign languages has been concerned with the beginning stage where it is somewhat easier to define the starting point and the order of steps that are to be followed. This program can give some idea of how more advanced work may usefully be supplemented and accompanied by a series of small selfcontained programmed units.

2) The remedial framework is the one that calls for the maximum use of branching based on the analysis of the responses that the student has made. It would be relatively simple to tie the

analysis subprogram into an initial teaching program, adding limitations as to the remedial subroutines to be used at various stages.

The pedagogical strategy of the program may be considered as consisting of four stages, the decision logic being shown in the flow-chart in Figure 12. 3.

STAGE I. Diagnostic frames (Box 1) The main track of the program consists of a number of diagnostic frames which test the student's ability to carry out all the operations in forming English verb phrases that the program deals with. At this stage, the student is presented with a frame of the type shown in Example 3.

Example 3. Sample diagnostic frame

FRAME NUMBER 1
MAKE THIS SENTENCE NEGATIVE: WE WENT.

The student types his response; if it is correct, the next diagnostic frame is presented. In the present state of the program, a set of diagnostic frames has been prepared manually, but this manual preparation will be replaced by the automatic frame generation procedure described below (section 5. 32).

STAGE II. Try again (Box 3) If the analysis routine discovers that there is an error in the student's response, he is asked to try again. This stage is included in order to allow the student to correct any errors he may have made in typing; it will also deal with spelling errors. If the second try is correct, the next diagnostic frame is presented. A statistics program, not considered here in any detail, would be included to keep track of the number of second tries that a student has made.

STAGE III. Cued response (Box 5) If, when it is analyzed, the second try is found to still contain an error, the student is informed of the type of mistake that he has made. The program will print out a clear cue such as:

YOU HAVE MADE AN ERROR. YOU HAVE NOT MADE THE SUBJECT AND THE VERB AGREE. TRY AGAIN.

The statistics program would keep a record of such cues, and would give extra remedial work when repeated cues have been needed for the same error.

STAGE IV; <u>Remedial routine</u> (Box 7) If the student still makes an error after a cue has been presented, or if it has been necessary to give him repeated cues for the same error, the program will present a remedial teaching routine which will show him how to form the correct response and which will give him practice in the appropriate form. An example of a remedial routine is given in detail later. The last step of this stage will be to present again the diagnostic frame in which the error was first made.

5.0 DESCRIPTION OF PROGRAM OPERATION

The program as a whole consists of the following sections:

1. Main routine
2. Analysis of student response
3. Preparation of frames
4. Remedial routines
5. Remedial frame generation
6. Statistics

5.1 <u>Main routine.</u> The decision logic for the main routine is shown in the flowchart in Figure 12.1.

5.20 <u>Analysis of student response.</u> The central part of the program is that part which analyzes the response that the student has typed, notes any errors that have been made in the formation of the verb phrase, and then compares the student's response with the correct response for the frame. This process involves coding the student's response into the format referred to in section 3.1 above. Example 4 shows a coded verb phrase.

Example 4. A coded verb phrase

We have not been asked

1. Subject pronoun : Plural
2. Concord marking : Plural or 1st person singular
3. Modal auxiliary : 0
4. Perfect auxiliary : 1
5. Continuous auxiliary : 0
6. Passive auxiliary : 1
7. Preterit marking : 0
8. Negative marking :1
9. Question marking : 1
10. Dictionary item : Past participle of ASK

The analysis falls into a number of subroutines described in the following sections.

5.21 <u>Abbreviations</u>. (For flowchart, see Figure 12.4) The
student's response is scanned for apostrophes; if they are found,
abbreviations are resolved using a dictionary that lists acceptable
forms and common errors.

5.22 <u>Tagging pronouns</u>. (For flowchart, see Figure 12.4) The
sentence is now scanned for a word on the pronoun list (HE, SHE,
IT, WE, THEY, YOU, and I); any pronoun found is tagged with the
appropriate concord marker (third person singular, plural, or first
person singular). Absence of a pronoun is interpreted as a mark
of the Imperative.

5.23 <u>Negatives and questions</u>. (For flowchart, see Figure 12.4)
The student's response is next scanned for the occurrence of the
word NOT; if it is found, the response is coded as 'Negative marking:
1.' The position of the tagged subject pronoun is now checked; if it
is found to be the second word in the sentence, the response is coded
as 'Question marking: 1.' If the pronoun is found to be in neither
initial nor second position, a notice of student error (Student error -
E11, misplaced subject) is recorded.

5.24 <u>Main look-up</u>. <u>Not</u> and the subject pronoun having been
tagged as no longer needed, each of the remaining words in the
student's response is looked up in the verb-form dictionary. This
dictionary contains all the forms of the auxiliary verbs that are
dealt with by the program, each marked with an appropriate grammar code (see Table 12.1). The grammar code marks the form as
being an auxiliary; identifies it as a part of one of the verbs BE,
HAVE, DO, CAN, MAY, MUST, SHALL, or WILL; notes restrictions
on its use in this form (e.g. AM is only used with the first person
singular; HAD is to be treated as a preterit of a past participle);
and gives restrictions on what suffixes may legitimately be attached
to it (e.g. AM may not be found with <u>ing</u>, <u>s</u>, or <u>ed</u>; BE may not be
found with <u>ed</u> or <u>s</u>). Also in the verb-form dictionary will be found
any forms of the verb or verbs that have been fed in with the frame
(see section 5.3 below on the preparation of frames). These forms
are similarly marked with a grammar code which here concerns
only restrictions on use and suffixes.

The main look-up routine is shown in the flowchart in Figure
12.4. As a word is looked up, its grammar code is entered in a
numbered coded word location, the first word going in Coded Word
Location I, the second in II, etc. If a word is not found in the verb-
form dictionary, it is checked for possible suffixes.

First, an S-stripping subroutine (shown in the flowchart in
Figure 12. 4) recognizes verbs that are in the third person singular
form.   This subroutine allows for various spellings of the third
singular present marker; it includes the possibilities of recognizing
two misspellings, the use of an S-form in the wrong position
(Student error-E21), and the use of an S-form in a question or a
negative sentence (E42).   If the marker is found, the code 'Third
person singular' is entered under verb concord of the Coded Word
Location.

If the word that has not been found in the verb-form dictionary
does not end with S but with ED, an ED-stripping subroutine (in
Figure 12. 5,   distinguishes between   preterits and past participles, [7]
recording notices of any errors that the student may have made in
spelling or information, and deciding the appropriate information
to be entered in the Coded Word Location.

Finally, an ING-stripping subroutine deals with any word not
so far identified; giving notice of wrongly formed present participles,
and of identifiable and unidentifiable spelling errors.

As a word is identified, its grammar code, sometimes as
modified by the stripping subroutine, is entered in the next empty
numbered coded word location.

5.25 Subject-verb concord.   In the next stage (shown in the
flowchart in Figure 12.5), the information in the first Coded Word
Location relevant to concord is entered in the coding of the response;
the concord marking of the pronoun and the concord marking of the
verb are now compared, any discrepancy being noted as an error.
All Coded Word Locations are now checked to see that there is no
word in an auxiliary verb position that is not marked as an auxiliary
verb, appropriate error notices being recorded if necessary.

5.26 Auxiliary verbs.   Each of the Coded Word Locations that
have been used is now checked in numerical order, and appropriate
information is recorded in the coded response location and in the
notice of student error location.   The coded response location has
the form shown in Example 4 above.   The recognition of a modal verb
leads to its presence being noted in the Modal auxiliary column; a
check is then made to be sure that the word in the following Coded
Word Location is a base form.   Similarly, subroutines deal with
the Perfect, the Continuous, and the Passive auxiliaries.   Finally,
a subroutine deals with the occurrence of the auxiliary do.   Notices
of student errors detail incorrectness of position or use of incorrect forms after an auxiliary verb.

5. 27 <u>Comparison with correct response</u>. The student's response has now been completely coded into the format shown in
Example 4, the information having been entered in the coded response location. The contents of the coded response location may
now therefore be compared with the correct response code, any
discrepancies leading to the appropriate error notices.

5. 30 <u>The preparation of frames</u>. The diagnostic frames referred to above (section 4, State I) may be prepared manually.
The format of a frame is shown in Example 5.

<u>Example 5.   Format of a typical diagnostic frame</u>

Frame number: 107
Instruction Code: 10000   (Interpretation: REPLACE THE
                                            SUBJECT OF THIS SENTENCE BY
                                            THE WORD 'HE')
Content: WE HAVE NOT BEEN ASKED.
Correct Response Code: Subject Pronoun: 3rd person singular
                                    Concord: 3rd person singular
                                    Modal: 0
                                    Perfect: 1
                                    Continuous: 0
                                    Passive: 1
                                    Preterit: 0
                                    Negative: 1
                                    Question: 0
Dictionary item with its grammar code: ASK base form
Remarks: Go to next diagnostic frame.

Manually prepared frames such as that in Example 5 could be
checked, by item analysis, for their usefulness, and a set of them
could form a diagnostic program.

5. 31 <u>Automatic generation of frames</u>. While the program will
be able to function satisfactorily with a set of manually prepared
frames, its value can be greatly increased by making it generate
its own diagnostic frames. This will mean, firstly, that the student
will not be limited to using a finite set of prepared frames, but can,
if necessary, come back and use the program again and again; and
secondly, as will be shown below in section 5. 50, the generation
strategy proves to be an effective way of dealing with the problems
of the remedial subroutines.

The basic concept on which this automatic generation is based
is the use of a randomly-generated code number, the interpretation
of which is restricted in certain ways.

A frame generation program consists of three main parts:

I.   The first part of a frame generating program is a store of randomly-generated numbers, each consisting of 36 binary digits. This number of digits suffices for the purposes of the present program, but more would be needed for a more sophisticated program. The interpretation of these digits is shown in Figure 12.6.

II. The second part will be a subroutine (shown in the flowchart in Figure 12.7) which takes the first six digits, looks them up in the instruction code (see Table 12.2), and sets certain of the other digits as determined by the code list. For example, if the first six digits are 000000, the instruction code interprets this as 'Make this sentence negative:'; the digit in the random number that will be interpreted as 'Negative' for the correct response code is therefore set at '1', while the digit that will be interpreted as 'Negative' for the content generating code is set at '0'. No other digits will be changed unless some other restriction has been imposed for this stage of the student's instruction.[8]   Table 12.2 gives full details of the alterations that will be made to the randomly-generated numbers.

III. The third part of the frame generation program generates the frame as follows:

1. It allocates a number to the frame and prints it out.
2. It prints out the instruction that was looked up in the previous part.
3. It generates and prints out the content.[9]
4. It takes the appropriate digits in the randomly-generated number (as modified by the previous part), and prepares the correct response code.
5. It adds the dictionary item that has been used for the frame, together with its grammar code, to the verb dictionary.
6. It adds remarks to the frame giving the address of the next frame to be presented after this one.

5.40 Remedial routines. When any notices of student errors have been recorded, they are first ordered and then treated in accordance with the strategy explained in section 4 above; the student is first asked to try again, then given a precise cue, and finally a remedial teaching program is presented. A remedial teaching program consists of a number of manually prepared frames (see example 7) and of instructions to generate other frames (see next section).

5.50 <u>Remedial routine generation.</u> As has been seen, the
basic frame generation program described above introduced the
concept of combining the use of a randomly-generated number with
certain restrictions on its interpretation. This concept is carried
on in the remedial routine generation program, where the same
randomly-generated numbers are used, but added restrictions are
placed on their use. Thus, the remedial frames include not only
these restrictions, but also preset remarks which control the path
to be followed before returning to the diagnostic frame or dealing
with other errors. The working of this principle is made clearer
if one considers the specifications for one such remedial teaching
routine. Each of the following sections details a part of this
routine; it will be seen that not all routines will include all the
parts.

5.51 <u>Precise identification of error.</u> In certain cases, it is
possible to identify the error with more precision than has been
done by the main analysis routine. The main program, for instance,
identifies a student error in concord (Student Error-E32, subject
and verb do not agree in person and number). A short subroutine
(shown in the flowchart in Figure 12.8) decides which of six possible incorrect combinations has been used, recognizing for instance
that a third person singular verb has been used with a first person
singular subject pronoun, and gives the address of the appropriate
remedial teaching routine.

5.52 <u>Further testing.</u> It is next advisable to check that the
identification has been right; that the student's error has arisen
from the precise problem that has been identified rather than from
a combination of elements. It is also desirable to know how generalized is the error. One or more frames are therefore presented
which will call on the student to carry out the instruction in isolation.
The specifications for this part of the routine are given in Example
6; it will be seen that this sample routine consists in effect of instructions to generate frames from randomly-generated numbers
that have to be modified to suit the special purposes of the frames.

<u>Example 6.   Three sample frames for testing of error</u>

Address of this routine: E3222 (subject is plural, verb is third
                                             person singular)
Generate remedial frames, from randomly-generated numbers,
subject to the restrictions detailed:
Frame number: E3222 1

Instruction set as: 10100 (Interpretation: Replace the subject
                                   of this sentence by the word they)
Content: Set all modals and auxiliaries at 0. Preterit 0.
Correct response: Modals, auxiliaries, Preterit all 0.
Remarks: If right, print 'RIGHT. AND THIS.' and then go to
              E 3222 2.
              If wrong, print 'NO. LOOK AT THIS.' and then go to
              E 3222 4.
Frame number: E 3222 2
Instruction set as: 10011 (Interpretation: Replace the subject
                                   of this sentence by the word 'we.')
Content and Correct Response: Modals, auxiliaries, preterit,
                                   all 0.
Remarks: If right, print 'RIGHT. AND THIS.' and then go to
              E 3222 3.
              If wrong, print 'NO. LOOK AT THIS.' and then go to
              E 3222 5.
Frame number: E 3222 3
Instruction set as: 10101 (Interpretation: Replace the subject
                                   of this sentence by the word you.)
Content and Correct Response: Modals, auxiliaries, preterit,
                                   all 0.
Remarks: If right, print 'GOOD. THE LETTER "S" IS NOT
              ADDED TO FORMS OF THE VERB AFTER THEY,
              WE, YOU. NOW TRY THIS AGAIN.' and present
              the original diagnostic frame again. If wrong,
              print 'NO, LOOK AT THIS' and go to E 3222 6.

It will be seen that the first of the frames in Example 6 calls on the
student to replace the word he by the word they in a sentence that
contains a simple tense form. If he does this correctly, the next
frame will call for the use of we and the third for you. The third
frame, if answered correctly, will include a restatement of the
rule that has been broken in the diagnostic item. Each of these
identification frames has, as its address in the case an error is
made, a remedial instruction frame.

5.53 Remedial teaching. We have seen in the previous two
sections that the error noted in the main analysis routine has been
identified as precisely as possible, and that the program has decided which rule the student failed to apply. The remedial teaching
frames are now used to present this rule and to drill the student
in its application. The specifications for this part of the program
are illustrated in Example 7.

Example 7. Three sample teaching frames

Frame number: E 3222 4
Print out: HE EATS.
             THEY EAT
             WHAT LETTER DOES THE VERB AFTER HE END
             WITH?   (Allow space for student to respond)
             IT ENDS WITH THE LETTER S. DOES THE VERB
             AFTER THEY END WITH THE LETTER S? NO.
             THE LETTER S IS NOT ADDED TO FORMS OF
             THE VERB AFTER THE WORD THEY.
             Go to E 3222 1.
Frame Number: E 3222 5
Print out the same material as in E 3222 4, substituting WE
for THEY.
Go to E 3222 2.
Frame Number: E 3222 6
Print out the same material as in E 3222 4, substituting YOU
for THEY.
Go to E 3222 3.

These remedial teaching frames may take the form, as was
shown in Example 7, of simple linear constructed-response
items, or they could be built as multiple-choice items with
branching for incorrect replies. However, to have remedial
teaching frames that call for constructed responses that will
need to be analyzed by the main analysis routine would call
for more complication than is justified in the early stages of
the development of the program.

5.54 Practice. The final section of a remedial routine is a
number of practice frames. In the example given, these are the
same in form as those that were used to identify the error, but
the random generation will ensure some variation in content. It
will be noted that the final frame of a remedial routine states the
rule that is in question and then calls for the diagnostic item in
which the original error was made to be presented again.

5.60 Statistics. Reference has been made earlier to the possibility of building in a statistics program. At a more sophisticated
stage, this could be used to control various parts of the main program, so creating a greater degree of program flexibility and
allowing for individual student differences. In an early stage,
however, it would be valuable to set up a program to collect the
following information:

a. Information about the student (name, native language, standard).
b. A list of frames that have been presented to each student.
c. A list of errors that have been recognized by the program and
    that the student has corrected 1. on the second try;
                                    2. when a cue has been given; and
                                    3. after a remedial instruction
                                       routine.
d. A list of errors that have been recognized by the program but
    that the student has still not corrected after a remedial routine.
e. Details of remedial teaching routines that have been used.
f. A list of misspellings or of words that have been so labeled.
    This list, correlated with the information about the student's
    native language and standard, would serve later as the basis
    for planning a way to build into the program the ability to offer
    remedial spelling teaching.

6.0 CONCLUSION

The aim of this paper has been to show that it is feasible to
set up an automated teaching program that will permit branching
on the basis of responses that the student constructs himself. The
crux of the matter has been shown to be in the analysis program,
and the problem has been shown to be solvable through a linguistic
analysis of the material being dealt with. That is to say, given a
workable method of analyzing input texts and coding their elements
so that they may be compared with desired inputs, it is possible
to use this process of analysis and comparison as a method of
identifying errors that the student has made in his responses to
diagnostic questions. It has also been shown that this analysis
program lends itself to the requirements of a frame generation
procedure that will form part of a program to prepare material
that can be used to teach the desired behavior.

It will still be necessary to show that such a program as has
been proposed here will be effective in use; such proof must wait
until the program is tried out in practice.

It would also be most interesting to consider the theoretical
implications of the program. There has been much debate on the
criteria for a good grammar: frequently the term 'pedagogical
grammar' has been loosely used to justify a grammar that cannot
be rigorously defended. A sounder definition is that a pedagogical
grammar is one that is to be used in teaching a language to a native
or nonnative speaker. A pedagogical grammar would then be considered to consist of a number of linguistic statements,[10] and its

validity might be established by its ability to fulfill the requirements of a given language teaching program. This paper makes
it clear that such a statement must make it possible to code any
response that the student may construct to a given stimulus in
such a way that it may be compared with the code of the correct
response which is required and that specific errors in the student's
response may be unambiguously recognized, and it has shown that
a linguistic statement of the form of the English verb phrase as
set out in the paper does lend itself to such a purpose.

NOTES

1. The intrinsic program that Norman Crowder has devised
is not in fact a pure branching paradigm, but rather is based on the
idea of letting the student's choice of answers to questions that are
included in the text direct him to remedial material when necessary.
See, for example, Norman Crowder, 'On the difference between
linear and intrinsic programming', Phi Delta Kappan (March, 1963).

2. See James G. Holland and Douglas Porter, 'The Influence
of Repetition of Incorrectly Answered Items in a Teaching-Machine
Program', Journal of the Experimental Analysis of Behavior 4. 305-
307 (1961).

3. See John B. Carroll, 'Programed Instruction and Student
Ability', The Journal of Programed Instruction, 2:4. 7-12 (1963).

4. As is done in Crowder's AutoTutor. See Norman A.
Crowder, 'Automatic Tutoring by Instrinsic Programming', in
A. A. Lumsdaine and R. Glaser (eds.), Teaching Machines and
Programmed Learning, Department of Audio-Visual Instruction,
NEA, (1960).

5. See A. Maher, 'Computer-Based Instruction (CBI): Intro-
duction to the IBM Research Project', IBM Research Report RC-1114
(March 6, 1964); also John E. Coulson, Programmed Learning and
Computer-Based Instruction (New York, 1962).

6. This state diagram is of the type that has been developed
by Jean-Paul Vinay.   See Canadian Journal of Linguistics, 9:1. 57
(1963).

7. This distinction cannot always be made for there is sometimes ambiguity. Ambiguities may be treated in two ways: each

of the possible solutions may be accepted in turn and carried
through until an error is found, in which case the other solution
is tried, or a notice of ambiguity may be given, asking the student
to say which of the possible interpretations he intended.

8. In the early stages of teaching, for instance, a restriction
might be set so that the student would not have to deal with more
than one or two auxiliary verbs in a sentence.

9. This section of the program was developed for a seminar
on computational linguistics conducted at the Université de Montréal
by Professor J.-P. Vinay. It was coded for computer operation,
as part of the Language Data Processing Seminar, by James Stone.

10. See Albert Valdman, 'Linguistic Statement and Language
Teaching', Proceedings of the Ninth International Congress of
Linguists, Cambridge, Mass. 1962 (The Hague, 1964).

Table 12.1 <u>Verb-form Dictionary</u>

AM	Aux BE	1 p. s. only	Not Pret, Past or Pres. Part.
ARE	Aux BE	Pl.	Not Pret, Past or Pres. Part.
BE	Aux BE	Not finite	Base form; not Pret or Past Part.
BEEN	Aux BE	Past Part.	Not base, Pret, or Pres. Part.
CAN	Aux Modal CAN	Base form	Not Pret, Past or Pres. Part.
COULD	Aux Modal CAN	Preterit.	Not base, Pres. or Past Part.
DID	Aux DO	Preterit	Not base, Pres. or Past Part.
DO	Aux DO	Base form	Not Pret, or Past Part.
DONE	Aux DO	Past Part.	Not base, Pret. or Pres. Part.
HAD	Aux HAVE	Pret or Past Part.	Not base or Pres. Part.
HAS	Aux HAVE	3 p. s.	Not Pret, Pres. or Past Part.
HAVE	Aux HAVE	Base form	Not Pret. or Past Part.
IS	Aux BE	3 p. s.	Not Pret, Pres. or Past Part.
MAY	Aux Modal MAY	Base form	Not Pret, Pres. or Past Part
MIGHT	Aux Modal MAY	Preterit.	Not base, Pres. or Past Part.
MUST	Aux Modal MUST	Base form	Not Pret, Pres. or Past Part.
SHALL	Aux Modal SHALL	Base form	Not Pret, Pres. or Past Part.
SHOULD	Aux Modal SHALL	Preterit.	Not base, Pres. or Past Part.
WAS	Aux BE	1 p. s. or 3 p. s. Preterit.	Not base, Pres. or Past Part.
WERE	Aux BE	Pl. Preterit	Not base, Pres. or Past Part.
WILL	Aux Modal WILL	Base form.	Not Pret, Pres. or Past Part.
WOULD	Aux Modal WILL	Preterit.	Not base, Pres. or Past Part.

Sample verb-forms that will be added as dictionary items by a program:

ASK	Base form	
CAME	Preterit.	Not base, Pres. or Past Part.
COME	Base or Past Part.	Not Pret.

Table 12.2 <u>Interpretation of Instruction Code</u>
(First 5 binary digits)

Configur-ation	PRINT OUT	Correct Response	Content
00000	MAKE THIS SENTENCE NEGATIVE	Neg 1	Neg 0
00001	A QUESTION	Q 1	Q 0
00010	PAST	Pret 1	Pret 0
00011	PASSIVE	Pass 1	Pass 0
00100	FUTURE	Mod 1	Mod 0
		Modal 001 or 010	
		Pret 0	Pret 0
		Perf 0	Perf 0
00101	PRESENT	Pret 0	Pret 1
		Mod 0	Mod 0
00110	SUPPLY THE APPROPRIATE PAST FORM OF THE VERB IN PARENTHESES.	Pret 1	Base Form (inf in parenth.)
00111	PRESENT PASSIVE	Pass 1	Base Form
		Others 0	
01000	PRESENT	All 0	Base Form
01001	PRESENT PERFECT	Perf 1	Base Form
		Others 0	
01010	PRESENT CONTINUOUS	Cont 1	Base Form
		Others 0	
01011	PAST CONTINUOUS	Pret 1	Base Form
		Cont 1	
		Others 0	
01100	PAST PERFECT	Pret 1	Base Form
		Perf 1	
		Others 0	
01101	PAST PASSIVE	Pret 1	Base Form
		Pass 1	
		Others 0	
01110	PERFECT PASSIVE	Perf 1	Base Form
		Pass 1	
		Others 0	
01111	PERFECT CONTINUOUS	Perf 1	Base Form
		Cont 1	
		Others 0	
10000	REPLACE THE SUBJECT OF THIS SENTENCE BY HE.	Subj 000	Subj 011
10001	SHE	Subj 001	Subj 100
10010	IT	Subj 010	Subj 110
10011	WE	Subj 011	Subj 000
10100	THEY	Subj 100	Subj 010
10101	YOU	Subj 101	Subj 001
10110	I	Subj 110	Subj 000
10111	ADD TO THIS SENTENCE THE WORD CAN	Mod 1	Mod 0
		Modal 000	Pret 0
		Pret 0	

Table 12.2 (p. 2)

Configuration	PRINT OUT	Correct Response	Content
11000	ADD TO THIS SENTENCE THE WORD <u>MAY</u>	Mod 1 Modal 011 Pret 0	Mod 0 Pret 0
11001	MIGHT	Mod 1 Modal 011 Pret 1	Mod 0 Pret 0
11010	COULD	Mod 1 Modal 000 Pret 1	Mod 0 Pret 0
11011	WILL	Mod 1 Modal 010 Pret 0	Mod 0 Pret 0
11100	WOULD	Mod 1 Modal 010 Pret 1	Mod 0 Pret 0
11101	SHALL	Mod 1 Modal 001 Pret 0	Mod 0 Pret 0
11110	SHOULD	Mod 1 Modal 001 Pret 1	Mod 0 Pret 0
11111	MUST	Mod 1 Modal 100 Pret 0	Mod 0 Pret 0

INTERPRETATION OF SUBJECT CODE   (6-8th binary digits)

Configuration	Subject Pronoun	Concord Marking	
000	HE	(c)	
001	SHE	(c)	3 p. s.
010	IT	(c)	
011	WE	(b)	
100	THEY	(b)	Pl.
101	YOU	(b)	
110	I	(a)	1 p. s.
111	0 (Imperative)	(b)	(Imperative)

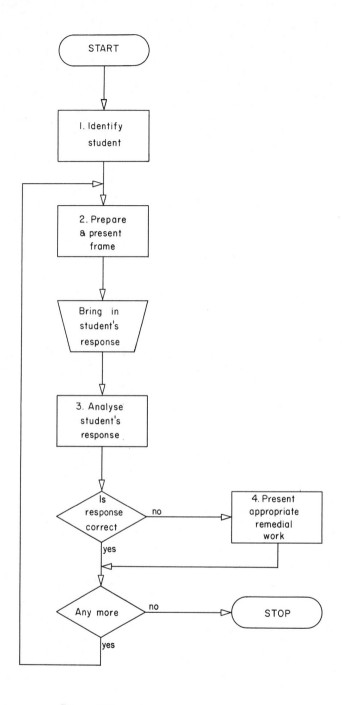

Figure 12.1   General Program Strategy

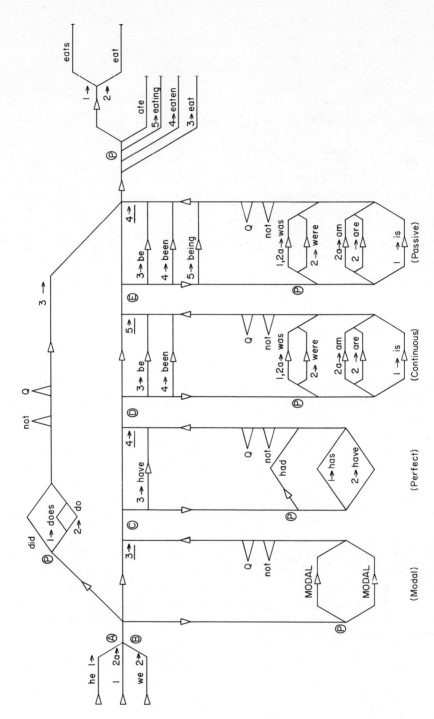

Figure 12.2   A State Diagram of the English Verb Phrase (with switching convention)

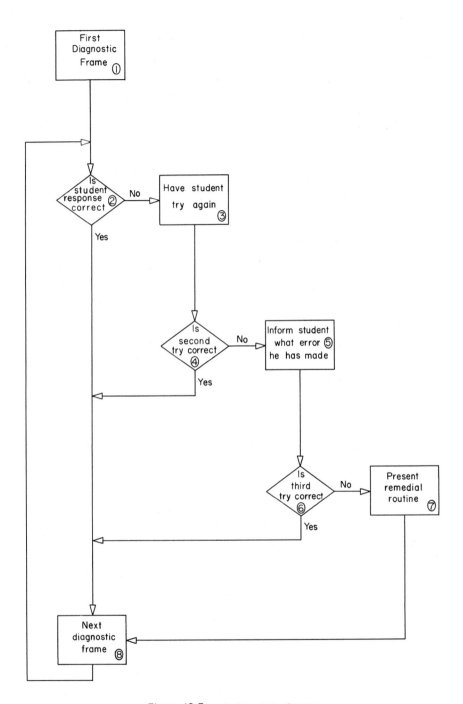

Figure 12.3   Pedagogical Strategy

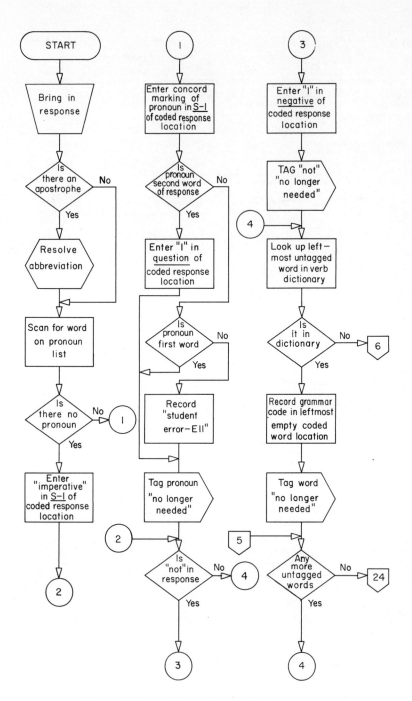

START

Bring in response

Is there an apostrophe
No
Yes

Resolve abbreviation

Scan for word on pronoun list

Is there no pronoun
No → 1
Yes

Enter "imperative" in S-1 of coded response location

2

1

Enter concord marking of pronoun in S-1 of coded response location

Is pronoun second word of response
No
Yes

Enter "I" in question of coded response location

Is pronoun first word
No
Yes

Record "student error—E11"

Tag pronoun "no longer needed"

2

Is "not" in response
No → 4
Yes

3

3

Enter "I" in negative of coded response location

TAG "not" "no longer needed"

4

Look up left-most untagged word in verb dictionary

Is it in dictionary
No → 6
Yes

Record grammar code in leftmost empty coded word location

Tag word "no longer needed"

5

Any more untagged words
No → 24
Yes

4

Figure 12.4   Analysis and Comparison

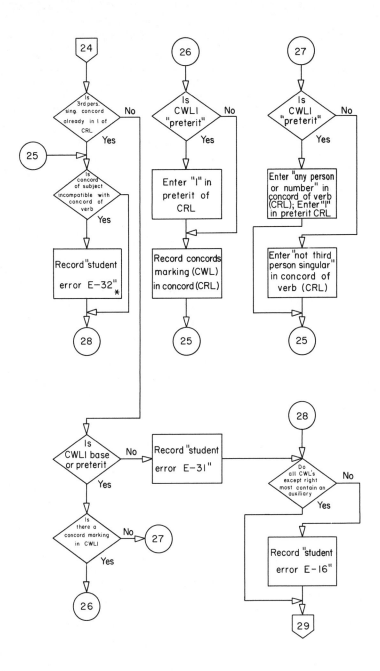

* See Figure 12.8 for treatment of this error in detail.

Figure 12.5   Analysis and Comparison

Figure 12.6 <u>Frame Generating Code</u>

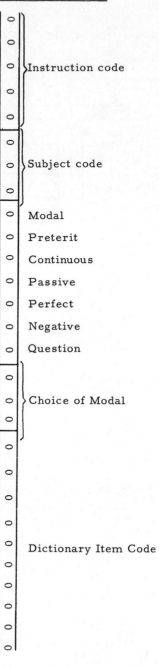

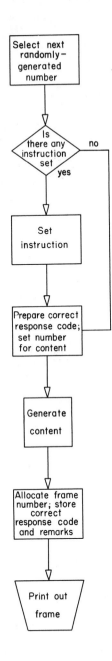

Figure 12.7   Decision Logic for Frame Generation

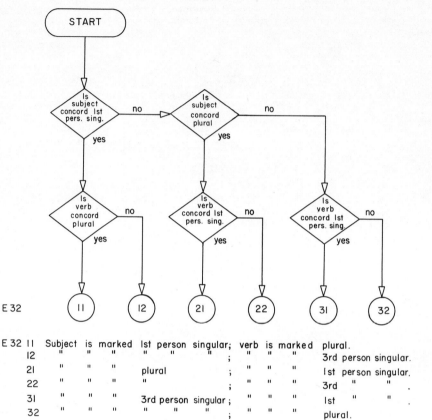

E 32 11	Subject	is	marked	1st person singular;	verb	is	marked	plural.
12	"	"	"	" " " ;	"	"	"	3rd person singular.
21	"	"	"	plural ;	"	"	"	1st person singular.
22	"	"	"	" ;	"	"	"	3rd " " .
31	"	"	"	3rd person singular ;	"	"	"	1st " " .
32	"	"	"	" " " ;	"	"	"	plural.

Figure 12.8   Error Notice E32*

(subject and verb do not agree) has been given;

what is the precise error ?

*See Figure 12.5 where this Error Notice originates.